GILBERT CANNAN
A Georgian Prodigy

Gilbert Cannan

A GEORGIAN PRODIGY

By
DIANA FARR

1978
CHATTO & WINDUS
LONDON

Published by
Chatto and Windus Ltd.
42 William IV Street
London WC2N 4DF
*
Clarke, Irwin & Co. Ltd.
Toronto

British Library Cataloguing in Publication Data
Farr, Diana
    Gilbert Cannan.
    1. Cannan, Gilbert – Biography   2. Authors,
    English – Biography
    828'.9'1209   PR6005.A48Z/
    ISBN 0–7011–2245–5

Printed in Great Britain by
Cox & Wyman Ltd.
London, Fakenham and Reading

To
DENNIS
with love

Contents

Illustrations

Foreword

MY mother was Joanna Cannan, one of Gilbert's second cousins. But they were friends only briefly at the beginning of the century when she was a little girl. During my childhood Gilbert's name was mentioned occasionally without affection. Our parents thought we might feel threatened by his madness and imagine a streak of schizophrenia within ourselves. Regrettably, as children we possessed little understanding or sympathy for mental patients, who were for us either a joke or a frightening phenomenon to be avoided. We talked of loony bins and yet thought romantically of Charles and Mary Lamb.

Poor Gilbert, not one of his books stood among the hundreds on our shelves, for he had alienated himself long before his final break-down, not by any sexual indiscretions or notions of free love, which probably would have been understood, but by acts of bad taste and disloyalty to members on our side of the family who had been kind to him, and perhaps also on account of his pacifist views which were anathema to my father. Yet he remained for me essentially a romantic figure, for had he not eloped (as it was wrongly said) with Mary Barrie and known D. H. Lawrence, and been singled out as a white hope of literature and the theatre? I think that even as a young girl I sensed a poignant tragedy, a story which had been too thoughtlessly swept under the carpet.

In 1952 I bought a tattered copy of *Pugs and Peacocks* for a shilling in a Reading bookshop. Looking for symptoms of insanity and shocking sexual elements, as well as indications of genius, I missed the subtleties and failed to recognise Bertrand Russell as the original of Melian Stokes. Indeed the novel seemed disappointingly tame considering that it came from the black sheep of the family.

In 1955 I decided out of curiosity, and I hope cousinly altruism, to visit Gilbert who was now in Holloway Sanatorium, where visits from his relations were allowed. Feeling that I must go through the older generation I spoke to my Aunt Dorothea, wife of Dr. John Johnson, Printer to the University of Oxford, who immediately said she would like to accompany me. A meeting was arranged in June, but sadly we were too late. By the middle of the month Gilbert, now an old man, was in the throes of his final illness, and in no state to make new

9

acquaintances. Our proposed visit was cancelled, and the opportunity had gone for ever, to our lasting regret.

In 1956 I asked an Earl's Court bookseller to look out for Gilbert's books for me. They came thick and fast and, after paying twenty-five shillings for a signed copy of *Noel*, I asked him to stop. It was getting too expensive for one who, at that time, could afford coffee only as a treat. This was a short-sighted decision on my part, for now most of his works are unobtainable.

In 1967, married and living in Glasgow, I started my research for a biography realising that before long some of those who had known Gilbert would be dead. I approached this task diffidently, but I need not have worried, for those who had known Gilbert were immensely kind and helpful. I visited Sir Compton Mackenzie in his house in Edinburgh and, moving south, lunched with Martin and Sylvia Secker at Bridgefoot and enjoyed tea with the Swinnertons at Cranleigh. Dame Sybil Thorndike talked to me of Gilbert on the telephone, and Sir Felix Aylmer sent me his copy of *Everybody's Husband*. With two young children to care for my time was limited, and sometimes I was defeated by death: Milton Rosmer, for one, dying while my letter was on its way to him, and Countess Jowitt before I could get down to see her.

By 1973 the first draft was half-written and discarded because it had become a saga of the Cannans rather than the story of Gilbert's life. By now I had received much welcome help from various American institutions where Gilbert's letters had been accumulating, and I was convinced his biography could throw fresh light on many of the remarkable men and women he had known. I saw in his life all the tragedy, the poignancy and the strange quirky brilliance that I had suspected, and knew without doubt that he had wanted to be remembered.

Seeking advice at the beginning of my researches I had met little enthusiasm for my book. 'Who reads Cannan now? Who even knows of Cannan?' I was asked. But when I advertised in *The Times Literary Supplement* for relevant papers, my ailing confidence was marvellously revived by a letter from Herbert van Thal, in which he stated his interest in the period and asked whether he might handle the biography for me if I had not already put it in the hands of an agent. Since then I have benefited immensely from his judgement and constructive and kindly criticism.

My other mentor to whom I wish to record my gratitude and thanks has been Martin Secker, who has read my book section by section as it was written. In him was a link of incalculable value, for here was a man who had read much of Gilbert's work in manuscript, a publisher who had known Gilbert so well that he could say 'Yes, you have brought him back to life', and I could believe him. For me, Secker possessed also the inestimable advantage of having known, not only Mary Barrie, but many of Gilbert's friends who were to appear in my book.

Thirdly, there was Gilbert's sister, Margaret Rideout, a determined old lady who had kept all that remained of Gilbert's papers in a wardrobe, and wanted him brought back to life. His letters had been destroyed, his books had disappeared, but there were many pages of manuscript, mostly written in his small precise hand, which she put in order. Margaret's memory was failing, but before it went she wrote me long letters about the family, their childhood and what she knew of Gilbert's later life and final illness. My debt to her is immeasurable.

I have also received help and encouragement from my husband, Dennis, who in the early stages of the book patiently played the part of resident tutor, having infinitely more academic experience than myself. But for him many a probing letter would have been unwritten; the footnotes would have been fewer and the language less exact.

Not being a drama or literary critic, I have attempted no serious academic assessment of Gilbert's work and have discussed only those plays and books that relate directly to his personal life. In the interests of brevity I have not examined all the facets of Gilbert's life as deeply as would have been justifiable in a longer work, deciding reluctantly, for example, only to touch upon his visits to North America and his pacifist activities. At the request of the publishers many letters have been cut and forms of address and signature usually omitted. The full name of one person and the surnames of two others have been left out to spare living people possible embarrassment.

In two chapters I have used Gilbert's novels, *Peter Homunculus* and *Time and Eternity*, to illuminate love affairs when surviving written evidence has been inadequate to describe his emotional state at the time, but on each occasion I have made it clear that this is so. I have also based some assumptions on events and emotions described in *Little Brother*. With the possible exception of *Devious Ways* and *Pink Roses*, I believe that all Gilbert's novels are based on real characters and events. (Indeed he has stated clearly that the name Lawrie, which appears in six, stands for Cannan, and Stephen for Gilbert.) Every check I have made supports this view and it is my opinion that future biographers of Gilbert's friends and colleagues may find useful material within the novels, just as those writing on Mark Gertler have drawn enlightenment and inspiration from *Mendel*. Here perhaps lies the greatest immediate value in his work, along with the recreation of the flavour of the times through which he lived.

Gilbert's working life as a writer spanned only fifteen years, during which time twenty-seven of his books were published, and at least fourteen plays written as well as many articles, short stories and columns of dramatic criticism.

Towards the end of his free life he divided most of his work into four sections, listing them thus (I have added dates of first publication in Britain):

The Lawrie Saga	Novels of the New Time
Little Brother (1912)	*Pugs and Peacocks* (1921)
Round the Corner (1913)	*Sembal* (1922)
The Stucco House (1917)	*The House of Prophecy* (1924)
Three Pretty Men (1916)	*The Soaring Bird* (in preparation)
Time and Eternity (1919)	
Annette and Bennett (1922)	

Letters and Social Studies	Stories and Plays
Noel (1922)	*Mendel* (1916)
Windmills (1915)	*Mummery* (1918)
The Anatomy of Society (1919)	*Pink Roses* (1919)
The Release of the Soul (1920)	*Peter Homunculus* (1909)
Letters From a Distance (1923)	*Old Mole* (1914)
Satire (1914)	*Four Plays* (1913)
Samuel Butler (1915)	*Seven Plays* (1923)

He omitted *The Joy of the Theatre* (1913), *Adventurous Love and Other Verses* (1915), *Devious Ways* (1910) (a novel he later disliked), *Old Mole's Novel Love* (1914) (a strange little fable), *Young Ernest* (1915), and two slim volumes, *Love* (1914) and *Freedom* (1917). *The Soaring Bird* was never completed. In addition he translated, during those fifteen years, *John Christopher* by Romain Rolland (4 vols.) (1910–13), *The Memoirs of Heinrich Heine* (1910), *A Yoke of Pity* by Julien Benda (1912), *With the Russian Wounded* by T. A. Aleksinskaya (1916), with S. S. Koteliansky *My Life and Other Stories* by Chekhov (1920), *A. O. Barnabooth: His Diary* by Valéry Larbaud (1924), (with Mme. A Strindberg) *The Savage* by M. K. Artsybashev (1924), and a play (with Francis Keyser), *The Right to Kill* by Pierre Frondate (1915).

While writing this book, I have received much help and information from the following people to whom I express my sincere gratitude: Professor Antony Alpers, Mr. Carl Baron, the late Hon. Mrs. Vera Birch, Mr. Andrew Birkin, Professor J. T. Boulton, the Hon. Dorothy Brett, Mr. Noel Carrington, Mr. Dennis Cole, Mr. Edward Craig, Mr. Nicholas Davies, Mr. David Garnett, Mr. Luke Gertler, Miss Sharon Goode, Mr. Michael Holroyd, Mr. Richard Kelly, Lord Kennet, Major Charles Mendel Kohan, Mrs. Marjorie Kostenz, the late Sir Compton

Mackenzie, Mr. Colin Murry, Miss Cathleen Nesbitt, Miss Georgia O'Keefe, Mr. Oleg Polunin, the late Harold Rubinstein, Mr. R. S. Sauter, Mr. John Stephens of Hungerford, Mr. Frank Swinnerton, the late Dame Sybil Thorndike, Mrs. Igor Vinogradoff, Mr. Alec Waugh, Dame Rebecca West.

I am also grateful for assistance and advice from the following Cannan relations: Mrs. F. A. Atkins, Miss Elizabeth Cannan, Mr. John F. Cannan, Mrs. M. D. Johnson, Mrs. Kathleen Lee, Mrs. John Lewis, and the late Mrs. M. Slater (May Wedderburn Cannan).

I have benefited greatly from the research facilities and scholarly expertise of the staff of the following university libraries: Cambridge, Birmingham, The Bodleian, Harvard, Illinois, McMaster (Mills Memorial), New York, The Humanities Research Center, Austin, Texas, and Yale, including their Beinecke Rare Book and Manuscript Library. In addition I am grateful to the staff of the British Library, Birmingham, and Manchester Central Libraries, New York Public Library and Salford and Solihull Public Libraries, and also to the late A. N. L. Munby of King's College, Cambridge, Mr. J. A. McCorquodale of Manchester Grammar School, and the staff of the British Theatre Museum.

Finally, I should like to thank the following people for generously providing me with useful details about Gilbert's forbears; although not all their information has been used in this book, each piece has been essential to complete the family jig-saw which proved invaluable in my assessment of Gilbert's background and inheritance: The Reverend John Alexander of Carsphairn Parish Church, Mr. Alan Brown of Cholesbury, Mr. M. G. Brown of the County Library Headquarters, Castle Douglas, Mr. Peter Cook, Rector of the Kirkcudbright Academy, Major O. M. Greg, Canon J. R. Jose of St. Stythian's Parish Church, Cornwall, the Reverend D. Wyatt of St. Paul's, Pendleton, and the Reverend D. H. A. Wilson, Vicar of Topsham.

Acknowledgement is gratefully made to copyright holders and others for permission to quote from the following works:

Gilbert Cannan, published and unpublished letters, memoirs, articles, poems and books, M. K. Rideout.

Dora Carrington, *Letters and Extracts from Her Diaries* and one partly unpublished letter, David Garnett, the Sophie Partridge Trust, Noel Carrington, and Jonathan Cape Ltd.

Ford Madox Ford, *It Was the Nightingale*, the Ford Madox Ford Estate.

John Galsworthy, letter, the Society of Authors as literary executors of the Estate of John Galsworthy.

David Garnett, *The Golden Echo*, the author and Chatto and Windus Ltd.

Mark Gertler, *Selected Letters*, Noel Carrington and Rupert Hart Davies; unpublished letters, Mrs. Marjorie Kostenz.

Michael Holroyd, *Lytton Strachey*, Vol. 2, the author and William Heinemann Ltd.

Kennet, Lady (Lady Scott, Kathleen Bruce), unpublished letters and diaries, *Self-Portrait of an Artist*, Lord Kennet and Sir Peter Scott, C.B.E., D.Sc.

D. H. Lawrence and Frieda Lawrence, *Fantasia of the Unconscious*, *The Priest of Love* by Harry T. Moore, *Collected Letters* and *Not I But The Wind*, William Heinemann Ltd., Laurence Pollinger Ltd., and the Estate of the late Frieda Lawrence.

Compton Mackenzie, *My Life and Times*, *Octave Four* and *Octave Five* and *The South Wind of Love*, Lady Mackenzie and Chatto and Windus Ltd.

Ottoline Morrell, *The Early Memoirs of Lady Ottoline* and *Ottoline at Garsington*, both edited by Robert Gathorne-Hardy, Mrs. I. Vinogradoff and Faber and Faber Ltd.

John Middleton Murry, *Between Two Worlds* and his unpublished *Journal*, Jonathan Cape Ltd., and the Society of Authors as literary executors of the Estate of John Middleton Murry.

Romain Rolland, letter, Mme. Rolland.

George Bernard Shaw, letters and *Fanny's First Play*, the Society of Authors on behalf of the Bernard Shaw Estate.

Frank Swinnerton, *Background with Chorus* and *Figures in the Foreground*, the author and Hutchinson and Co. Ltd.

Alec Waugh, *The Early Years of Alec Waugh* and *My Brother Evelyn and Other Profiles*, the author and Cassell and Co. Ltd.

H. G. Wells, letters, the Estate of the late H. G. Wells.

Lastly, my thanks are again due to Mrs. Rideout, this time for photographs of Gilbert and Mary Cannan, and to Lord Kennet for the photograph of Kathleen Bruce.

I

'A Very Special Nature'

Kathleen Bruce

ON the evening of April 14th, 1908, a young man of remarkable appearance walked by devious routes from Cheyne Walk to his rooms in the Temple, his mind in turmoil.

Tall and thin with thick fair hair, crooked mouth, large blue-grey eyes and a nose fit for a Roman Emperor, he had nevertheless for many years considered himself ugly. Now for the first time he believed himself deeply in love; the cynicism which had been nibbling away at his romantic idealism was in retreat. Sexually aroused but unsatisfied, and emotionally at sea, he climbed at last the stone steps to his rooms which looked out across pleasant gardens and a square of green turf. He found pen and paper. In a small, fluent hand he wrote:

1 T.G. [Temple Gardens]
Monday night.

My dear K, Quite quite impossible to sleep, after I left you I wandered miles and miles—*and* miles, exactly where I don't know; through mean streets and prosperous streets, vulgar streets and streets gentle, ... streets where the people were not asleep but all dead, and streets where there was God. N.B. all these beautiful reflections are of subsequent date. The cause of the wanderings was the wonderful you, the maker of beautiful things, the creator sole and without male assistance of enough lovely babies[1] to stock the whole world civilized and uncivilized—though I imagine that in the babies' kingdom there is no knowledge of civilization or they would surely refuse to visit civilized men and women . . . What about you? Oh! yes. That you should have—have—have—I don't know—given me so many hours of yourself, liked my works, liked me. Ye Gods. It seems incredible.—Do I sleep, do I dream, is (*sic*) babies about? There must be babies about and one of them has closed a little pink dimpled hand round my crooked and rather dimpled forefinger and led me clean out of myself, and everything that I have ever known before, into a dream. No. Everything before is the dream, drunken grandfather, political economist and all,[2] and all the reality of all the world is concentrated in you! . . .

Perhaps I have only dreamed it—never mind, I'll hug the dream and that

15

won't be any nuisance to you as the reality might be, most precious of persons. I feel better. By the next time I see you I shall hope to have discovered whether I am standing on my head or my heels. Goodnight.   G. C.

K was Kathleen Bruce, a sculptor, informally engaged to Robert Falcon Scott, the explorer. Born in the Rectory at Carlton-in-Lindrick, Nottinghamshire, on March 27th, 1878, she was the youngest of eleven children. Her father, the Reverend Lloyd Stewart Bruce, was Canon of York, fourth son of Sir James Bruce, second Baronet of Downhill, Londonderry. Her mother, Jane Skene, half Greek and granddaughter of James Skene of Rubislaw, Sir Walter Scott's friend, went blind when Kathleen was born, and 'for the brief time that she lived afterwards' (actually eighteen months) 'she lay gently feeling her last lusty baby's face, tracing the small features. Even a dozen had not, it seemed, taken completely from her the sense of the miraculous.'[3]

The frequent tracing of features by loving hands, so much part of the sensuousness of this first vital relationship, may well have affected Kathleen Bruce's whole life. Feel was of special significance for her, one of the most important elements in the sense of the miraculous which she had inherited. She loved the feel of sand running through her toes, the wind in her face, dewy grass on bare feet, clay in her hands, young men's hair between her fingers. Best of all she loved the feel and presence of baby boys and secondly beautiful intelligent males with whom she normally desired a loving but platonic friendship.

In her book, *Self-Portrait of an Artist*, she wrote:

1888. Already in nursery days appeared a trait of character which lasted me a lifetime. I had a quantity of dolls, all female save one, a sailor boy with blue eyes and brown curls. The girls I put kindly but permanently to bed with measles. The boy went everywhere with me, and was my idol, my baby, my love. So through life, let all females be kindly and comfortably disposed of, so that my complete preoccupation with the male of the moment be unhampered![4]

After her father's early death, Kathleen spent part of her childhood with her Presbyterian lawyer great-uncle in Edinburgh and, when he died, a cheap convent school was her 'next adventure'.

Here her religious devotion was rewarded with a vision also described in *Self-Portrait of an Artist:*

There were no half-measures for me. There, to be religious was to be good; to be ecstatically religious was to be very good. Very well then! I would be very good. Some of the girls at the Convent worked themselves into such a state of religious over-excitement that they saw visions. To some an angel would appear. To a chosen few the Figure would descend in compassion from the Cross. To me, a full-hearted child, the little, fat baby once came down from the Madonna's lap and snuggled warmly into my yearning, immature arms. That day I was deified. How could I explain what made me late for the cold, dreary supper? . . . My little breasts were still warm where the baby had lain. I could still feel his little fingers on my lips.[1]

Warm-hearted, charming but not conventionally beautiful, Kathleen Bruce's attraction lay as much in the originality and liveliness of her character as in her appearance. Indeed, although her eyes were fine and blue, early photographs show a somewhat heavy-featured girl with a rather large, slightly up-turned nose and a long, pointed chin. But she was, above all, a witty and exciting companion. As a young woman she had gone to Paris, to study with Rodin, and afterwards to Macedonia, where she worked in a hospital after the revolt in 1903, so gaining a width of experience unusual in a girl of her age. She was never dull; she appeared strong and healthy with an appetite for new experiences and a great capacity for friendship. Such a woman, living alone in London, chaste, feminine, maternal, without coquetry, yet caring deeply for her art, was a rarity in Edwardian England and to the young men, recently down from university, an entrancing change from the girls they met in London drawing-rooms, who were often inhibited by parents on the look out for prospective husbands. However, on further acquaintance these young men were to find that Kathleen was also at times irrational, impulsive, patronising and unreliable, a wildly attractive mixture to the immature susceptible males searching for both lover and mother.

G. C., Gilbert Eric Cannan, was born on June 25th, 1884, at 25 Cheetham Street West in Broughton, Manchester, in a red brick terrace house with a mean yard at the back. He was the second son of Henry, an ill-paid shipping clerk, and Violet Cannan. An academically bright but strangely unmotivated child, given to long bouts of crying, he won a scholarship from Board School to Manchester Grammar School, before going on to Cambridge to read Modern and Mediaeval languages.

His mother was the daughter of Francis Hill Arbuthnot Wright, the High Anglican Vicar of St. Paul's, Paddington, Salford, and Martha Brand, a well-connected, indolent woman from the West Country. His father was the son of James Cannan, a bearded Scot, who had left his native Kirkcudbrightshire at sixteen to make his fortune in business in Manchester. Even twelve years as a bank clerk did not, however, succeed in teaching James simple economic sense. Illogical, generous, with a weakness for whisky, his special love was for the theatre and he finished up an impecunious journalist, writing on the cotton market for the *Weekly Examiner*, dramatic criticism for the *Manchester City News* and provocative articles, many against the Establishment, for an *avant-garde* Mancunian periodical, *The Sphinx*. James's wife, Agnes, was the daughter of John Storrs Smith, author of a book on Mirabeau and two volumes of poetry, and founder with James Cannan, Edwin Waugh and Francis Épinasse of a literary coterie known as the Shandean Club. Church-going and puritanical, Agnes disapproved of the theatre and was embittered by her husband's failure to support her in the manner she expected. She withdrew gradually from the world, modelling herself on Queen Victoria under whose portrait she sat day after day growing increasingly fat.

Gilbert spent many hours of his early childhood in his paternal grandparents' house. By 1886 James and Agnes were no longer on speaking terms and it was often Gilbert's lot to carry the notes by which they communicated from the cold dining-room in which James worked (his wife never allowed him a fire) to the upstairs drawing-room where Agnes existed in a state of permanent disapproval. For a small boy it was a perplexing situation.

In his memoirs Gilbert wrote:

I do not know how much time I spent in that house, but my life was caught up in it to an extent which I did not realise till many years later. Perhaps I and my grandfather loved and understood each other, but he died before I knew him clearly and I only remember him faintly as a very handsome very shabby old man who smelled of nicotine and had a drawer full of treasures, a box of dominoes and wonderful scrap books.[6]

It is probable that Kathleen found in Gilbert a capacity for love and friendship, a well of feeling, which few of his contemporaries knew or suspected, for his manner was frequently off-putting. Frank Swinnerton mentions (in his book, *Background with Chorus*) an 'air of aloofness'. Major Charles Mendel Kohan, barrister, poet, and historian, who knew Gilbert both at Manchester Grammar School and King's College, Cambridge, went further in a letter to me:

The cast of his features was, as popularly conceived, aristocratic, his manner inclined to be patronising: even at school, and more so at Cambridge, where he was taken up by some of the well known intellectual characters, in our occasional encounters.

In 1906 Gilbert had been called to the Bar, had devilled, and then turned away from the Law to writing. He had met many leading figures in the world of literature and drama, becoming honorary secretary of the Society for the Abolition of Censorship, through the good offices of Mrs. Granville-Barker.

This Society had been formed as a result of the Lord Chamberlain's refusal to grant a licence for Harley Granville-Barker's play, *Waste*. One of the pioneering and most powerful spirits behind this campaign was James Barrie, who must have viewed Gilbert's appointment with some relief for on November 4th, 1907, he had written to his friend

Sylvia Davies: 'I am having a life of it over this censorship business. Receiving committees, telephones, telegrams etc., all day and every day.'[7]

Inevitably in his new post Gilbert was to come to know the Barries increasingly well, until Leinster Corner became almost a second home to him. But at first they were just two of the many friends he shared with Kathleen, whom he had met through Granville-Barker in September, 1907, and 'found' in his rooms that Monday night six months later.

From the beginning these two were experiencing friendship at very different levels. Gilbert was definitely sexually aroused and ready for consummation, Kathleen was determined to preserve her chastity. He had little experience of love. She had rejected many suitors. Superficially his life had been mainly that of an ordinary middle-class man. Hers had been unconventional and unsheltered for the last seven years. But although her life style in the climate of the time might suggest a loose woman, when it came to the sexual act, as opposed to kissing and caressing, Kathleen became again the Rector's daughter and the Convent's child. This attitude is confirmed in her comments on the pregnancy of the then unmarried dancer, Isadora Duncan: 'I was torn and shattered. All my inborn prudery strengthened by my convent upbringing was terribly affronted.'[8]

She might live among those termed Bohemians, but she was never to be one of them.

In 1908 sex for Kathleen was to be solely for the procreation of a legitimate male child. The most important question in her life was not whom she most desired but who would make the most worthy sire for her son, which accounts to some extent for Gilbert always referring to sexual drive as the 'father in me' in his letters to her.

Both Gilbert Cannan and Kathleen came from highly fertile families. Gilbert's parents' youthful, passionate and pre-marital affair had led to a secret wedding, nine children and life-long economic difficulties. Though he was the odd man out in his family, a second son who had come too soon after the adored first to receive his full share of loving attention, his background had not in itself lacked warmth. From an early age he had witnessed a permanent, passionate if sometimes disorganized relationship between his parents. His mother, full-hearted, intelligent and impulsive, bore no grudges and to the end declared that her failed husband was a man of rare talent and character. For them kisses meant courtship and love. Only the base caressed without deeply caring, and, still within the sphere of their influence (however much he might deny it) Gilbert appears to have taken Kathleen's demonstrations of affection and maternal love more seriously than she intended. Probably lacking at this time any deep sexual awareness, she could not

19

know how she tormented the objects of her feminine, cat-like adoration.

With Scott her relationship was very different, less maternal, more controlled. He was already celebrated and she wanted to impress him, yet he was neither beautiful nor young, as she makes clear in her description of their first meeting.

He was not very young—perhaps forty, nor very good-looking, but he looked very healthy and alert, and I glowed rather foolishly and suddenly when I clearly saw him ask his neighbour who I was. I was nobody and I knew his neighbour, my hostess, would be saying so . . .

And describing a second meeting some ten months later she wrote:

I was sitting in a stiff uncomfortable chair with an ill-balanced cup of tea, and being trivially chaffed by this very well-dressed rather ugly celebrated explorer. He was standing over me. He was of medium height, with broad shoulders, very small waist, and dull hair beginning to thin, but with a rare smile, and with eyes of a quite unusually dark blue, almost purple.[9]

However, she did not feel that her informal engagement to Scott should inhibit her friendship with other men

There were two young men amongst my intimates, two young men physically not unalike, both tall, thin, fair, lithe, and of the same age, but in all other respects very different. One was a law student without family, later a well-known novelist, who lived on two hundred a year and what little extra he made from writing. He was no older than I,* and was confident that he was made for me. I adored his vivid vitality, but was less confident than he. The other was a young diplomat, rich, spoilt by an adoring mother, titled with the world before him. This young man was also confident that he could not do without me. What could I do? The law forbade me to marry them all! I loved them for loving me. I wanted greatly to take care of them. I wanted to prevent them from being hurt.[11]

Over ten passionate and disorganised weeks, Gilbert wrote forty-one letters to Kathleen Bruce, sometimes three in one day; many were delivered by his hand, so desperate was he that his thoughts and expressions of love should be conveyed to her without delay. His need to reiterate his devotion over and over again was increased by the existence of his famous rival, who possessed the crucial advantage of having proved himself. Kathleen wanted above all a courageous father for her son and Scott's earlier expedition to the Antarctic had shown that he did not lack that quality. Yet Kathleen's attractions were such that she could not 'take care of Gilbert' without arousing him sexually.

This was Gilbert's first real love affair, and while suffering all the

* Kathleen Bruce was six years older than Gilbert.

pangs of unrequited love, he was to show himself to be persistent, ardent, reckless and egotistical, but not selfish. He never entirely lost sight of Kathleen's own feelings and needs and, apart from a few fleeting moments of anger, there was none of the hatred which can occur in frustrated infatuation.

He knew at twenty-three that he could only find the maturity he was seeking through passionate involvement with a woman, yet deep inside himself he also knew that he was unready for any permanent tie, whatever he might say aloud to the contrary. When he met Kathleen, he had been, like many another young man, on the look out for the great 'she' who would arouse his love and end his reluctant celibacy. Where such an affair would lead him he left more or less to fate, just as his ardent, disorganised but less intelligent father had done before him.

The impression Gilbert made on Kathleen Bruce was unforgettable and poignant. He was, she subsequently told her sons, and James Barrie, 'one with a very special nature'. Gilbert's letters she kept, along with those from Asquith with whom she was to have a close friendship in later years. And it was on this admiration, this feeling that he was a special person, that Gilbert built his slender hopes. He could not believe that she did not also desire him.

Suppose you give yourself to a good man who loves you and I myself to a good woman who loves me (he wrote on April 22nd), there will be a want for the you in me and the me in you, which will never die however much we reason and reason and argue and argue. I see the bitter difficulty of it for you and I know that I should not try to influence you but there's a cold bread and butter for me too, and I think it cannot altogether be extreme youth that refuses to have any real misgivings about the future . . .

And, quick to play on her longings for a son, equating his own desires with a baby actually asking to be born, he continued:

It is the child which has called to us, our child; we may make other children, but that child, if we shut our eyes to that cry, will be lost and left crying in the void, for ever wandering until in another state we come together again, and finally and for ever together. What is it that you lose by taking?

The last question suggests disingenuousness. Kathleen would of course have lost Scott, and she would also have lost her virginity, which she was determined to keep for the man to whom she wished to commit herself for life.

While Gilbert was pressing his case in high-flown sentences, Scott was consolidating his position in a more restrained and dignified manner. On April 18th, he had written to Kathleen Bruce, giving notice of the dates she must keep free for him in May. He mentioned sadly that naval duties would keep him tied until after May 7th, except for weekends, and, after the middle of May, even those would not be free.

Well, it's no use grumbling. After Wednesday next I shall certainly go to London, if not asked to Farnham. It will be necessary to restart the sledge matters.*

On April 19th he wrote again from H.M.S. *Essex*, more possessively:

Here is a little note to meet and greet you in London. If you've not done so on the instant, take pen and paper and write to your devoted man. Here is our programme with more definition.

A list of naval activities followed with asterisks showing that in May, Scott could be free only on the 8th and between the 16th and 20th. He finished:

I am very depressed to think that I shall see so little of you, but when I can come I must be always with you. Do you understand, these are clear orders. Goodbye, take care of yourself, and you are *not* to go without lunch again. I must be getting ready to mount my bicycle and trundle to the country where spring is in the air.—Oh, but I must have a day with you in the country.[11]

According to her pocket engagement diary, Kathleen dined with Gilbert on April 23rd, but on the 24th she met Scott at Victoria Station and presumably spent much of the day with him, while an anguished Gilbert wrote her three letters, from which I quote the more poignant passages:

Oh! If there is goodness in it you should be all mine—for love is only love when wedded. There is knowledge and no knowledge. Without that in the two, soul is soul and body body; with that the two are for ever and indissolubly, beautifully, magically one. So by God's alchemy human beings are turned to gold.

And believing Kathleen Bruce to be choosing between Scott and himself:

Oh! my love there is a point beyond which madness is the only sanity; and in my silly brain there turn you and me and the other. It is as though I had three pebbles to drop into the well of truth. Each sinks far far and the rings spread over the water so that I cannot see. The bubbles rise, beautiful bubbles that look silvery truth, but at the surface they are no more and again there are three pebbles in my hand, and until you come to throw one away there will be three. Which?

Of the evening spent with Kathleen Bruce on the 23rd he wrote: 'The wonder of last night will be with me always. Real lovers!' by which it

* Concerning Scott's Antarctic Expedition.

must not be assumed that there was consummation, but rather that they made romantic love in intensely romantic circumstances: the barges with their red and green lights moving on the river, the April moon sailing the night sky, and all the spring smells of the shrubs of Cheyne Walk floating up through the flat's bow window.

For Kathleen Bruce the mad see-saw of these letters and the love they revealed, were both a stimulus and a reassurance of her own personal magnetism. In her autobiography she sums up with the wisdom of hindsight, in late middle age, her reaction to the arrival of the first of the three, and of Gilbert's letters in general.

Pushed under my door were four letters. I leapt out of bed. One came every morning from the law student, which was to me as the morning sun, as the fresh breeze that ruffled my hair, something to put fresh eagerness in my work, new glory into my play. That one was there; but I read the others first, and then dressed, ate my roll and got my work all ready before reading it, like a lioness being fed at the Zoo. A lion when thrown his hunk of raw meat attacks and devours it at once; a lioness will often lick and play with her portion and relish it for a long while before eating it. So with me. My letters from the young law student must be relished before as well as after reading.[12]

So still in two minds Kathleen continued to try both to keep Gilbert and to send him away. But Gilbert was far too idealistic to deceive Scott. He hated underhand behaviour and wanted to act 'decently'. The explorer must be told all. Some time on the 25th an arrangement was made for the three of them to discuss the affair the following day, so giving Kathleen a chance to compare the two men in the same room, an event which afterwards prompted another letter from the younger man.

1. T.G.
26 April, 1908.

Dear You, I'm so glad R.S. came up this morning. He's a dear clean thing and, 'cept that he don't see things and never will, 'right'. He could laugh although he was being hurt all the time. You laughed too and I laughed and laughing all together it seems perfectly ridiculous that you can't have both of us since you are so rapacious that the love of the one you love isn't enough for you . . .

It really is gigantically funny that you should give everything and nothing to me, and to him nothing and yet everything. Sheer cussedness because it's you and is part of you. It's like a child when a sixpence and a penny are offered to it choosing the penny because it is comfortably large. Somewhere out of it all we shall get some sort of happiness, and I pray that it may be the best and greatest; and yet how afraid I am of urging you to it, from a fear of seeming a personally minded egoist . . .

... Mine or his—and which the better friend? You'll hurt him – yes. But hurting him, you will not wrong the world. For you can be to him only a thing made of men: else, a singing instrument of God-made forces, lightnings and tides made by the saints, the real lovers ...

But whether Scott was hurt or not the victory appeared to be his.

Dear you are quite wrong, but you can't help the wrongness, [wrote Gilbert in a letter dated 26th, but probably written the following day]. You mustn't leave me. Just the great womanliness I can have, and there are things in me which you need. I wrote another letter to you last night which I will post. There are things in it which may help you—also I enclose a letter from Galsworthy to whom I wrote on Friday night: 'I am crumpled up with a thing which has happened to me.' It will help you too. . . .[13]

But if Kathleen had really hoped that the meeting with Scott would settle matters, she was mistaken. The letters continued to fall on her mat.

Dear light o' the Sun . . . [begins a typical one of two written on the 28th].
   I've been ridiculously happy ever since I left you standing there. I think it is because I know that you know that whatever happens you belong to me, and that no blazing folly that you choose to commit can alter that. . . .

Of which Kathleen Bruce was to write:

Confidently I waved away the young law student so teeming with vitality—confidently for I was certain now that he understood and would accept, only to receive the next morning this upsetting letter . . . and I struggled to mock. But no mockery would come. I wrote to him that he had never been my lover; that he must not let his wild mad imagination fly on and up; that he must calm down his exuberance and face realities; that it was a pedestrian girl who was going to cease to hold his hand. But, with his tall thin form, his crooked smile, his shock of straight, corn-coloured hair, it seemed woefully hard to throw it all away; and his constantly repeated, 'With you I can conquer worlds, without you I shall be nothing', clanged through my mind with a tiresome insistence of conviction. The perfect father for my son is not there, I thought. 'Corn-coloured hair and a crooked smile, maybe, but not the father for my son.'[14]

Gilbert, of course, sensed her hesitation and, more important saw that she was not in love with Scott, a fact she confirmed when, after the birth of her first son, she wrote:

One week later he was born. Very large, very healthy, quite perfect was my boy-baby; and then a strange thing happened to me. I fell for the first time gloriously, passionately, wildly in love with my husband. I did not know I had not been so before.[15]

While Kathleen was making up her mind Gilbert was expanding his social life. Mary Barrie and Lillah McCarthy, Granville-Barker's wife, had noticed his vitality and the charm of 'corn-coloured hair and a crooked smile'.

J lunched with Lillah today [he told Kathleen]. Her fondness for me is a sickening thing: nothing of the child in it at all; and such I shall only have offered to me except by you, always. Have you read the letters of Abelard and Heloise? The world aches with pity for the waste of lovers, great lovers as are you and I. The waste! 'It isn't that I'm thinking of – and grief's no good. It's the waste of a good man. Oh! the waste.' Those are the last words of Harley's play; but he only meant the waste of a politician which doesn't matter much.

On April 30th, Gilbert announced in one of three postscripts at the end of a long letter to Kathleen that Mary Barrie had invited him to go to a Private View with her and he asks 'What does she want of me?', adding that he was not amusing. He decides however to accept, not having been to a Private View before.

But, as well as getting to know people, Gilbert was trying to advance his career and here Granville-Barker had attempted to help. But Shaw, who was backing the Granville-Barker Vedrenne Management financially, had proved a powerful adversary from the beginning. He disliked both Gilbert and his work and on February 7th, 1908 had written testily to Granville-Barker:

Cannan must do better than F and S* if we are to spend all the money on producing it. It is very promising but it is too boyish to offer to grown up people. There are limits even to the encouragement of the young. It is like Kipling's boy imitating his parent.

And later on March 8th when Granville-Barker had obviously made a second attempt:

Let Cannan send in his wretched play. He can write one if he likes – or will grow into it presently.

These letters, possibly shown to Gilbert by Granville-Barker, were to mark the start of an hostility which was to smoulder between the two men until Gilbert's final incarceration.

On April 30th, Gilbert and Kathleen Bruce visited Granville-Barker at his place near Haslemere, arriving in time for lunch. Granville-Barker knew of course something of the affair, which he must have welcomed if it kept Lillah, whom he had married only the previous year, away from Gilbert. One wonders indeed how he felt

* I can find no play with a title appropriate to this abbreviation and assume that it was not performed or preserved.

about her 'sickening' fondness for the struggling playwright. A talented actress, effusive, rather overwhelming but undoubtedly pretty, she appears to have found him an unsatisfactory husband at an early stage. It would be surprising if Granville-Barker had felt no stirrings of jealousy, and when Gilbert's infatuation with Kathleen was dying down it was he who acted first as chaperone in the liaison with Mary Barrie which followed.

Thirty-one years old, handsome, immensely gifted, a man without formal education after fifteen, Granville-Barker was already a figure of some importance in the theatre world, while Gilbert was still groping at the bottom of the ladder. It is possible that the naïve twenty-three-year old saw the older man as an elder-brother figure while Granville-Barker was to some extent only trying to protect his own marital life.

By now Gilbert appears to have accepted for a time, Kathleen as a maternal figure rather than a lover, and to prove it he signed his letters to her 'Your Boy'. But one written from Masefield's, at 20 Maida Hill West where he stayed on the night of May 1st, shows that he had not yet given up hope. Indeed the day spent in the country had only increased his passion.

Grass and your feet, strong, stumpy feet, so strong. Strength that I love in you ... Oh everything I love. Oh! me, mother of me, wife, sister of me, and woman of me. Hair! Sunshine and water and something of the wind— (another quotation). Sweet, my sweet. I have swum for you. You are mine. You are me.

Meanwhile, Mary Barrie was turning an acquaintanceship into friendship. To Gilbert's surprise she seemed to be taking him under her wing. On May 6th he mentioned in a letter to Kathleen that he was going with the famous playwright's wife to see George Meredith.

Oh! Heaven. It is too much. The great man his soaring done and the little young man with wings trembling to the flight.

The Barries, he wrote, had dined with him in the Temple the night before, 'Barrie, the dearest thing in the world.'

While Gilbert continued in pursuit, Scott worried about his own capacity to be a suitable husband for Kathleen and the right father for her son. On January 5th of that year he had expressed doubts that were to continue to trouble him for the next seven or eight months.

I want to marry you very badly, but it is absurd to pretend I can do so without facing a great difficulty and risking a great deal for others as well as myself.

If I was very young I should probably take all risks and probably win through.

I am still young enough to believe we could win through, but in facing poverty we should be living and believing in a better future. The old can only live in the present. My mother is 67—only a strand of life remains. She has had a hard life in many respects. I set myself to make the last years free from anxiety. I can't light-heartedly think of events that may disturb my decision.

Since my return I have always said that worry was to be put aside, and half in joke I added that if I married I would look out that the young lady had lots of money. In the uncertainty of life it is stupid to make promises, and though my mother would freely absolve me I cannot quite forgive myself.

But all this is only what you know, that things are difficult. If you care enough however we can put things right – I am convinced of that; but it can only be if you care enough, and heaven knows when I think of your future I don't want to force you to face a life of poverty.

When you say we are 'horribly different' it perhaps means that you would not now act with caution as I do. But if you really believe and think we are horribly different in all our ideas and thoughts, why of course it would make things impossible. I don't think this a bit; if I did I should not want to marry you. . . .[16]

Later, when Gilbert was still pressing his case, Scott again expressed his doubts in a letter from H.M.S. *Essex* dated May 11th, 1908.

I am sad tonight. It *is* difficult to know what to do, and all the time I am conscious of bringing unhappiness to you—disappointment in me, I think, though your sweet generosity wouldn't admit it. Kathleen, don't let your happiness be troubled. Sometimes when all the obstacles loom large, I wonder for the future; but always, always, I know that to take away that happy smile of yours would be the most dreadful thing in the world. Then fancy mounts for a gallop, and it seems that I have already sorely troubled the serenity of your life, and banished some of the sweetness. Don't let me be a trouble to you.

Yet oh my dear, there is another side of me, born of hereditary instinct of caution, and fostered by the circumstances which have made the struggle for existence an especially hard one for me. Can you understand? I review a past—a real fight—from an almost desperate position to the bare right to live as my fellows. Is is strange that I should hate to look at all the consequences of a fresh struggle? I know, as you will think, that this should be no attitude for the man determined to conquer. But, my dear, what I know, and you do not, is our service with its machine-like accuracy and limitations. It offers place and power, but never a money prize—so that it must be poverty always.

I am a coward to write like this, but it is late and I have been thinking much. You are the only woman to whom I can tell things. I try to tell you and somehow it is comparatively easy. Will you see in the midst of my despondency that I tell you of my sadder thoughts, of the difficulties before us, as well as of the love I feel for you and the longing I have that you should be always near me?

And now goodnight. Give me of your patience.[17]

The fight had been financial ever since Scott's father had lost his money in the family brewery and Scott had felt obliged to contribute to the family's welfare. Now, since his father's death in 1897 and his brother's a year later, Scott had been responsible not only for his mother, but also for a time for two sisters.

But Kathleen Bruce still could not throw Gilbert away. Her diary for the first twelve days of May reads:

May 1st More Granville-Barker, a little G.C!
May 3rd The Boy
May 4th Country with Con
May 12th Boy 7.15

Still she kissed, stroked and loved him as far as her scruples would permit, while at the same time paradoxically trying to break with him. 'Friday and last night! Well then—and then, and then. You will go back on the wonder of it though you ache for it . . .' he wrote in an undated letter in early May.

Then suddenly, the tables were turned, and when he tried to break away, she sought him out. On May 9th he wrote:

When, where and what on Monday afternoon. Of course I will come. . . .

The next rather stilted letter written on the 10th suggests that Kathleen may have at last considered Gilbert more seriously as a prospective father for her son, or perhaps merely pointed out that he was not financially capable of taking on that responsibility. Here his prose shows the influence of legal training and jargon.

Materially, and I am by no means blind to material considerations, the problem wears a different complexion, and it is necessary for me to tell you something of myself. My cousin, more than father indeed in anxiety and hen-like fussiness over my welfare, pays my rent here and allows me £200 a year —(nominally, for the sum is overpassed). That was the arrangement when I was pursuing a legal career. When we were brought face to face with the far-cical nature of that career we arranged that I should as soon as possible break away. I am rolling the log but not at present earning more than about 2d a week . . . Gilbert Murray writing of my work apropos of a remark of mine says, 'If you can get sun and earth into it, that is more cryingly wanted than anything else in the world.' Sun and Earth are just what by some miracle we have touched. It was in you before but not in me. I am not at the beginning of things and no (sic) dear are you. 24 and 28 are not Poles asunder . . .

Two further letters followed on the 11th, and then on the 13th came the first actual proposal of marriage in writing. He had just read Kathleen's notes on her work in the hospital in Macedonia.[18]

There is nothing of you that is not mine. I have read your wonderful notes and felt all that you felt. Your disgust, your joys. Your fears of death and your rejoicing in humanity. Oh! you. Last night I walked home and it was after three when I crawled into my bed. [Then after reiterating his claim that Kathleen belonged to him, he continued:] My blessed—I ask you to marry me. Please do.

The next paragraph suggests that they had decided their position should be discussed with a third person.

I couldn't tell H. G. B. this morning as he was too worried with business and his own affairs: but in the middle of this letter the other 'hope' came up. Lowes Dickinson, who knows all about me. I put the case I think fairly. I told him that your chief concern was with the child, but that you couldn't see it clearly, it was a matter that affected the soul's welfare of both of us— and I told him that you were at present insisting on marrying Con. Well then—he said nothing. But as he was going he said: 'Of course I can't tell really any more than you can, what reason is at the bottom of her but I think she ought to be stopped.'

But by now the unpredictable Kathleen had decided definitely to announce her engagement to Scott and to escape from Gilbert by leaving the country. She would go on a walking tour in Italy, sleeping out like a vagabond. As a protector she took her brother Rosslyn's friend, Hugo Law, son of the Irish Chancellor. A married man with three children, he was recovering from a bout of severe neuritis and went at the suggestion of his wife, Lota—one of the few women Kathleen Bruce found charming and likeable. He took along a guitar slung over his shoulder and played at the inns and in the villages, while his companion sketched those who listened. Accustomed in early youth to the protection of her brothers, Kathleen was entirely happy with this kind of arrangement.

Scott, who appears to have been the least jealous of men, took news of her plans well. His reply was more or less: Write to me often and don't stay too long. 'A grand man', she recorded in her autobiography, 'no suspicions, no querulousness, no recriminations. Perfect man.'

Gilbert reacted badly at first, as much because she had broken a date with him as at the thought of her absence. But his eye was already wandering and in the end he took her absence rather better than either had anticipated. Gradually Mary Barrie was taking Kathleen's place. In one of his five letters to Kathleen during her absence, Gilbert wrote of a visit to the Barries' Black Lake Cottage.

We played croquet, wandered in the woods, which yet were wonderful though wanting you—the precise you. Still there was much of you lingering there under the heron's nests. There were baby herons, and we saw a mother wild duck with two soft brown babies. Everything was young. Oh! good, all of it, good. We motored back to town, H. G. B., Mary Barrie et moi, under the moon, a lantern-hanging moon, so near that one could touch her, so large and warm that one could cry for the kindness of her—and Harley went to sleep!! Oh! hideously practical pose. Well, well. What more. I'm getting on with Macedonia. It is good so much of it and I think clear—there's no grey stuff in it so far and less of the aching me. Trees is (*sic*) wonderful and so is grass, an' so is water, water most of all—there's courage in water. I told Mrs. Barrie Ripley Lake was an acre of courage. She was pleased with that. More than ever she is my friend and she is becoming more real. She likes to be liked—that is all. Likes it so much that she has often missed it— too often. Yesterday she talked to me about babies again. Well, wonder lady —well—well—well. Is it well with you? I am brown.[19]

Kathleen's influence on him had been deep and lasting, as every first real love must be. But now the ideal of a monogamous affair concerned him less than the desire to give pleasure to those who needed him (although this assertion could have been a rationalisation of his own need to satisfy his desires). Yet, in spite of her rejection, he still felt that Kathleen was generous to share him with others. Nothing it seemed would persuade him that she had 'kissed falsely'. Nor did he see their affair as finished or other women as a substitute for her.

Oh! Heavens, what need there is in me for you—you who can share me generously with all who want me. Can I share you? I don't know. Why yes, yes, yes!

A complaint from Kathleen that his letters seemed unreal brought forth on the 28th a long egotistical reply about his writing:

I can't do this journalism. It is pitiful. I cannot write from the point of view of the reader. Soit. There are so many tedious old fools—and yet I love them for being tedious and old. I love everybody . . .

and further on:

Oh! we are so alike. I like you rapacious, devouring—I cannot give myself to one, nor yet can you: but to all who ask—all who need—men, women, children, beasts I must be real, real—Or should I be? . . . Yesterday Lillah and Mrs. Barrie came and had tea—Mrs. Barrie suddenly began to talk to me like a mother. She really is a dear thing, and she seems to need a good deal of me—I feel the need and give—gladly. Can you share me with so many? You have made me grow—Oh! blessed one. Shall you see Isadora's baby in Berlin, a beautiful baby?

But although he was to beg again 'Come back to me soon, I have much need of you', his battle was really lost. And in a letter of June 5th, after her return, it is clear that he has submitted at last to the role of rejected lover.

How silly of us to pretend that we were used to each other! It was very horrid—Possibly your defensive instinct for the baby you want to make is right. To have a volcanic father and an equally volcanic and vagabond mother with about 2d. between them—! But we shall always make dream babies together, and out of your love for me, and my love for you there will be good things in the children that you make without me. You must make Con into a father, for children need fathers as much as mothers . . .

He wrote again calmly on June 25th, his birthday, and the following day. Then in a letter dated June 30th he asked to meet Isadora Duncan.

I must know her—can you bring her here—or me to see her—and will the baby come? And how are you and is my baby statue finished, or must I come to see exactly how crooked the boy's nose is?

It is not clear whether Gilbert's statue was to represent himself as a baby or to be Kathleen Bruce's interpretation of the baby they might have produced had their affair been consummated, or it may be that she described all her pieces of sculpture as her babies. The frequent mention of babies comes oddly from the pen of a young man, but it must be remembered that Barrie, with *Peter Pan*, had dragged children out of the Victorian nursery into the limelight. Meanwhile, they were becoming increasingly a subject for whimsical conversation and adulation in some fashionable circles.

The wedding was not to be until September 2nd. Scott had written on May 25th more optimistically from H.M.S. *Essex* to announce that he had accepted a new appointment, to a first-class battleship, H.M.S. *Bulwark* and would be on the '£832 scale or whatever the sum was we discussed'.[20]

On June 3rd, however, he expressed further doubts in a letter to Kathleen Bruce.

> H.M.S. Bulwark
> Friday night.
> 3.6.08

Do you realise you will have to change me, change me, infuse something of the joyous pure spirit within you? A year or two hence it would have been too late, I should have been too set to admit the principle of change. It is something that I acknowledge my shortcomings! But oh dear what a task you have before you.

All this because you have met Isadora Duncan, and I see you half-worshipful, wholly and beautifully alive, and I love you for it. Here is the antithesis of all that's worldly and conventional. I know this, I say to myself over and over, I love this—but oh the grinding effects of a mechanical existence—in the end I am half fearful. Shall I satisfy you? Keep, oh keep, all you think of the beauty of life—of the wonder of its renewal.[21]

It was not perhaps in Scott's nature to be a joyous and exuberant winner. He had seen too much go wrong in life to believe in or expect complete harmony and happiness.

But now Gilbert was determined to be a good loser, to act 'decently'. On July 24th he wrote his congratulatory letter to Kathleen which she was later to send to James Barrie with a message scrawled in her large hand at the bottom. 'You must love this boy too, because I do. His is one of the very fine natures. Don't destroy the note. I like it.'

Kathleen dear, I don't know the date of your marriage and I'm going to France at the end of next week. I do wish you and Con all the widest and most vivid happiness—and make a splendid, splendid baby—But you will —I know, I know. In the little house I see you next a great woman striding to her purpose. So?

Ever yours, and Con's,

It was over. He had lost. But he was not alone. His defeat had been seen by several of the more worldly people in whom he had confided. There were others ready to hold his hand, to talk of babies if that was what he wanted. Like splendid butterflies the lovely females hovered round him—Mary Barrie, Sylvia Davies, Molly Muir and Lillah McCarthy. For the Manchester boy who had never quite fitted in it was a strange and intensely flattering experience. Never again would he take kisses quite so seriously.

2

'A Rather Odd Party'

Peter Davies

'YOUNG, beautiful, quite charming, a genius for preference, and able to flirt.'[1] Those were the attributes Barrie needed for the girl who was to play the lead in *Walker London*, and through Jerome K. Jerome he had found for this part Mary Ansell, who was also to become his wife.

She had lost her youth when Gilbert met her, but not her charm and for him she became beautiful again. He had been brought up by his parents to admire actors and actresses. Both Violet and Henry Cannan had taken part in amateur dramatics and, when there was money to spare, they had found their greatest joy in the theatre.

They loved *actors* [Gilbert was to write later], and they thought nothing of waiting for hours to squeeze into the pit to see Irving or Alexander or John Hare or Forbes Robertson. They idolised these men and the two saints in my mother's calendar were Charles I and Henry Irving, whose yearly visits to Manchester kept romance alive in her in her cheerful struggle to feed, clothe and educate a family which grew faster than my father's income.[2]

And so for him it was particularly flattering to be taken up by Mary Barrie and, for a young man deeply involved in translating *Jean Christophe* and influenced by the passionate impermanent love-affairs of its eponymous hero there was a chance to gain experience and edge nearer to the maturity he needed both for his work and his own self-respect.

But his family, romantic and unworldly, saw at first only a famous man's wife being kind to a struggling young author. From Margaret Rideout I learned of their reactions and her own first meeting with Mary at Christmas 1908 when Gilbert was staying with the Barries at Leinster Corner before going with them in a party to stay at the Grand Hotel, Caux, which is above Montreux in Switzerland.

Of all Gilbert's brothers and sisters Margaret was the least impetuous and the least frivolous. It was as though, in making her, nature had ignored her parents and gone back two generations to model her on the lines of her great-grandmother, her namesake, the high principled

33

Margaret Kennedy who had stepped down a rung in the social ladder to marry the fiery young minister, Thomas Cannan, son of a tenant farmer.

In Mary Barrie's elegant drawing-room furnished with little regard for expense Margaret was on alien territory. The three people who met her gaze were from another world; Mary, blithe, theatrical, a little fulsome in her welcome to one brought up in the hard-hearted backwaters of Manchester; Barrie with his high, white marble brow crowned with pitch-black hair, his eyes dark in a tense face, his manner shy and diffident; and Gilbert, her long-worshipped brother, surprisingly handsome now, with a new sophistication foreign to his background and yet with the stamp of tragedy already on his countenance.

They gave her tea, Mary talking engagingly, Gilbert pleasant, perhaps a little patronising to this provincial sister. They showed her their Christmas presents, among them a grand dressing-case which was Mary's present to Gilbert. A more worldly woman than Margaret might have wondered, might have looked from the poised radiant ex-actress to the tall Hamlet-like young man with the large blue eyes and fresh complexion, and guessed.

But not Margaret; deeply conformist, she saw this dressing-case, which had obviously cost more than her mother spent on a week's house-keeping, as a mark of the Barries' esteem for her brother's literary talents. They loved him, she thought, as a son. The ugly duckling, who in youth had seen himself as a changeling, was turning into a swan. Knowing nothing of the snobbery and high living which created problems for a young man of the middle class with barely adequate funds, she supposed university had helped, leading him into exciting literary circles where at last his talents would be encouraged. If Margaret now thought about Gilbert's emotional future at all it was to suppose that, like everyone else, he would eventually marry and have a family. Gilbert loved children as well as babies. He played the piano for children, got down on his knees and was a bear; stories of fairy castles, goblins and giants rolled off his tongue as easily as an auctioneer's patter, although with a good deal more colour and imagination. The fact that at home, as a child, Margaret had championed Gilbert against the claims of his tough elder brother, Angus, now afforded her a sense of triumph.

That evening Gilbert took his sister to *Peter Pan*, with the Barries.

Ellen Terry and her young husband were in a box one side of the theatre and the Davies family opposite [she recalled to me in a letter in 1969]. Gilbert took me with him to speak to Ellen Terry who was perfectly sweet and made me sit next to her.[3]

Next day, innocently happy, this somewhat inhibited physical training instructress sped away by train to Oxford bearing good news of her brother to his ex-guardian and adoptive father, their middle-aged cousin, the eminent economist Edwin Cannan.

The party to Switzerland was made up of James and Mary Barrie, Gilbert Cannan and the recently widowed Sylvia Llewelyn Davies with her five sons, whom Barrie had informally adopted. The trip was Barrie's Christmas present to the boys, who had inspired *Peter Pan* and become a focal point in his life, lively and delightful beings on whom he could lavish his affection and share his boyish sense of fun. George, Jack, Peter, Michael and Nicholas, he loved them all with an intensity and possessiveness abnormal in a grown man.

Their mother, the third child of George du Maurier and sister of the distinguished actor, Gerald du Maurier, was for Barrie an archetypal mother-figure even before her marriage to the hapless classicist, Arthur Llewelyn Davies, a barrister with a fine profile and diffident nature, who had died of cancer on April 19th, 1907. Sylvia, the model for Grizel in Barrie's book *Tommy and Grizel*, was a graceful beauty, her charm enhanced by the endearing crookedness of her mouth and a tip-tilted nose which the playwright found a special attraction. Her skin was white, her shoulders wide and splendid; her hair very dark, a fine frame for that pale face which in repose had a noble almost Grecian quality. But perhaps Sylvia's most remarkable feature was her eyes, set wide apart with a serenity which attracted the young, the shy and the hesitant.

Mary Barrie came from humbler beginnings. An uncle was butler to a member of Parliament, her mother kept a boarding house on the South coast. The daughter of George Ansell, a licensed victualler, she had tenaciously made her own way in the theatrical world, first with a touring company in the provinces, then with Norman Forbes's company at the Globe Theatre, before getting her big chance when Barrie offered her a leading part in his play, *Walker London*. In the world of the theatre and literature, social shibboleths were few and Mary had slipped easily into the role of a famous writer's wife. In a number of memoirs and autobiographies covering the period reference will be found to her charm as a hostess. Increasingly, though, Barrie had been absent from her parties. He preferred to see his friends on their own, to retreat from them without giving offence when his mood was for silence. Whereas his wife, an inveterate talker, liked to surround herself with those she found charming and witty, to share if she could some of their vicissitudes. As a former actress, she needed especially a defined role to play in life now that she was no longer on the stage. Although Barrie frequently humiliated her in front of their friends, although he found her conversation irksome and her

35

company unexciting, she continued to play the part of a celebrity's wife.

Mrs. J. Comyns-Carr, who knew Mary soon after she married Barrie, wrote in her *Reminiscences*:

I remember her as a very charming hostess in her pretty home in Hereford Square. Mrs. Barrie had furnished it with all the coquettish arts of an attractive woman. There were comfortable velvet chairs and rosy pink lampshades and flowers everywhere.[4]

The Mary whom Gilbert grew to love had lost some of her coquettishness and discarded pastels for primary colours and white. He saw her as a woman 'worn by flattery, hungering for love'. And, as he had written to Kathleen, he 'gave gladly', for he realised quite soon that Barrie could not satisfy that hunger and was indeed partly the cause of it.

Peter Davies, the third of Sylvia's sons, wrote (in his *Notes* to the collection of his mother's letters) that when Barrie felt attracted to people, he wanted 'at once to own and to be dominated by them'. Mary could dominate, she could manage a man's affairs, choose his houses, plan his gardens, entertain his friends, but ownership there could not be without sexual love. After seven years of empty marriage, shut out from Barrie's confidences, the hoped-for children unconceived, the nuptial bed an embarrassing failure, she moved to a room of her own and sought consolation with more virile men, leaving Barrie to play romantic if platonic court to other women how and when he pleased. These, and the love affairs she mentioned to two of Gilbert's relations, kept her on an even keel and enabled her to play out the charade of her marriage for another seven years after the move to separate rooms.

Now on the eve of this trip to Switzerland, Mary was undoubtedly in love again. She, who could only love 'clever men', had captivated one younger than she had dared to hope for. For Mary as for Kathleen the closed face opened; for a time it seemed that she alone could pierce the reserve and detachment which seemed to imprison him, that soon she could be admitted to that 'cupboard' where he kept 'his cleverness'.[5] Absurdly chivalrous, this enigmatic man now used a tongue which could reveal a remarkable cynicism and bitterness of soul for one so young.

In appearance Gilbert was Barrie's opposite, tall, and slim, likened by Alec Waugh to Siegfried Sassoon.[6] Heads turned when he entered a room, second glances, prompted by that slightly tragic air, followed. He was noticed wherever he went, whereas the tiny pale, Scottish playwright was unremarked upon unless his identity were known.

It had not been long before Mary took the easiest way of developing her friendship with Gilbert by offering to help him with the increasing correspondence connected with the Society for the Abolition of Censorship. Soon some of this went down with them both to Black Lake Cottage, where in the pine woods conditions for the flowering of romantic love were nearly perfect. Suspicions were not at first aroused because it was quite usual at that time for great men to take up the young and promising; many lesser men than Barrie took a special pride in recognising talent and encouraging it. Literary London saw, like the Cannans, that the Barries were being kind to a raw young barrister with fine aspirations, and applauded.

Through the campaign, which was to lead eventually to the formation of the League of Dramatists, Gilbert met most of the leading playwrights and literary figures of the day. One of the most important of these new friends was that kindest of men and literary critics, Edward Garnett. Born in 1868, the second son of Richard Garnett, Keeper of Printed Books at the British Museum, Edward Garnett helped and encouraged many young writers. Most of Garnett's working life was spent in the employment of Gerald Duckworth and later Jonathan Cape; he also reviewed novels for *The Speaker* and *The Nation*. In his biographical note on his father in Edward Garnett's *Conrad's Prefaces* (1937), David Garnett writes:

Having discovered an author and got his first book published, Edward felt it his job to cajole and persuade him to persevere and to develop his talent. Usually tolerant of vanity and egotism, he treated young authors as the ideal producer has to treat theatrical stars.[7]

Frank Swinnerton has described Garnett as a 'big, purblind, shaggy-haired, baggy-tweed trousered man, whose overcoat pockets seemed to have been made like Swiss Father Robinson's, a giant size'.[8] These pockets were full of manuscripts. Garnett could criticise without offending because behind that criticism could be sensed the burning enthusiasm untempered by personal jealousy or egotism which made him so impelling and excellent a champion and reviewer. His own plays and books include *Friday Nights, Literary Criticisms and Appreciations* and a three-act play called *The Feud*. His wife was the distinguished translator of Chekhov, Turgenev and Dostoyevsky.

Gilbert's letter to Edward Garnett on the forming of a Dramatists' Society quickly led to friendship. A correspondence between these two men of very different temperaments followed, a little of which has survived. With Kathleen at last slipping into the background, on July 21st, 1908 Gilbert had written from Temple Gardens:

My dear Garnett,

Many thanks for the nice things you say about the Clara play. Lapage has returned it to me and I send it to you herewith.

I began a short story about a little slavey the other day which grew and grew until it is now a portentious length and nowhere near the end. I am afraid I can't come next Friday and the end of the following week I go abroad for a month to get away from things and people and myself, but I will come and fish you out to lunch on Thursday if that suits.

I have heard nothing yet from Heinemann.

Gilbert returned from France to more financial and literary problems, and disappointment, as we see in his next letter (September 7th, 1908) to the long-suffering and good-natured Edward Garnett.

I saw Heinemann yesterday. He didn't give me much encouragement but has kept the stories and will try to make various editors take them. It's a nuisance as I wanted to get something done so as no longer to be working in the dark. Things have taken a serious turn with me, as my silly family's affairs have gone bust and I must earn money.

Gilbert's father, Henry Angus Cannan had been retired in his early forties on a pension of £120 a year. On this he had to support his wife and the four younger Cannan children who were still at home. Having no other source of income, he relied on legacies to keep his household going. When these did not materialise as expected, or relations were tactless enough to live longer than anticipated, he ran into financial difficulties, and usually moved house. In September 1908 the Cannans decided to rent a pleasant stucco house, 68 Cecil Street, in Moss Side, Manchester, probably having found it difficult to keep up payments of rent at their previous home. (Once the family moved into a house which, unknown to them, had been a brothel, and much embarrassment was caused to them by male callers.) When financial crisis threatened, Angus, now working for a large shipping firm in Kowloon, normally came to the rescue, generously sending money to his parents. This time Gilbert must have been called upon to contribute and, in spite of Edwin Cannan's generosity, found himself in no position to do so.

The family's difficulties were just another complication in that emotionally exhausting summer. But in those days literary London was quick to rush to the aid of talented young men and such a cry from the heart would not go unanswered. It may well be that the subsequent commission to translate Heinrich Heine's *Memoirs* came Gilbert's way through the Garnetts as a consequence of his perilous financial position as well as on account of his talent as a translator.

Mary and her friends continued to find him good company and it appears that he was now often invited to stay at Blake Lake Cottage, where the women flattered him with their attentions and advice. Set in pinewoods deep in the countryside, the cottage provided Mary with an idyllic escape from the gossip and wear and tear of London. Barrie brought down many friends, among them A. E. W. Mason, Arthur Quiller-Couch, Maurice Hewlett and of course, Sylvia Davies.

Barrie had now begun a fresh flirtation, this time with Millicent, Duchess of Sutherland. On September 17th Barrie wrote somewhat archly to his new friend:

Dear Duchess,
I like you for writing about the play—also for other reasons—and I hope you will write something soon, as you enjoy writing, but if I were you I wouldn't bother writing, there is something else you are good at, I won't say what it is, but it's What Every Man Knows.[9]

In September, Gilbert was putting the finishing touches to his first novel, *Peter Homunculus*, which went to Heinemann for consideration. Frank Swinnerton has described this book as an autobiographical, and, although not consistently so, it is as important a work in considering the Barrie-Cannan triangle as Gilbert's novel *Mendel* is in any study of the life of the artist Mark Gertler. The main characters are jerkily presented like puppets on a stage. Mary Barrie is called Mary Dugdale; Gilbert, with some of the writer E. V. Lucas's background, is the hero, Peter Davies. James Barrie possesses an E. V. Lucas terrier and is called Murray Wilson. Sylvia Davies is Cynthia Basset-Crewe, with three children, Hob, Patch and Jane. In addition Mary Barrie's cat, Peter Cat, plays a part and is known as 'Peter with the Orange Eyes'.

The inclusion of facets of E. V. Lucas is interesting, for Gilbert was to claim later that Lucas had been one of Mary Barrie's lovers. Editor, publisher's reader, novelist, essayist and author of a number of travel books, E. V. Lucas had started life poor, had been apprenticed to a bookseller in Brighton, where he worked until he was left £200, with which he had paid for his education at King's College, London.

In some ways E. V. Lucas must have resembled the man Barrie would have liked to have been: virile, lively and at times extrovert, but inside Lucas was complicated too, trailed forever by an unconventional and strange childhood; a womaniser who never found contentment. Barrie writes of Lucas in a letter to Sir Arthur Quiller-Couch, dated January 6th, 1906:

I am going on Monday with E. V. Lucas (one of the few men I see much of) to Coventry to Mason's election. He is loved all over the place and gets wound up by big meetings to great effect. I have been reading a bit of his next novel. His heroines (Mrs. Couch will be interested at last) are always drawn from the lady he is then in love with and by the time I see the proofs it is always off, but he keeps her in and roars his great laugh when attention is drawn to the circumstances.[10]

Lucas was also in the habit of 'keeping every conceivable company' and may have been used by Gilbert partly as a model for Bertram Bond, Mary Dugdale's first husband, in *Peter Homunculus*. Both Lucas and his wife, Elisabeth, remained good friends with Barrie throughout his life.

The first draft of *Peter Homunculus* was probably finished before Mary and Gilbert became lovers in November 1908. In the story Peter Davies retires when Mary Dugdale decides to marry the other man, the silent pipe-smoking Murray Wilson, who suddenly discovers his virility. It is a young man's book, clumsily constructed, lacking in craftsmanship and erratically written. The precociousness ascribed to it by one reviewer is probably a comment inspired by the sudden and true flashes of insight into human nature and its predicaments, the underlying cynicism and literary observations based on the wide and cosmopolitan reading of its author. Seen in these terms it was a fine achievement for a young man of twenty-three or four, but gives some indication of Gilbert's emotional immaturity at that time. He might smile with worldly condescension at his provincial hero's perplexities and romantic entanglements, but he could give no remedies, putting much down to 'growing pains'. The whole story, flirting with reality, seems to suggest that Gilbert never lost himself in his love for Mary Barrie and it is perhaps significant that he never used his affair with Kathleen as material for a novel.

There has been no explanation for Gilbert's decision to name his hero in *Peter Homunculus* after Sylvia Davies' third son (another character is called Scott); possibly he saw the choice as a form of dedication to the most literary of the Davies boys. More likely it was a wilful quirk intended to tantalise, for in other novels, too, he mischievously played around with the names of friends and relations, sometimes causing offence, at least in his own family. Peter of the story has a large nose, loose mouth, literary aspirations and, like Gilbert, an aptitude for writing tolerable verse to those with whom he fancied himself in love. Before going to London University he works for a bookseller[11] who leaves, on dying, a manuscript about a girl called Clara which Peter tries to place with a publisher. Gradually, Peter moves up the social scale and finds himself on the country-house-party circuit, staying in the same house as Mary Dugdale. Peter's weaknesses are Gilbert's weaknesses exaggerated. Poseur and phrase-maker, he is malleable in the hands of Cynthia and Mary, two perceptive and sophisticated women ready to exploit his egoism and treat him tenderly.

In the novel there is no explanation for Cynthia's sympathy with these lovers who were crossing the barrier of a generation. But for Sylvia Davies, frequently in Barrie's company, widowed and short of money, the affair between Gilbert and Mary offered possibilities of a more formal and financially helpful association with the inhibited playwright. Ambitious for her sons, unaccustomed to making small tedious economies, and harbouring within herself the seeds of a fatal disease, she was very vulnerable. Her own relations showed little inclination to help; her husband's were not in a position to do so; the future was frightening and uncertain. She could not have been blamed if, knowing Mary's frustration and temperament, she had hoped that a breakup of the Barrie marriage might ease her own difficulties.

Many years later Gilbert alleged that Sylvia encouraged and abetted his affair with Mary Barrie, making it easy for them to meet and see each other unknown to Barrie. She was a woman of great diplomacy and charm in whom one suspects it was easy to believe. For some years she had trodden a perilous path keeping both her husband's love and devotion, and Barrie's romantic adoration. If Gilbert's allegation is true, one could argue that there was wisdom as well as expediency in her actions, that for a time everyone involved gained from the affair. For a jaded, neglected wife the love of a young man hardly more than half her age can be the finest tonic in the world.

In considering the relationship between his mother and Mary Barrie, Peter Davies commented:

I don't know what the relations were between her and Mary Barrie, whether they loathed each other, were bored by each other, got on quite well together, tolerated each other or what. That she must have had many thoughts about the whole affair and about the possible effects on her own and our future goes without saying.[12]

Bearing in mind that Gilbert was capable of remembering conversations verbatim and incorporating them in his novels, perhaps we may find a clue in this extract from *Peter Homunculus*, when the gauche but charming Peter, bewildered by the strength of his feelings for Mary Dugdale, asks of Sylvia Basset-Crewe:

'How old is Mary?'
She, startled into truth, said 'Thirty-one'.
Peter, at his most whimsical, rejoined: 'She is not old enough to be my mother.'
He waited still for comment.
All she said was, as she stroked his head—he was sitting at her feet—'There is no practical issue to discuss. It is time for bed.'
'If only', said Peter, 'I had a mother like you.'
'If only,' she said, 'Hob may grow a little like you.'
As Peter reached the door, she said: 'Mr. Wilson is forty-four.'
The remark filled Peter with dismay. Passing the door of Miss Dugdale's

room, he saw that she was not yet asleep, and he had an insane desire to call to her: 'Mr. Wilson is forty-four.' He controlled the impulse and as he passed along the corridor to his own little room, he thought 'He is forty-four, just twice my age. That he will never be again.' This reflection struck him as enormously clever and he chuckled.

The age differences of those two in the book's triangle are interesting. Gilbert was twenty-three or four when writing *Peter Homunculus*. Barrie must have been forty-seven or eight. Mary's exact age is in doubt, no birth certificate having been found for her, but according to Janet Dunbar in her book, *J. M. Barrie, The Man behind the Image*, she would have been forty-three or four in 1908. However, she gave her age as forty-one on her second marriage certificate in 1910, and her obituary notice in *Who's Who in the Theatre* states that she was eighty-three when she died in 1950, which would make her forty-one or two in 1908.

In the novel the age difference is a recurring problem; it nags at the back of the lovers' minds like the thought of an overdraft to somebody about to buy something expensive. There is also the unhealed wound of Mary's childlessness. For her time is running out; soon she will be too old to conceive.

Here are the novel's lovers in Kensington Gardens, a place of enchantment to Mary Barrie.

Behind them a boy and a girl lay in the grass reading.

'We have invaded their Eden, Peter.'

The intrusion was soon forgotten. There were childish caresses and embraces.

'You, too, are young,' she sighed.

'I am remarkably old,' he said.

'And wonderfully young.'

'Old,' he said, and to show his knowledge and the depth of his thoughts he recited what he could remember of the story of the King's son, and his quest for the purple sorrow. Here in the sun, and with this kind of splendid lady, the story took life again and seemed a fine thing. Of the recurrent phrase she said:

'Why purple? Surely grey.'

'Grey,' said Peter. 'Grey as the sorrow of the childless woman.'

Mary Dugdale's reaction to this reference to childlessness is immediate and baffling to the unthinking Peter. She lowers her sunshade, turns her face away to hide the hurt which she knows he will detect in the expression of her eyes. Peter chatters on until at last he notices that she no longer listens: then, with the supreme egotism of youth, he, too, is hurt.

The Mary of the book is, in Kensington Gardens, 'a brave solitary little figure in blue, a gallant blue feather in her hat, her parasol of scarlet—a flaming, flaunting woman'. But she is not without conscience.

A love-affair with an experienced middle-aged woman can be a liberation for a serious young man, especially when he has suffered a previous rejection, if eventually it can be allowed to die a natural death. It can teach him so much in the art of living and loving. A once solitary child in a large family, Gilbert as we have seen needed perhaps above all in 1908 the love and sympathy of a mature and compassionate woman. Yet deeply embedded in the Edwardian state of mind was a distrust of 'cradle-snatchers' and the Mary in the story is full of doubts. Reluctantly Mary Dugdale runs away from it all to struggle with her conscience.

If the love between Gilbert and Mary Barrie dawdled during the long summer, it came to life as autumn approached with a new intensity. For Gilbert it was a time of growth in several directions. The translation of *Jean Christophe* commissioned by Heinemann was a challenge he enjoyed. It was indeed high recognition for so young a man to be entrusted with the translation of a long and brilliant work by a future Nobel Prize-winner.

In the Foreword to the American edition, Gilbert wrote:

I was twenty-three when I began translating Jean Christophe. I was twenty-seven when I finished it, so that my growing years were fortunately for me illuminated by the closest possible contact with a masterpiece with the result that already in 1910 I began to write and indeed to live as though I were living in 1920. Romain Rolland was probably doing that in 1900...

Another author who influenced Gilbert deeply at this time was Stendhal, just then the subject of much debate and discussion among the literary young. The similarity of his situation with that of Julian the provincial tutor in *The Scarlet and the Black* did not escape him and probably added a certain *cachet* to his love affair with Mary Barrie. His attitude to women became increasingly continental rather than British. His reading encouraged the romantic notions of chivalry which had been so much a part of his early youth. He felt no disloyalty towards Barrie in loving Mary, for the playwright clearly did not want her, and without love she would fade as a flower with neither sun nor water.

Peter Homunculus was finished. The hero had crept away from his Mary after seeing her with Murray Wilson and hearing the venerated author cry out as if in pain.

'Aye, you can laugh and you can laugh...'
And Mary laughed the more. Furiously Wilson turned on her.
'I'm just a man like the rest...'

Mary laughed no more.

'Oh Buntie . . . does it hurt?'

'No,' said Wilson, a sort of flinging triumph in his voice.

'No, no—but I'm so glad of it.'

They laughed together, and Peter hugging Herbertson (his dog) yet tighter, clutching his muzzle, stole downstairs and out into the street . . .'

In real life any retreat by Mary's young lover was temporary and brought only a need for greater intimacy. Early autumn mists lay on the Thames. His rooms needed redecorating. Mary with her passion for interior decoration longed to lighten them with white paint. He could come, she said, to Black Lake Cottage while the work was done. She would arrange for female friends to accompany them as chaperones. Barrie would remain in London. It was all quite simple, an open invitation, and Gilbert would return to find his flat transformed.

It was November, a time for wood fires, cosy chats around the hearth, the early drawing of curtains against the cold. It was very quiet down there at the cottage where the Tilford road wound its wooded way through the misty valley. The leaves had fallen; the pines and firs stood unchallenged against the winter sky, jagged and dark. The gardener was busy clearing up; the evergreens paled and lost their gloss, the lawn yellowed. It was a novel situation for Gilbert, isolated in the large black and white cottage on the edge of the woods with two or three women, a far cry from his many different homes in Manchester and from living with Uncle Edwin, in rooms above the coal merchants' office in St. Giles, Oxford. The female friends were probably chosen because they were sympathetic to the lovers, but at first it seems that Gilbert did not intend to be seen going in and out of Mary's room by the door; that would indeed be too mundane and expected for one who believed himself different from other men.

Gilbert, influenced surely by Stendhal, chose to go to Mary by ladder, crawling over the window sill, after dark, an action perhaps typical of his literary and continental approach to love. Sex for him was not to be a 'farmyard' matter. It was to be shrouded and enhanced by all the romance he could muster and arrange. He had seen so much of the other kind in the yards and courts of the poorer parts of Manchester. Sex, he believed, should give 'love, liberty, truth, tenderness, warmth, kindness, honesty, chivalry, all the manly and womanly virtues'. It was a tall order, but he later claimed that such was the sex he was fortunate enough to know.[13]

But although Gilbert's idealism was fervent, that practical turn of mind, known as common sense, was never one of his strong points. The ladder might save him from discovery by indoor staff and other guests, but, leaning up against the wall, it told its own story to those who rose at light of day to work in Mary's cherished garden. One morning, Gilbert must have left Mary after dawn for he found the ladder gone. The gardener, Mary told Sir Compton Mackenzie years later, had taken it. The gardener bided his time; he held a weapon which would keep until an appropriate occasion; he knew and soon the other servants knew, but they all remained loyal to Mary for the time being. It was doubtless a little chilling for the lovers, but no more, for their attitude to the sanctity of marriage was growing increasingly unconventional.

Outwardly Gilbert kept his head. If anything he worked even harder. In November Herbert Trench bought his one-act play *James & John*. This was a big stride forward, although it was not to be staged for many months. The greatness which, in moods of optimism, Gilbert expected one day to grace his name seemed to inch nearer. A tiny thread of thought which whispered 'genius' challenged the alternative voice, the voice of his mannikin which said, 'Tiny man!' and 'Grow big!' Work was becoming an addiction from which he would never escape. Words flowed from his pencil on to the paper; short stories, plays, articles and the translations of *Jean Christophe* and Heinrich Heine's *Memoirs*. Like all addictions its hold was to tighten, until at last it turned into a destructive rather than a creative force. But now it bore him on a gentle wave towards a golden shore.

By this time the attractions of Kathleen had definitely slipped into the background. An invitation to dine with her on December 11th had been coolly declined by Gilbert:

There is a dear man, who has been having a dreadful time with his babies, coming to be cheered up during the weekend [he wrote, by way of excuse]. I go to Oxford on Tuesday for a day or two and on the 24th to Switzerland for three weeks.

Scott was away serving on H.M.S *Bulwark*, with Kathleen's statuette of Gilbert on his cabin table. It is not clear whether she had given him this or whether he had chosen to take it as a distinguished example of her work, one of her babies. A letter from his ship dated December 8th, shows that he had not at first been aware of the identity of the sitter.

I am a slow thinker—what news for you! It's an increasing joy to have your work before my eyes. There's something so astonishingly fine about your work, such truth and vigour, that you must go on . . .

Strange, isn't it? that I never really guessed the close likeness of your man—it's wonderfully true in spirit and now to me each touch is significant. But the man oughtn't to be going to tea parties if he's *that*.[14]

Switzerland was also mentioned in Gilbert's letter to Garnett of December 16th, from the Temple.

Very many thanks. You are very loyal to those same short stories which are in possession of the 'orrible Pinker.[15] I have written to him to tell him to send them to you. I hope something will happen. I'm lost in a new novel[16] which I am going to take to Switzerland next week.

Writing of the Swiss holiday, Peter Davies comments:

The boys all enjoyed themselves hugely . . . I remember 'luge-ing' and ski-ing in a clumsy but exhilarating fashion; I remember a pair of very high yellow brown lacing boots of Mary B's which somehow impressed me. It must have been a queer quartet of adults who conversed together after the boys had gone to bed.[17]

Barrie, who was quite capable of carrying on two flirtations at once, wrote to the Duchess of Sutherland on January 9th:

This world is given over the Lugeing (*sic*). I don't know if you have a luge, you have everything else. It's a little toboggan and they glide down on it for ever and ever. And evidently man needs little here below except his little luge. Age annihilated. We are simply ants with luges. I say we, but by great good luck I hurt myself at once and so am debarred. We are returning in two or three days and I hope you are to be back and that I am to see you soon and explain you to yourself.[18]

It seems that the company of no one beautiful woman could satisfy Barrie, that he must always be looking forward to seeing another. Rebecca West wrote to me in 1972 that Mary had been 'unbelievably pretty, really exquisite', and Audrey Lucas, daughter of E. V. Lucas, has left us in her memoirs a passage in praise of Sylvia Davies' looks:

Beautiful as a word for Sylvia Davies is all but miserly, yet what other word is there? Hers was a beauty so arresting and so rare that even now, as one exhibits some old photograph album, there is no need to apologise, to say of her 'she was considered lovely then, but, of course, clothes were so un-becoming . . .'[19]

But Barrie was caught for ever in that vacuum between adolescence and manhood. He could love his idea of the woman to whom he was attracted, romanticise them, worship them, amuse them, flatter and flirt with them, but their bodies, or their true, imperfect, vulnerable selves, he could not fully love. Perhaps it was this inadequacy that prevented him from suspecting the truth about Mary and the men she loved, that made him quite happy to invite Gilbert to amuse Mary while he played at courtship with the lovely and perceptive Sylvia.

Denis Mackail's views, expressed in his book *The Story of J.M.B.*, were probably shared by others who knew the distinguished quartet.

A rather odd party in a way, though. Almost three generations in a sense. The Barries and Sylvia all in their forties; the boys ranging from five to fifteen, and Cannan only twenty-four. One sees who Sylvia's chief companion would be and who would be left over among the grown-ups. Yet Cannan not only had an intense admiration for the host's genius and attainments, but was extremely popular with the boys; he told stories, too, and perhaps—for he was brilliant and keen enough—he would follow in other footsteps as well.[20]

In Switzerland Sylvia Davies was taken ill, her alarming symptoms the first obvious signs of the cancer which was to lead her to an early death. There were desperate moments when she could not get her breath, but Gilbert has left us no comments on this episode. As far as I know, the holiday features in none of his work; perhaps he lost himself at last in the deep snow and the biting air tearing down the slopes on one of those little toboggans. Maybe he was briefly no longer a spectator of his own pleasures, but wholly involved in his love for Mary. With Barrie debarred by his injury, Sylvia ill and weak, the way was left clear for Gilbert and Mary with only the unperceptive children to witness the signs of a liaison.

Many people were later to question whether Barrie suspected the truth about his wife and the young man who appeared to be so talented. His book *Tommy and Grizel* shows how well he understood his own predicament. Perhaps the answer lies partly in a Rectorial Address, called *Courage*, which he gave late in life at St. Andrew's University, in which he suggested that future generations would criticise his generation believing that their:

. . . avoidance of frankness in life and the arts is often (but not as often as you think) a cowardly way of shirking unpalatable truths.[21]

3

'The Only Person in the World for Me'
Mary Barrie

AFTER the Swiss holiday the love-affair continued, while Barrie worried about Sylvia's health, lamented that he could not see more of the boys ('I feel they are growing up without my looking on and I grudge any blank day without them'),[1] and considered whether or not to write a biography of his old friend, George Meredith. He also continued to work, with Gilbert's secretarial assistance, for the abolition of censorship and the formation of a club for dramatists, of which Sir Arthur Pinero became the first President.

Meanwhile, when not working for Barrie, Gilbert was covering hundreds of sheets of small, thin paper in his well-formed hand with stories, plays, essays, and articles, writing with the speed and dedication of a missionary who suspects his life may be cut short, still disturbed by a sense of not being as other men, a legacy from childhood, he thought, perhaps even from his moment of birth.

There are times indeed when I doubt whether I succeeded completely in being born, so insistent has my instinct been on holding aloof from that particular part of the world in which I made my appearance. When I was a child this used to make me weep for days together, and I could never explain what was the matter, nor could the doctor.

I was very early aware of being detached from my family and used to imagine that I was born in some peculiar way and was some kind of changeling, ideas from which I suffered the greatest remorse, but they remained with me nevertheless.

Life did many strange things and I knew very early that life was heading for disaster, though I could not have told a soul what I knew or why I knew it. The knowledge was there.

My grandmothers shook their heads over me; and my great aunt, gazing ominously at the bumps in my forehead, mentioned something about water on the brain.[2]

So Gilbert wrote of himself perhaps exaggeratedly, certainly despairingly, some ten years later. And his father, the passionate yet weakwilled Henry Cannan, did nothing to dispel his second son's particular anxiety, as these verses written by the father for his awkward, perplexing child's thirteenth birthday clearly show:

> *We join this twenty-fifth of June*
> *In birthday wish sincerest*
> *To Gil! Our family buffoon*
> *Of all boys he's the queerest.*
>
> *Long may his ox eyes on us beam*
> *Though we grow old and grey*
> *But still with strawberries and cream*
> *Share we his Festal Day.*[3]

Gilbert had his own comment on this.

Not to be what is expected is difficult especially in a large family and I solved the problem, raised by my refusing to be a boy, by being a buffoon. That was a relief, provided by the theatre to which my mother took me to see John Hare in *Caste*.[4]

Now in early Summer 1909, his first novel just published, his first play, *Dull Monotony*, a satire in two acts, under consideration by the Stage Society, Gilbert still sought advice from the ever-patient Edward Garnett, and, no doubt, moral support from Mary, whose happiness in her new-found love was becoming apparent to many of her friends. At this time much of Gilbert's writing was being returned by publishers, editors and theatrical managers. The reviews of *Peter Homunculus* were not as encouraging as he had hoped, although some critics, sniffing around for new talent, scented future possibilities in his work. The anonymous reviewer in *The Times Literary Supplement* of May 13th concluded, after giving a précis of the novel:

There is plenty of matter and good matter in the book; yet hardly a scene or character among the diverse marionettes really moves us and we are weary of Mr. Cannan's jerky dialogue. Nor is there any end to the story worth speaking of, save that Mary, the actress, marries the other fellow.

Some undated letters addressed to Garnett from Temple Gardens give further indications of Gilbert's struggle to become firmly established as an author. He writes here of several unpublished stories:

If you can bully some publisher into issuing them I should be grateful as I think I had better have some sort of status, however small. I have one or two other stories lying about somewhere, and have already sketched out one or two more as a result of reading those I sent you. Will you therefore hang on to them?

And on another occasion:

My dear Garnett, I'm glad you like 'Birth'—I want to put it first and call the volume by its name. Sorry Duckworth is of little faith. If necessary we must bribe a publisher, but I hope it won't be . . .

And in a brief, telling note:

Enclosed received from Chapman. Shall 'ere (*sic*) try Elkin Mathews.[5]

One of Gilbert's virtues at this stage was his ability to take criticism of his work gracefully. Indeed, he improved both his dialogue and his characterisation after the publication of *Peter Homunculus* and we do not find such jerkiness and sloppiness of construction in later novels. The following letter to Garnett is further evidence of this humbleness unsuspected by those of his contemporaries who found him supercilious and aloof.

Many thanks for the 'Feud'. I am sorry you had expected more from Peter than you find in it, but I am looking forward to your criticism and wish I had had it before I began the new novel which is now nearly finished.

I hope you will come to see my 'Dull Monotony' and that I will see you before Shaw shoots me because of it.

There don't seem to be any masters worth going to just now.

Dull Monotony was eventually put on by the Stage Society as a special performance at the Hotel Cecil.[6] The play was never published and I have been unable to trace a copy or to discover who the cast were. It seems likely that it contained a portrait of Shaw, or that it caricatured his work in some way. Shaw's portrait of Gilbert, as the supercilious dramatic critic in *Fanny's First Play*, may have been his revenge. Still antagonistic towards Gilbert, Shaw made clear that he opposed the production of *Dull Monotony* in a letter he wrote on March 21st, 1910, to Sir Arthur Pinero:

I speak feelingly for I have superseded you of late as the whipping boy of the youthful educator of the public in the higher drama. Hankin swore by me and went for you. Arnold Bennett went for you but did not exactly swear by me. But now the still younger generation knocking at the door knocks on my nose. Gilbert Cannan who when he first heard that I opposed the performance of his first play (*Dull Monotony*, 1909) by the Stage Society, exclaimed 'Christ betraying Judas!'[7]

Meanwhile there were many house parties at Black Lake Cottage. A. E. W. Mason, Quiller-Couch (to whose daughter, Foy, Barrie was Godfather), Maurice Hewlett and E. V. Lucas were among the guests. Mary, vivaciously in love, was a lively hostess, and if her perfectionism irritated the servants they were not to be cowed, for in their hands they still held the trump card. They had only to summon the courage to speak to their silent, inscrutable master and she was ditched.

The rhododendrons sprang into life with summer, the great trees shaded the sloping lawn. Peaty paths, dark as chocolate, led away through the pines and fern into the woods. This place found and leased by Mary had become her little heaven from which she could hardly drag herself away. Gardening had become a passion, each shrub and tree a friend, each plant a separate being to be cherished. She grew as knowledgeable as the gardener who was employed by Barrie, and more particular, and this in the end was her undoing. Had she not cared so much about the garden, common sense might have caused her to hesitate before criticising the work of the man who had removed the ladder and knew of her adultery. But Mary had grown hot-headed, over-confident and, perhaps, a little domineering towards her servants and they, with all the snobbery of the English servant, class, were not likely to kow-tow to an ex-actress of humble origins, and an adulteress to boot.

Resentful, smarting from rebuke, spurred into action at last, the gardener chose to speak of her treachery at a moment when Barrie was alone at the cottage and Mary in London. Barrie immediately tele-graphed Mary to say that he was returning. His chauffeur drove him swiftly to Leinster Corner. White-faced, hurt and bewildered, he faced his wife who appears to have remained poised and confident, glad to admit to a fact which had enlivened her whole life, glad to bring it out into the daylight.

Barrie had been brought face to face with an unpalatable truth from which there was no retreat. His attempt to make a lasting and happy marriage with a dashing young woman was to be exposed as the folly he had long ago suspected it would be. All the early fears of his youth, his terrible sense of inadequacy, must have seemed all at once to be justified. Now that he was about to lose Mary she suddenly became more important to him and, with all the contrariness of human nature, he seemed to want to win her back. He offered terms: if she would give up Gilbert, promise never to see him again, he would forgive her all. But Mary wanted no return to the old claustrophobic life. The man she had once admired so much had become a pathetic and vulnerable human being, his greatness the product of a twisted personality. She was actually sorry for him. And now that she had captured the love of a younger, more virile, genius, a man she supposed she would bring also to greatness, her path was clear. She would marry Gilbert and perhaps even produce a child, a baby to nurse, as the Mary in *Peter Homunculus* had nursed for a brief moment the charcoal burner's infant in the pine woods. Her self-confidence grew into a determined force that bore the lost, vacillating men along. She alone knew exactly what she wanted, a fairy-tale ending which could have no place in reality.

Barrie, desperate at the thought of the law's cold light illuminating his private life, took Mary to see his friend and solicitor, Sir George Lewis, in the hope that perhaps this fashionable and persuasive man could induce her to change her mind. But no warnings of scandal, ostracism or future unhappiness caused by disparity of age, would make her think again. She was adamant and that strain of recklessness which shows so clearly in early photographs of her, ensured that she ignored the warnings. Such decisiveness must have seemed to Barrie to put the seal of truth on many of his innermost fears. In youth he had found it hard to see himself as a married man, had loved himself too little to suppose that he could be lovable to others, knowing too well that in his mother's heart he had been second until his adored, elder brother died. Only success and wealth had gradually led him to believe that he might marry happily after all, for if his manliness fell short, his wealth and fame could compensate.

His meagre figure had been one factor in his lack of confidence and self-appreciation, as mentioned in his autobiographical description of a Scot of twenty-seven coming to London to seek his fortune (in *The Greenwood Hat*). 'Ladies have decided that he is of no account, and he already knows this and has private anguish thereanent.'[8] Physically he could not expect to compete with Gilbert. Indeed Barrie had nothing to offer but his wealth, his wit, the shadow of his fame and the art of his flattery. Yet pathetically he continued to try, turning to all the romantic, tender and affectionate attentions a nearly impotent or otherwise abnormal man has to offer his wife, which can sometimes be enough.

Conferences were held at which Gilbert, according to Denis Mackail, 'made strange proposals of his own',[9] which were ignored by Barrie, who, encouraged by Lady Lewis, wanted Gilbert to leave the scene immediately, to be cut by Mary from her life forever, or face divorce and all the scandal of being the co-respondent. And Gilbert's cynicism now quarrelled with his romanticism, his British sense of honour with his continental approach to love and sex. In addition, an innate kindness towards women made it impossible for him to leave so devoted a lover in the lurch. Refused the possibility of sharing this woman and thereby playing a bizarre role and blazing the path of Free Love, he took the old-fashioned part of knight-errant and agreed to a marriage he did not really want.

He bowed to all Mary's wishes and left London for Wellington Square, Oxford, where Edwin Cannan now lived with the cousin he had married in 1907, and their small son, David. Gilbert's sister Margaret, a fellow guest in that gloomy house, was the first Cannan to hear of Gilbert's entanglement, an experience she described to me in a letter.

When we met at Edwin Cannan's in the summer of—would it be 1908 or 9?—he asked me to go for a walk and we went off and then he told me. He was in a state of misery and exaltation and told me that Barrie was applying for a divorce. I was astonished. 'But she is old enough to be your mother,' I said. And then he told me that Barrie was not normal and that Mary had always wanted children, and was most unhappy in spite of all the wealth. He seemed to feel that he could give her happiness, even a child perhaps. He did not seem to think about money or anything.

I said 'You will have to tell Edwin. It will be dreadful for him.'

'Yes,' he said. 'That's what I came down for.' I couldn't believe that he would have dreamt of making love to anyone so old, almost old enough to be his mother.

After dinner I went to bed, saying that I was tired, and the next day Gilbert had gone and Edwin asked me if I knew about this and I said 'Yes, he told me when we went for that walk. Will Barrie really divorce her?' and Edwin said, 'I hope not. I shall go and see him. It will be the ruin of Gilbert, these damned theatrical people!' But it went on. Barrie wanted her away. He must have known it would wreck Gilbert's life.

It was not perhaps so dreadful for the little economist who went to see Barrie, as Margaret had anticipated. Life had made Edwin a stoic. His father, David Cannan, dogged by fate as any Hardy character, seemed to attract tragedy and by the time Edwin reached Balliol, he had already lost the four people nearest to him; mother, stepmother, father and his Aunt Agnes who had cared for him until her death when he was three. There had remained, however, his elder brother, Charles, Dean of Trinity, Oxford, later to become Secretary to the Delegates of the Clarendon Press, and his Aunt Margaret (whom after her death Gilbert was to replace temporarily), one of three daughters of the manse, a thrifty Presbyterian who tended Edwin with the obsessional care of a lonely woman for an only son. There was no laughter in Aunt Margaret's life, no sudden flashes of merriment to lighten the gloom of the rooms in St. Giles and the influence of her perpetual presence on Edwin's attitude to life must have been profound and in time affected Gilbert. Edwin grew to prefer the ugly, the grey, the necessary things of life to the frivolous, the bright and the light. His favourite walk took him round the Oxford Gas Works. He had been appointed Professor of Political Economy at London University in 1907, the same year as he married his cousin, the shrewish tiny Mary Margaret Cullen known in the family as Rita, the daughter of the Deputy Surgeon General, but continued to reside in Oxford. By 1909 he had become an authority on Adam Smith, had written several books on economics and lectured extensively. A radical who sported a red tie and refused to wear a dinner jacket, Edwin was unconventional enough not to condemn Gilbert for his adulterous liaison; his aim in seeing Barrie was to extract from a difficult situation the young man who had once been his charge.

The Cannans and the Barries were both lowland Scots. Edwin's great-uncle, another David Cannan, had been Minister in Barrie's parish of 'Thrums' and Barrie's accent probably reminded Edwin of his paternal aunts, who had retained their Kirkcudbrightshire accents all their lives. The two small men who eventually faced each other at Leinster Corner in July 1909 shared an inability to discuss their emotions but little else. Edwin believed absolutely in common sense and practical solutions; whimsical flights of fancy were foreign to his nature. He asked Barrie not to divorce Mary, pleading Gilbert's youth and inexperience in contrast with the lady's sophistication and knowledge of affairs of the heart. He hinted at cradle snatching, pointed out that such a scandal could ruin a young man at the beginning of his career, that Gilbert's foolishness should be dismissed as the mere hot-headedness of youth. Barrie appeared awkward and difficult. He could not bring himself to explain his wife's obdurate attitude, for this would have injured his pride too deeply and reinforced Edwin's suggestions that the force behind the affair was Mary's. Instead he was stubbornly silent, gave not an inch and showed himself in the worst possible light.

When Edwin returned to Oxford he could say no more than 'What a horrible little man!' And no doubt in London Barrie was thinking in the same terms of Edwin, for both it had been a painful and infuriating experience, which had got them nowhere. Gilbert, on the other hand, in his own words, 'always exonerated the women'. He might later become exasperated with Mary, but he rarely uttered a truly unkind word against her. He usually stopped in time, sometimes leaving a sentence half-finished.

So there was no escape. His conscience, his sense of honour, a nicety he would mock in others as a mere bowing to convention, his weakness towards women and dislike of hurting them, a characteristic inherited from both his grandfathers, all drove him into the net of marriage.

On September 24th we find him again writing to Edward Garnett, from Temple Gardens.

I've a rather startling announcement for you—I'm to be married next April to Mrs. Barrie. She will be divorced next month. It has been a mighty thing and she's splendidly happy, as I am. Wish us well.

But there is little doubt that Garnett would have already heard of the impending divorce on the literary grapevine. H. G. Wells had known for some time, and an undated letter from him to Mary makes it clear that rumours had been around.

My dear Mrs. Barrie,

How are things with you? I'm concerned with vague rumours that everything isn't well between Barrie and you. Can't someone do something? I don't like to think of you as getting poor and embittered and that's the turn the stories give things. My best respects to Cannan, too. I've had rather a bad time. Amber and I are being forced never to see or write to each other. I suppose it's the same thing in the long run—except that I rather hanker after bolting—but it hurts horribly and leaves one the prey to all sorts of moods. Anyway, we've brought a jolly little daughter into the world.

      Good wishes to you.

Mary retreated to live at Black Lake Cottage with her Newfoundland dog Luath, and Peter the cat. Wells visited her there, for who better to consult and confide in at such a time than a fellow adulterer who had been caught up in more than one marital entanglement? And in spite of Denis Mackail's assertion to the contrary, it appears that Wells persuaded Mary to negotiate for options other than divorce and subsequent marriage, although probably she did not press very hard for alternative solutions but followed again her own desires. This letter is undated, but refers to her second meeting with Barrie and his solicitor.

Dear Mr. Wells,

Things are exactly where they were when you left. My overtures were rejected because I could not perjure myself by saying that not only would I give up G.C. but I must promise never to *think* of the past or long for it, but give myself up to loving J. and accepting his loving advances. He seems to have developed the most ardent passion for me now that he has lost me; that frightens me. I could go back to what I was but to fight that, in the circumstances, is more than I can promise to do. Poor thing, he is distracted and I am dreadfully sorry. He says he knows I would be happier with G.C. and that we ought to marry, one moment, and the next clamours for me. Anyhow I am to have money and that will help things somewhat, but I have no fear of my happiness, none at all, and it all seems too good a thing to be true. You have been a dear friend, I shall never forget it. Don't mention a word, will you, to anyone.

A grateful Gilbert wrote appreciatively to Wells on August 16th from the Temple:

I want to thank you for your letter to Mrs. Barrie, which she has sent on to me. I am more glad than I can say that she has found in you so fine a friend.

    One can really say nothing in a letter but thank you, and I hope that when you come to London I may see you.

An undated letter from Mary Barrie, scrawled diagonally across a sheet of Black Lake Cottage paper, suggests that Gilbert as a result of his letter visited the Wells's at their Hampstead house.

Sunday.

Dear Mrs. Wells.

How very kind of you to write. It has all been so awful, but now I have only a happy future to look forward to and I long for the six months to go. I am afraid I shall not be in London just yet, but presently I shall ask you both to come down and see me, and get a little fresh air when London becomes unbearable. I aim to live here always. I long to see your house. Gilbert Cannan tells me it is lovely, and as for your boys he is never tired of talking about them. You will have to bring them down here for me to play with.

My remembrances to your husband.

Gilbert in his own words was then 'dreadfully sentimental about children'. He believed passionately that nothing mattered but the begetting and rearing of them ... He was not conventional about marriage ... 'but he had simply no idea of the meaning of marriage or its appalling difficulty in practice'.[10]

He was, in fact, still too immature to take on any lasting commitment. And it can be argued that if Barrie had really wanted to keep his wife, he would not have made his terms so impossible for her, and that Mary's second letter to H. G. Wells supports Gilbert's sister's view that Barrie 'wanted her away'. Most likely he did not know his own mind, as Mary suggests, and swerved from one extreme to another, and that his desire to win his wife back was spurred on by possessive jealousy and the fear of scandal.

On September 30th we find Gilbert again writing to Garnett from Temple Gardens:

I think I could come on Wednesday next week though my plans are a little unsettled just at present, as we are rather busy. We've less than a fortnight to wait now.

I've sold myself to the Star as dramatic critic.

Now there was a fortnight to the divorce and then the long wait before marriage, and the need always for money. The hunt around for a more regular source of income, which had resulted in the appointment to *The Star*, was just the beginning of a long struggle to provide for a wife by someone barely able to provide for himself. But if Gilbert felt any trepidation, if he wakened in the early hours to worry about money, he appears to have told no one. Most likely he was allowing life to bear him along, as according to his memoirs he had in childhood:

I was a passive resister and let life do what it liked with me while to my conscience I disclaimed all personal responsibility.

And he still watched himself from the sidelines, believing with Stephen in *Little Brother* that:

Every man is three persons . . . Himself which is Godlike; Himself which is bestial; and Himself which looks on at and applauds the struggle between the other two. The first is moral, the second is non-moral, the third is immoral and despicable.

There were, however, consolations. Undoubtedly Gilbert must have felt he was beginning to make a little headway with his writing. The founding of *The English Review* by Ford Madox Ford (Ford Madox Hueffer) in November 1908 had provided a new outlet for writers' work. Its L-shaped office was used by some of them as a meeting place; indeed it was so often full of young aspiring authors, and a few established writers too, that Ford Madox Ford was obliged to spend his evenings in a nearby music hall where he could correct proofs and do editorial work in comparative peace. Sometimes Ford, Galsworthy and Gilbert would meet for a walk before breakfast. Occasionally they were accompanied by Ezra Pound.

Ford mentions Gilbert several times in his autobiography, *Return to Yesterday*. He was there in the L-shaped room when Ford gave a rather dismal party for Thomas Hardy. Ezra Pound was then looking after the cakes, Miss Thomas, 'large, very blond, invariably good-tempered, presided over the tea table'. There was a red-purple divan, a present from Ford's mother on which sat side by side, three men 'dumb as milestones', their legs stretched out,

their ankles were clothed, as to the one in emerald green socks, as to the next in vermilion and as to the next with electric blue. Merely to look in the direction of that divan was to have a pain in the eyes. The young men kept their hands deep in their trouser pockets and appeared to meditate suicide. Ezra did not eat any cakes. *He* had the toothache. Next to him was Gilbert Cannan: he had just been served with papers in a disagreeable action. Next to Cannan was Mr. Hugh Walpole. He had just published a particularly admirable novel called *Mr. Perrin and Mr. Traill*. But he was suffering agonies of fear lest his charming mother, who was the wife of the Bishop of Edinburgh and hidden round the corner [talking to Thomas Hardy], might hear something that should shock her.[11]

Galsworthy, Ford recorded, was helpful with *The English Review* but did not appear very approving, feeling that it should be more philanthropic and less literary. Gilbert, on the other hand, was the most silent man Ford ever knew.[12]

On the whole, literary people are not noted for harsh or derisive judgements on matters of moral and social implications, and many of Barrie's friends were sympathetic to all three parties in the approaching divorce, fearing most, however, for Barrie, lest the scandal might seriously damage his sensitive nature. A. E. W. Mason and Arthur Quiller-Couch, both close friends of Charles Cannan, appear however to have blamed Gilbert, feeling that he had bitten the hand that fed him. Stealing another man's wife was a dirty deed whatever the circumstances, but when that man had befriended you, paid for your holidays, and given you frequent hospitality under his roof, the adultery was unforgivable. Once the news broke Gilbert was never again invited to Magdalen Gate House, where he had gone from time to time to play the piano for the three Cannan girls. There were no more teas for him in the day-nursery where the nurse, Miss Ellen Hall, had watched him with ill-concealed disapproval, having been told that he was never to be 'left alone' with her charges, for what reason she knew not, only it was rumoured that he had taken out a servant girl in Manchester while barely fourteen. Now Gilbert's affair with an ex-actress had confirmed Charles Cannan's wife's earlier suspicions. He was a black sheep whose name was never again to be mentioned within earshot of her daughters. It was several years before the elder of these, Dorothea, learned from Lady Quiller-Couch of the divorce, which appeared, after all, to be quite a small crime compared with those which had grown in the girls' imaginations.

Lord Esher, George Alexander, William Archer, Edmund Gosse, Maurice Hewlett, Henry James, A. E. W. Mason, Arthur Pinero, Beerbohm Tree and H. G. Wells sent a letter to the editors of the national papers in an attempt to protect Barrie from the publicity they feared might devastate him.

The divorce suit for Barrie v Barrie & Cannan is down for hearing at the Michaelmas Term. The plaintiff in the suit was in early life a distinguished journalist. More recently his work in fiction and the drama has given pleasure of a high order to hundreds of thousand of readers and spectators wherever the English language is spoken. He is a man for whom the inevitable pain of these proceedings would be greatly increased by the publicity. Therefore, it is hoped the Press, as a mark of respect and gratitude to a writer of genius, will unite in abstaining from any mention of the case beyond the briefest report of the hearing. The suit is undefended, and, apart from the eminence of the plaintiff, raises no question of the slightest public interest.[13]

The divorce which was heard on October 13th, was reported in all the leading British newspapers, the *Daily Mail* and the *Daily Telegraph* giving two of the longest accounts.

The case was heard in the Divorce division before the President, Sir John Bigham. Mr. Barnard, appearing for Barrie, said the petitioner's marriage had been happy until eighteen months ago. In November 1908 Gilbert had gone for two or three weeks to Barrie's Black Lake

Cottage while his flat was under repair. He had been visited by Mary with 'lady friends' and in July 1909, a statement had been made by one of the servants to Barrie as to what had taken place on November 2nd and 25th.

Under examination, Barrie agreed that the gardener, Mr. Hunt's revelation on July 28th, referred to only one occasion in November.

He said his wife took up tea in the morning to Mr. Cannan and he was not in his room. She then went with tea to my wife's room and knocked at the door, but got no answer. Presently she heard my wife say, 'Gilbert, Gilbert!'

Did you tell your wife what Mr. Hunt had said?—I told her and she said 'it is all quite true'. I said. 'If it is quite true, I must go and see Sir George Lewis about it.'

Sir George was not only your solicitor, but the friend of both of you?—Yes.

Did you and your wife both see him?—Yes.

What took place at the interview?—My wife said it was the only time it had ever taken place, and they had both been in a state about it. I said 'If you will come back I will forgive you. No one would ever know anything about it.' She said it would be all pretence, I should be thinking of her all the time, but he was the only person in the world for her.

The President: She meant that she was in love with him?—Yes. She said it would be a much more ignoble thing to go back to me in those circumstances.

Mr. Barnard: Did you then offer to separate by deed if she would promise to have nothing more to do with him?—Yes. And she refused?—Yes.[14]

After the calling of Mrs. Hunt's evidence, in which she gave a more detailed description of taking round the morning tea and confirmed that she had often seen Gilbert coming out of Mary's room in the early morning, a decree nisi was granted with costs. In an undated letter to H. G. Wells, Mary claimed that Barrie lied at the hearing:

J. came out badly in court. 3 lies. First, never said it was the only time. 2nd, it is *my cottage*, lease is in my name and I bought it with my money. 3rd. It is seven years since we separated and that does not spell happiness until 18 months ago. This had damaged us a lot in the eyes of the public but with our friends, well, they all knew better.

Mary had her supporters too. On November 9th, George Meredith had written to Charles Scribner, the American publishers:

The whole truth is that Mrs. B. is a woman—with a woman's desires—which for many years she has controlled. (And she had no children, which made it harder.) Barrie is a son born to a mother long after the rest of her family—and as so often is the case—with genius but little virility.

Now—people are saying that Mrs. Barrie had many lovers. This is false—
I am certain of it—I have good authority. There was no rumour of it until
this divorce came as a surprise. She was, as it happens, overcome by this
man for whom she has left Barrie. She loves the man as a young woman
loves a man—and still loves Barrie as a mother loves a helpless child.

But if Mary told the truth when years later she announced to
Gilbert's sister, Margaret, in a bitter moment that he had not been the
only lover, but simply the one who was 'unlucky enough to be caught'
(and there seems no reason why she should have lied), then the rumour
had a very firm foundation, and it seems most likely that Edwin
Cannan was right when he claimed that Mary had set out to captivate
the young man.

Certainly none of the three players in the drama could be relied upon
to tell the truth. They all had their secret selves to guard against
exposure, their public fronts to protect. And for a time Gilbert was still
concerned with keeping up an appearance of decency as another sentence
in an undated letter from Mary to H. G. Wells confirms:

The Horror is over and I am living a lonely life down here. G. and I are to
be separated until we marry in April. We are playing the game for the look
of the thing, but it is very dull.

H. G. Wells gave his advice in an undated letter from 17 Church Row,
Hampstead:

Sillies you are! Go and live together and get babies as soon as you can like
two sensible people. One could think there was Magic in Marriage. Fancy
you and your old friends conspiring to glorify the Damned old Fetish. Also
—and this is impertinence—I wouldn't marry if I were you unless you know
you are going to have babys (*sic*). No earthly reason why you should for if
so be you soon should disagree, it gives you both amazing powers of making
Hell for one another. So take an old Sinner's advice and *tell* them you are
married when the time comes, and don't marry unless there is a child to
legitimate. I'll always say I know you are and declare I was a witness at the
Registry Office if you want confirmation.

But J. A. Hammerton in his book, *Barrie, the Story of a Genius*,
probably spoke for many who deeply admired the cuckolded playwright:

Literary success does not always nor often imply that those who enjoy it
find a straight and easy path to the hearts of their readers, but perhaps the
most unusual feature of Barrie's extraordinarily successful career has been
the way in which the personality of the man has drawn forth the affections
of his literary admirers. It is not too much, therefore, to say that when, on
October 13th, 1909, he had to sustain the ordeal terrible to one of his extreme

sensitiveness, of bearing witness in a case before the President of the Divorce Division which resulted in the dissolution of his marriage, he was the subject of universal sympathy. No good service would be served by dwelling upon this most regrettable but entirely creditable episode in his life beyond the simple statement I have made but this I would venture to add, that in the later development of the circumstances which led to so unhappy an ending the attitude of the lady, whose highest honour it had been to share his life for fourteen years, was not altogether unwanting of respect.[15]

The other side had been put earlier and sparingly by Gilbert in a letter to Kathleen Bruce dated February 25th, 1910:

I want to explain that my indignation is not against J.M.B. but against the current sycophantic idea of him—as I told you there need have been no split. It should have been possible for people to say, 'I am his friend and her friend. I am glad for her because she is happy and I believe that he will be the happier and the better for living away from a woman whose happiness he could not procure'. Instead of that the limelight was turned on. He became the puppet of Lady Lewis, with the result that you know. What is between the three of us is our affair and ours only and people do not go through the sort of thing that we have done unless no other solution is possible. I cared for nothing and do care for nothing but her happiness: and that should have been first with him. It was not so, and therefore the current idea of him is monstrous. One cannot break it but one can in course of time show that he has not a monopoly of success. The whole of this mess I think comes from his having a vulgar idea of what a great man and a genius is. I believe he used to see Carlyle when he was a boy and so he has aped the rottenness of that other sham great man and been infinitely more vulgar.

However, 'nuff said. Please don't talk about things unless you come up against a wildly foolish story which you are able to contradict. There is nothing to be done but to throw my work in the scale against his. I am 25, he is 48 or 9. I have that to the good. I am happy and full of life; he is wretched and rotten through to the bone, a poor sick beast with a poor sick soul.

That's all.

4

'An Empty Bucket'

Lytton Strachey

THE waiting was too long. On March 5th Gilbert wrote a postcard to Edward Garnett.

> Black Lake Cottage,
> nr. Farnham,
> Surrey.

Above is our address after 10th. Four of my sketches are to appear in the English Review April and May![1]

So for Gilbert it was goodbye to the stone stairs, the lonely white chambers overlooking the quad, and the walk by the Embankment past the statue of Isambard Kingdom Brunel, whose sons Gilbert's Great-Aunt Mary had prepared for school. Turning his back on much of the setting for *Peter Homunculus*, he came into the all-embracing warmth of Mary's cottage and garden which were so much an expression of her own personality.

According to Denis Mackail, Mary was

> to keep the cars, the chauffeur and Luath. She had refused his (Barrie's) suggestion of an allowance—and it wasn't until some years later when she was in serious need that he learnt of this, and would be generous here also for the rest of his life.[2]

From her own books, *The Happy Garden* and *Dogs and Men*, it seems that she kept Luath and a little car of her own, but not the chauffeur for he was too expensive for Gilbert, who learned to drive himself.

At first Mary's love was to bring a great change in Gilbert's circumstances. Never before had he been master of a house, a garden and servants. Coming to Black Lake Cottage with all his books and chattels, he was not only greeted by an enraptured woman but also by two dogs and a smoky blue Persian cat, another Peter. The second dog, Billy, a bob-tail sheepdog, had been given to Mary by a neighbour who feared that she was lonely waiting for the divorce to become absolute.

The four acres of garden were enclosed on all sides by trees; carefully planned zig-zagging paths led to secret bowers, rockeries, a

Japanese garden and a pond with lizards and goldfish. There was a little tea-house lit on summer nights by Chinese lanterns. Behind the house beyond the garden, tall pines marched up the hill to meet the horizon. A study awaited Gilbert, Barrie's study, the last room to be built-on under Mary's supervision. It was upstairs at the end of a passage hung with Japanese prints and a Wellington mirror. Light and sunny in spring and summer, it faced south and west and had been somewhat pretentiously planned for a 'master'. Low leaded windows looked out across the garden, their seats cushioned in green, a colour repeated by the hearth rug which decorated a white painted floor partly carpeted in black. Over the fireplace, more leaded panes let light into the passage through green net curtains with the 'Winged Victory in miniature striding through them'.[3] Soon Gilbert's books lined the walls, replacing Barrie's:

Shakespeare and Meredith, and the New Dramatists, all rather hurt by J. M. Synge's preface to the 'The Tinkers Wedding', with all its disrespectful reference to their Ibsen. And Kipling hobnobs with H. G. Wells, while Tennyson shudders as far away from Swinburne as he possibly can. 'Jean Christophe' denounces mountebanks, and protects himself from Stendhal on the one hand and Balzac on the other, with the lives of Beethoven and Tolstoy written by his Godfather, Romain Rolland. 'Don Quixote' finds himself sandwiched in between 'Roderick Hudson' and the 'Bluebird', and never dreams that they are anything but books of chivalry . . . Stevenson and Henley are united in wondering when literature is going to digest the mess of sociology which it gulped down so hastily as soon as their protecting presences were removed. And Robert Burns roars at them all: 'man to man the world o'er, shall brithers be for a' that'.[4]

On the green cushions Billy would lie, head hanging out of a window, 'watching the shadows come and go, listening to the cars going by on the road'.[5] Here Gilbert continued his mammoth translation of *Jean Christophe*, starting *Little Brother*, and reviewed drama in *The Star*.

The tell-tale gardener had been replaced by another, a young 'man of the Earth', with a wife and baby who, unlike his predecessor, used the greenhouses for the good of the garden rather than the cultivating of show chrysanthemums. Since the divorce, laurels had been cut down, the way cleared for a little brick court, the setting for hydrangeas in tubs, a wooden seat, a cool corner for reflection near the house. At last the garden seemed to be truly Mary's. A basic frustration had disappeared. Until now she had felt in the position of an Anglo-Indian mother whose children are in England.

In the winter and spring you snatch a Sunday here and there to see how your flower-children are growing up: all is not well: you have fearful presentiments; they are not what you had planned and dreamed and hoped! Your gardener crushes you with his expert professional knowledge; he discounts your enthusiasm as severely as a tutor discounts a mother's love.

But now she seemed to have the answer:

If you are a woman, then marry an artist, an author or a clergyman and make it clear to him that your garden is to be the central idea of both your lives, stipulate for an adequate allowance to meet the temptations of the autumn catalogues, select your friends, discard your acquaintances, and set to work.[6]

Gilbert appears to have had no objection at first to such stipulations. Indeed, he learned to build stone walls and make seats and bowers himself, and, perhaps more important for marital harmony, he gave Mary the courage to write *The Happy Garden*, a book which, with its references to Nietzsche, the Social Conscience and Bernard Shaw, bears the stamp of his influence. Yet in all ways the house was Mary's, never his own. Its interior was chintzy, feminine, fussy, full of knick-knacks, from Mary's past. Above her bed hung Botticelli prints in Italian frames: 'best of all the Carpaccio boy from Venice: the perfect angel playing a lute'. A narrow Gothic aperture led through to the dressing-room (mentioned in the divorce case), across which a curtain could be drawn for greater privacy.[7]

Here, for seven weeks, they lived together, except on those occasions when Gilbert had to spend a night in London after seeing a play for *The Star*. His first signed notice for this paper had appeared on December 2nd, over his initials G. C. It was a review of *Mrs. Cummin*, a play based on Mrs. Mary Mann's *The Englamere Portraits* put on at the Playhouse. Five days later his notice of Maeterlinck's *The Bluebird* at the Haymarket was published. That month he reviewed in all seven plays for *The Star*, some of his notices being as long as fourteen column-inches. A noticeable exception was *Peter Pan* at the Duke of York's Theatre, which was covered by another critic. So a pattern was set which was to last all through the summer, a pattern which was only broken briefly after his marriage to Mary.

This civil ceremony took place at the Holborn Registry Office on April 28th, a quiet affair without any relations present. Gilbert gave his address as 7 New Square, Lincoln's Inn, an address which, according to the Post Office Directory for 1910, belonged to no less than thirty-three people. None of the names listed there or on the electoral roll of the time appears elsewhere among Gilbert's letters and papers, but it is quite probable that Gilbert knew a lawyer with rooms or chambers at number 7. Elizabeth Worsley, his daily help, was a witness, together with Douglas MacKeurton.[8] Both Mary and Gilbert described their fathers as being men of 'independent means'.

Much later there was a rumour spread by Mary, and mentioned to me by the late Harold Rubenstein, the libel lawyer, that Gilbert had kissed another woman passionately while on his honeymoon, but there is no supporting evidence and, in later years, it was to Mary's advantage to show Gilbert up in a bad light. Even so, the rumour does suggest that the pair took a holiday after the marriage—no more than a week, for on May 5th *The Star* printed a long review by Gilbert on George Paston's *Nobody's Daughter*, which was playing at Wyndham's. In this he singled out for a special praise the performance of Gerald du Maurier, Sylvia Davies's brother.

Taken as a whole, his notices were encouraging rather than destructively critical. He still liked whimsy, but what he cared most about was *soul*. In a review of *The Dawn of Tomorrow* by Hodgson Burnett, at the Garrick, which appeared on May 14th, we find him defending a particular type of play, which was also likely to appeal to Mary if we are to take seriously the sentiments expressed in her three books. He wrote:

It is easy to sneer at these plays with a purpose. They are sincere and, after all, they do bring a God on to the boards even if he be only a second rate God. Some day it may be possible to give the public a first rate God, and then the Theatre will be really serving its purpose.

His review of *The Bluebird* contains the following admission: 'We do believe in Fairies and we do believe that there is a soul in everything.'

But, like many others, he never defined soul, although for more than a decade he was to continue to look for it in work and life. Brought up on Lang's *Fairy Tales*, nurtured by Celtic fantasy as a child, he had often escaped from the perplexities and sordidness of late nineteenth-century Manchester into the world of make-believe. It is also easy to see the influence of Barrie, that 'Dearest thing in the world' in some of Gilbert's reviews. Perhaps, because he often felt unreal and was never absolutely sure of his own identity, he was particularly vulnerable to cults, movements and new philosophies.

. . . an empty bucket [Lytton Strachey was later to call him] which has been filled up to the brim with modern ideas—simply because it happened to be standing near that tap. The good thing about him is a substratum of honest serviceableness—but that is not enough in my line to excite me. *He* no doubt found me far too rarefied for him. I daresay if I took the trouble I could induce in him a culte (*sic*) for me which would replace the one he at present has for Rupert [Brooke]. But of course I shan't.[9]

There is probably a small grain of truth in this arrogant assessment. It is also clear that Gilbert could only feel *real* through a close and loving association with another human being, and the cry, 'without you I am nothing', which echoes through his letters to Kathleen, suggests that he may have appreciated that fact. Alone he was lost.

Mary understood little of Gilbert's character when she married him and, in time, was to make surprising and unexpected discoveries. She was probably also largely unaware of his inherited characteristics and the environmental forces which had shaped his nature. She does not appear to have appreciated the basic sense of inferiority sometimes alternating with a feeling almost of genius, which often lurked behind a façade of aloof self-confidence. He needed constant reassurance that he was important to other people, and when he became aware of that he reacted with enthusiasm and generosity which was not without gratitude.

That you should have—have—have—have. I don't know—given me so many hours of yourself, liked my work, liked me. It seems incredible. Do I sleep, do I dream?[10]

Those words, overdramatic and emotional, were heartfelt, and such feelings do not fade easily, even with fame and recognition. Basically Gilbert did not expect to be liked. Aged twelve, he had been amazed when Edwin had presented him with a bicycle when they were both staying at his Great-Aunt Mary's house, The Shieling, Grasmere. His sister, Margaret, told me he had found it hard to believe that anyone should wish to give him so handsome a present. The event occurred before Gilbert's informal adoption, probably marking the beginning of Edwin's special interest in him, and suggesting that he felt the boy needed more affection and love, emotions that Edwin could only express to him through giving.

The cause of Gilbert's low estimate of himself as a likeable person can largely be traced back to his childhood, and to the obvious popularity of Angus, who for many years surpassed him in every field. Angus was expected to gain a scholarship to Manchester Grammar School. Gilbert was not; indeed Henry Cannan was against his second son entering for it. Angus wrote plays put on at the Grammar School, and also by the Ducie Amateur Dramatic Society with Henry Cannan as producer, all of which were well reviewed in local papers. Gilbert gained no such public recognition, although he was later to win an Exhibition to Cambridge on the strength of a brilliant essay on Schiller. As a youngster Angus was the centre of a group of marauding boys who swopped penknives and smutty stories and teased Gilbert mercilessly. His parents would not have handed Angus over to a cousin on any account. He stayed with his family, leaving school at sixteen (he could have gone on to university but he wanted to make money), and only left home when he was offered a good job out East in shipping.

The tremendous 'enthusiasm' of 1908 was, for Gilbert, an exception and was never again to return in such intensity. The reality of his marriage gradually destroyed his boyishness, the hopefulness in spite of everything, which had so irritated Shaw. By 1910 the charms of literary London, the kindnesses of the great ones, had begun to turn a little sour. Garnett's hands were clean, but others, including Granville-Barker's, must have seemed in retrospect a little sullied. He began to feel increasingly that they, the older ones, should have stepped in, rather than watch a young man walk blithely into a trap, which forced him for the sake of decency and honour to marry a woman to whom he had not intended to commit himself for life.

Had I known the strange destiny that awaited me I doubt that I should have been born [he wrote some years later]. Even the courage of an embryo would have quailed before it.[11]

Although this statement smacks of exaggeration and self-pity, it probably expresses in part his feelings about his marriage and the way it came about.

Life was not easy for Mary, either, at this time. Some of the problems she had endured with Barrie were reincarnated, for it was her tragedy to be attracted to insecure, intensely private men while her nature demanded spontaneity and lively male appreciation in response to her vivaciousness and femininity. She was a talker needing an admiring audience; she gave and desired confidences. And, as the weeks went by, Gilbert's ambition to prove himself, to confound those who had disparaged and disliked him, and to beat Barrie at his own game, became infinitely more important to him than the pleasing of his wife.

Paradoxically in this he was driven as much by hidden family influences, which he called 'Lawrieism', as by any sense of inferiority or thwarted pride. Successive generations of Cannans had been, from an early age, indoctrinated with the idea that they were somehow different and more remarkable than other people simply because they were Cannans. To be ordinary was, for them, to fail. Every Cannan was expected to make his mark and those males who were unsuccessful took to drink (a course followed by James Cannan and eventually by his three sons and possibly, in some degree, by Edwin's father, David Cannan). This is touched on by Gilbert in his Lawrie novels (Lawrie being the name he gave the Cannans in his books). He describes how the theory was started by his great-grandmother, Margaret Kennedy Cannan, and her servant, Martha (Tibby in the novels) whose influence on the talented, drunken, gregarious James Cannan was immeasurable. Martha survived into her nineties and never lost her faith in the superiority of the family, for whom and with whom she had lived since the age of fourteen.

In Bournemouth and Oxford, Charles and Edwin Cannan had not escaped indoctrination, carried on largely by their Aunts Margaret and Mary. But their twice-widowed father, David, saw that practical help was also needed, and that the university education he lacked was essential if his dear boys were to follow the brilliant careers in politics and the law, to which he hoped to guide them. He died of bronchitis, alone in a Limerick hotel, too soon to know of their adult successes. But typically his sister, Mary (of Grasmere), saw in the manner he had borne his many tragedies the spark of greatness she expected from a Cannan and wrote in her notebook beside the carefully pasted announcement of his death, 'High bliss is only from a higher state. But surely if ever afflictions borne with patience merit the reward of peace, Peace you deserve.'

In Oxford Ellen Hall had faithfully carried on the tradition set by Martha. Only here the link with the Wedderburns*, surely one of the proudest families in the Lowlands of Scotland, lifted expectations even higher, so that the three girls, one of whom was to make her mark as a novelist and another as a poet, were sometimes heard to say 'Us not like other children'. Although Gilbert analysed and described this Lawrieism, he had not escaped its influence. He might outwardly scorn the theory but inwardly it had settled in him like a seed in the soil that must send forth shoots.

In *Little Brother*, in which George Lawrie is based on Edwin Cannan and Aunt Phoebe on Margaret Cannan, Gilbert wrote of the attitude of the aunt to her nephew.

To her being his father's son, he was too precious ever to go to school or to have the ordinary experience of an undergraduate. She took him to the University, and lived with him in his lodgings. She never let it occur to him that there might be any other way of living, and fed him with that cardinal Lawrie quality which makes us all think everybody else is in the wrong and every other way of doing things is fantastic . . .

Added to this special feeling imbued in Gilbert before he reached eight (and confusingly contradicted by his own father's failures and poor opinion of this second son) was the sense of having cheated death, for twice as a child he had been expected to die. In his memoirs he wrote: 'I was certain that if I lived long enough the world would one day be to my liking, but no one else thought I would live long enough.'

Could it be then that God had spared him for some special reason? He had thrown over the established church long ago as a boy, but he fervently believed in a religious instinct and had never ruled out the possibility of a Deity. From an early age he had decided he was different from other boys. His brain was extraordinary in its ability to

* Charles Cannan's wife was Mary Wedderburn.

absorb knowledge without noticeable effort. As a child he felt apart, outside, nearly all the time, especially when thought came back suddenly with a click, as though he had been elsewhere, not in the world like other men. A fine linguist, he spoke three languages more easily than most men speak one. And gifts, he might argue, were given for a purpose; talents, his Presbyterian relations would have told him, should be developed for the common good. Britain was in a mess, caught, he thought, in a vacuum between the greatness and squalor, riches and hypocrisy, of the Victorian era, and the 'New Spirit' which he felt must come. Service was part of his family tradition. On both sides there were clergymen and Ministers, men of fire. There were also distinguished soldiers and sailors. If the world was not to his liking he must change it with the power of his art, with 'winged words' and 'force' and 'soul'.

With such an inheritance and upbringing it was clearly impossible for Gilbert to fall in with Mary's wishes and make the garden the 'central idea of his life', nor could he while away valuable hours between bouts of writing, talking to Mary about dogs, flowers and possible changes in décor. He needed silence and soon began to long for a work place away from the house, the sort of arrangement that Barrie enjoyed at Leinster Corner, where there was a building which he used as a study at the bottom of the garden. He began to envy a friend who had converted a cowshed into a work room. Like Barrie he sometimes fled from visitors.

For Mary it was a familiar problem. Once again, part of the life she had hoped to share was to be shut away from her, only this time she knew at once what to do and she bore no rancour. She turned to her dogs, resigned to the inevitable. It was no good complaining; this was simply a natural drawback of the marital state, the state which women always hoped would give them another half.

For, she wrote, a dog makes the most admirable accompaniment to a husband. He supplies those darling little ways, so near to a woman's heart, and so necessary to her well-being, that come tripping along gracefully before marriage but by the end of the first year have tripped away—less gracefully —into oblivion.

My woman readers will, I am sure, see my point at once. To quote an instance, those silent meals. Haven't most of us experienced them? When the mind of your man is elsewhere, Lord knows where, but nowhere in your direction. Just when the silence is becoming unbearable, your dog steps in and attracts your attention. He lays his head on your knee or he presses your hand, as it is in the act of conveying a succulent morsel to your mouth. 'Merely asking for food', you interrupt. Quite true. But to ask for anything is a relief . . . And with how much charm he does it, and with what an adoring glance he rewards you for the titbits you pop into his mouth. Your heart begins at once to warm up again. The whole balance of life is restored.[12]

Fewer and fewer titbits were to pass from Gilbert to Mary, as he became increasingly immersed in his work; although still kind and courteous, the spark of animation which had lit his face for her was becoming a thing of the past. And inside him was a growing impatience with much of the work of his fellow writers. He began to rail.

In spring he had written critically and pompously of Shaw and Granville-Barker, in *The English Review*, June 1910, attacking their plays *Misalliance* and *The Madras House*, both Duke of York Theatre productions:

One bad play more or less is no very great matter. What does offend and what does give to mourn is that the admirable fantastic talent of Mr. Shaw and the capital powers of observation and skill in recording of Mr. Barker should be vitiated and rendered impotent to please by an unhealthy and unwholesome preoccupation with the sexual relationship of men and women . . . These writers make their puppets talk as though it were possible for men and women by light of reason to choose whether they will be actuated by their sex-impulse or not . . . They make men and women deliberately and in cold blood pursue the creature of their desire and the spectacle is undeifying and not entertaining. It offends.

It is possible to dispose of sex, either by reason or any other contrivance of the mind. It is possible to abuse sex; but Nature is subtle and unrelenting in her vengeance. And so the sensualists—those who use their sex to feed their appetites and not in response to the call of their instincts—do little by little lose their dramatic sense, their perception, and instinctive knowledge of life, their capacity for experience, and in the end are captives in a prison house of their own building. . . .

By now he could criticise a little more confidently for his work had reached the West End, if only in a small and unsatisfactory way. At last Herbert Trench had put on *James and John*, his one-act play, at the Haymarket, but so discourteously that Gilbert could feel no sense of triumph, as he makes clear in a letter to H. G. Wells written on Good Friday 1910.

Very glad to have your letter about James & John; and I hope you have punched the right heads. Various persons have been behaving very badly about it including H. Trench. He bought it a year and a half ago, and as far as I can make out did everything he could to queer its production. He didn't even send us seats for the first performance and we paid each 2/6d. to see it. It wasn't quite as I wanted it to be—too slow and not quite alive enough. But it seems to have pleased many people worth pleasing, and I'm glad it has given you faith in my work. I knew your faith was wobbly, but I couldn't do anything. I'm not a novelist by intent, hope, faith, ambition or even conceit. I came to London to write plays and I wrote 'em until there came a point when I saw that nobody was really interested in me, or had the least intention of producing anything I did. So I wrote books. I write plays when I must, so hope to have enough to stock a repertory by the time people begin to discover, as they will, that tricks aren't necessary in the theatre.

James and John have walked off the Haymarket stage, and Trench hadn't the decency even to write to me about that: but he's quite logical in a way. He never wrote to tell me it when it was being put on so he can hardly write and tell me that it has been taken off. I feel strangely unresponsible for it all, but to have had your letter—and others like it from other people who count —helps me to realise that part of what I wanted to do has been done. Therefore, many thank-yous.

The play appears to have been a curtain-raiser for some performances of *The Blue Bird*, but was not advertised or announced in the national press. It seems likely that Herbert Trench and those 'various people' were sympathetic to Barrie and did not wish to be seen supporting the man who had cuckolded him. Possibly, too, Gilbert's misinterpreted silences and proud profile were making him enemies, as they would continue to do for the rest of his free life.

James and John, a slight play, is based on the relationship between Gilbert's grandfather, James Cannan, his wife Agnes, and their two mother-dominated sons, George and James, trapped and held together by their father's crime, which appears to be embezzlement, and the appalling possessiveness of their mother. Their house is the house in which Gilbert spent much of his youth, their plight the plight of his two strange uncles—one of whom was avoided when possible by the younger Cannans, who, with the instinct of children, scented insanity.

The play shows Gilbert once again trying to understand his grandfather, in whom he had felt so deeply the passion he was never to find again in any man. James Cannan's religious fervour had nothing to do with a conventional God; he loathed and decried in *The Sphinx* the hypocrisy of many churchgoers, describing with a bitter pen the congregation of the church his wife supported. But he was willing to give time and boundless affection to his grandchildren, to write them special poems for their birthdays. He was tolerant of the weak, judged no man and loathed prejudice. The letters he sent from North America when he went out as a young married man to report on the state of cotton show him as a loving father and husband, rather timid, very homesick, but already deeply attached to the theatre and well read in poetry and literature.

I never knew the truth about him. The poor man had somehow come to grief, but he handed on something to me which all the others stopped dead.

Wrote Gilbert in his memoirs, still puzzled, halfway through his life, by how and where that lovable man had gone wrong to be so scorned and forsaken by his sons and wife.

In 1910 Mary was determined to devote all her spare time to the garden and, keeping up the Barrie tradition, Gilbert invited interesting people down to Black Lake Cottage. Garnett was pressed to come in a letter of June 5th: 'I only go up to Town for the theatres and nothing will tear my wife away from her garden.' Whether all those invited came is not clear, but certainly Black Lake Cottage had lost none of its charm since Barrie's departure and everything was done to give guests a pleasant and relaxing time in beautiful and flower-scented surroundings.

We eat in the orchard (wrote Mary in *The Happy Garden*) lunch and tea; dinner attracts too many insects to be possible or pleasant. There is an old table and an old public-house settle under the cherry tree at the end of the privet hedge, where the della Robbia Madonna is enshrined.

An old flour-bin serves to keep the wind from the spirit lamp, over which the coffee is boiled. The whole family assembles for lunch including the tortoise, Everard, the second of his line, who is tethered by a long string and pegged down. His predecessor was slain by the Newfoundland dog, who was filled with passionate scientific curiosity.[13]

The Charles Cannan family would have been appalled by the net curtains in the house, considering them plebeian, a taste which marked Mary out as coming from a common background, but there is no evidence that Gilbert objected. The décor he left to Mary. He never felt that he had to set himself against a particular background, nor considered that he belonged to any special class which entailed keeping up appearances of a particular kind. Normally he dressed conventionally, not wishing to draw attention to himself, although Swinnerton told me that the first time he met Gilbert after the marriage he noticed that he was rather self-consciously wearing a large, very thick and colourful sweater. 'Mary put me in this as soon as we were married', he said, as though attempting to excuse some outlandish garment. And it is likely that the vermilion socks, mentioned by Ford Madox Ford, were also Mary's choice.

On September 16th *The Star* published a long piece by Gilbert entitled 'The Dying Theatre, a Plea for Humanity and Reality', in which he commented on the London summer season of plays.

I cannot remember who made the remark that it is the business of the critic to shake down the fruit from the tree of genius [he began]. There is truth in it. The critic has to decide which is the tree of genius, and, having done that, his work is forestry. He has to tend the good tree, assist it in maturing, lop

it here and there, destroy parasites and poisonous growths and cull the fruit
if there be any . . . This is a notoriously bad year for fruit.

There had been, he continued, two profitless adaptations from the
French, two very weather-worn American farces, a pageant based on a
play of which Shakespeare had been part author, a rehash of an old
morality play by Mr. Hall Caine, an adaptation at the Coronet, the
Follies entertainment, and a very inferior imitation of it at another
theatre. After discussing the plays to come he declared that the position
was lamentable:

To produce bad plays is not to meet the competition of the lower places of
entertainment: it is to court disaster. The success of those places which I call
lower in no disparaging sense, drives the theatre back upon a higher level,
if it is to succeed at all; and if it is to maintain its existence. If the theatre dies,
then these places in course of time will die also, for the lower forms of art
are fed from the higher.

The problem, he wrote, was also European. Quoting from a
Manifesto published in France in 1899 by 'certain young enthusiasts'
including Romain Rolland, he continued: 'Art is a prey to egoism and
anarchy. A few men have made it their preserve, and withhold it from
the people.' Developing this theme, he went on:

I shall be told that the public did not support the Court Theatre or the Repertory Theatre. Why should it? The programs (*sic*) of both those theatres fell
short of art. And, quoting from Mazzini, an artist in life who worked for the
people against privilege, an artist who so won and served the people that
80,000 men and women attended his obsequies: 'Analysis is egotism: syn-
thesis, a religion' . . .
A man of genius is neither more nor less than a human being who has the
courage of the religious instinct which tells him that he has to pay for his
life with truth: a human being who has the courage to be human, one who
believes in the collective destiny of humanity, and serves that destiny with his
individuality. Genius is not always articulate. It does not always find talent:
it does not always find the right talent.

He finished his long article with youthful optimism.

Emotion divorced from intellect is barren: intellect divorced from emotion
is barren . . .
We have arrived at a point at which we can see the sterility of both our
theatres. Having seen it I do not think it will be long before another movement arises in which emotion and intellect will live happily ever after. Then
the theatre will play a part in the life of the community which it has never yet
fulfilled. It will be the heart of the community: the centre of the imaginative

life. Those who give such a theatre to the community will be richly rewarded. . . .

Men and women are today striving with the same lofty ideals, but such an article in 1910 was not likely to make Gilbert many friends in the London theatre world. Established and powerful figures, who might have eventually taken an interest in his plays, resented such strong criticism. To condemn virtually all that had been performed during the summer was not an action likely to promote the young playwright's own efforts. However, Miss A. E. Horniman was to be an exception and probably by this time she had already expressed interest in his play, *Miles Dixon*, which she was to stage at the Gaiety Theatre, Manchester, in November.

Gilbert was also enjoying an exchange of letters with Romain Rolland, with whom he shared many ideals and aspirations.

Your splendid letter gave me great pleasure [Rolland had written from Schoenbrunn par Zug on September 9th]. Thank you for not being cross with yourself for having translated my books: it must be so tedious a thing to translate a work which is almost endless!

What pleases me most is not how successful *Christophe* may be, but that there may be so many of us in Europe who feel and wish for the same things. Everywhere the moral unease is the same: the very same, the need to react. I hope and I believe that we are at the start of an era more manly and saner in spirit than that we are leaving. Open all the windows and, as you put it, let a gust of air sweep away the miasmas. Let us do even better: let us go out of the house, and strive to rebuild a much larger and better ventilated one . . .

In spite of financial problems Mary and Gilbert continued to offer hospitality, and the Wells family visited them in November. It was one of the paradoxes in Gilbert's life that, although lonely and often angry in a general way with mankind, he liked to have people visit him and he invited them with little regard to the state of his bank balance or the housekeeping. It was simply for him the automatic and natural thing to do and in this way he resembled Violet Cannan's father, Francis Arbuthnot Wright, some of whose parishioners in 1884 accused him of using church funds to entertain his friends, knowing that his own finances were in a precarious state.

Galsworthy's friendship was another which survived the divorce. Indeed his kindly nature and social conscience assured that he was usually available to help if needed. In addition he was prepared to take seriously the naive political and philosophical theorizing of the young.

My dear Gilbert [he wrote on December 4th, 1910]. Well—perhaps. At all events you state a case. The other side of that case is that every ardent youth in every decade believes that he is in for a breaking up of the waters. And every decade sees its own ardent movement; which seems so little ardent to the next decade. I believe much more in the slow (sometimes invisible) continuous ferment, than I believe in definite sudden renascences. The slow continuous ferment, the impalpable change of thought and manners, throws up and feeds certain conscious creatures all the time, and these conscious creatures in the course of shaping their impressions form what we call movements by the power of the expressed consciousness. What we are inclined to forget is that though our fathers were nearer damnation and further from salvation as *we* conceive of them, they were closer to salvation and further from damnation than we are as *they* conceived of those two states. We fight for our own hands, of course; but the conscious of 2050 looking back will be just as hard on us as you are on the 19th century. And the only things he will not be hard on are those expressions of individuality (fed, if you like, on varying food), which are shaped and chiselled to the point of resisting time.[14]

Although Mary and Gilbert were living beyond their means, Miss Horniman's successful and well-received production of Gilbert's *Miles Dixon* gave them reason for hope that their fortunes were about to pick up. In this two-act play Milton Rosmer and Irene Rooke played the leading parts. The *Manchester Guardian* of November 23rd devoted 800 words to the play, rather more than the space given to Stanley Houghton's *The Younger Generation*, which followed it in the theatre. The piece began:

Miss Horniman's theatre has been the means of giving many new dramatists their first publicity; it has never shown anything better in achievement, nor with better hope for the future, than Mr. Cannan's play last night. Mr. Cannan is of course already known as a novelist; he has been (one mentions it with pride, for *Miles Dixon* gives the lie to an old discredit to our mystery) a dramatic critic. *Miles Dixon* proclaims him a dramatist of brilliant promise for our English stage. It is not merely that he has, surely and finely, the sense of drama, though that is all the more welcome because not a few of our younger dramatists, in their zeal for 'leaving Aristotle out', affect to despise the immemorial arts by which the theatre makes its special appeals to the imaginations of its audience. It would be scarcely possible to praise too highly the acuteness of technique which thrills us when the lover is talking to the husband and we know that the woman is crouching listening behind the door. But Mr. Cannan has something much deeper and more precious than his courage of the theatre. Right through his play—and this is notable because his is the first fruit of the inspiration—one could feel the imaginative reach of perception and the passion which was the burning gift of Synge.

Gilbert and Luath stayed in Manchester to attend rehearsals. 'He arrived each day', Dame Sybil Thorndike, who was one of the

Company, told me, 'with a large, very obedient dog.' For the black and white Newfoundland it was like a return to old times. The Master and the Theatre were different, but the circumstances were similar. Already a celebrity, having taken a bow in *Peter Pan*, an acknowledgement of his part as the inspiration for Nana, he was quite at home.

For Gilbert too, there was pleasure in working with the unique Miss Horniman. Tall and dignified, dressed always in mid-Victorian clothes, an oxidised silver dragon around her neck, she had gathered together a distinguished company, among them Iden Payne, Sybil Thorndike and Lewis Casson. Gilbert felt a special affinity with Milton Rosmer and Irene Rooke, both as skilful professionals dedicated to their art and as genuine people. He was less happy with the Cassons who found him 'reserved and difficult' although they considered *Miles Dixon* to be a 'marvellous play', an opinion that was still held by Sybil Thorndike sixty-five years later.

At Christmas, Gilbert's sister Margaret came to stay at Black Lake Cottage. She found Gilbert and Mary happy and cheerful, but noted sadly that no baby was on the way. A quiet life in the country did not appear to increase Mary's waning fertility as she had probably hoped (although later she was to rationalise her barrenness by saying that she never felt comfortable with babies and preferred dogs). Janet Dunbar, in her book on Barrie, suggests that Mary's failure to conceive as a young woman was due to Barrie's impotence. Middleton Murry, writing in his Journal on the occasion of Gilbert's death in 1955, put forward another view.

What we were given to understand by Gilbert and Mary was that Barrie was guilty of unmentionable sex behaviour towards Mary. Knowing Mary I should say that *any* sexual approach towards her would have come in such a category for her. And I am pretty certain that Gilbert had no sex-relation with Mary at any time. The divorce must have been a put-up job, Gilly, having got himself into the role of Perseus-Galahad rescuing Andromeda, had to live up to it.

But Middleton Murry was a surprisingly poor judge of character, as his first three marriages and his children's haphazard upbringing show. And Murry did not know Gilbert and Mary when they were first married, but only later, after the Black Lake Cottage era, when Mary may have been approaching or in the menopause and Gilbert had, for one reason or another, started to suppress or redirect his sexual appetite. In the early years of her first marriage Mary had been subjected to a small operation which may have been gynaecological. 'Mary is quite well', Barrie had written to Quiller-Couch in 1899, 'but unfortunately it seems that she must have one of those operations again, which depress me, though she makes light of it.'[15]

Now, however, there were certain small, if inadequate compensations; the delight both Mary and Gilbert found in the dogs and countryside, the beauty and character of the tame heron, the amusement they derived from the friendly lizards, which they named Mr. & Mrs. Robinson, who came into the sitting-room on summer evenings, the charm and interest of flowers and garden. And, more important, their writing. In a small way they were striving together with the garden and books and that gave the marriage some stability and happiness.

But Gilbert's earnings had not come up to expectations and together they were spending more than he could earn. By spring 1911 the days at Black Cottage were coming to an end.

The time came when I was compelled to sell my cottage (wrote Mary). This was about a year after my second marriage. We were poor and needed the money that the sale of it would bring in.

My heart ached at the thought of leaving my beloved garden. I had made every bit of it. It was my child. Created out of me and by me. Creation in some form or other must go on, even if one is unable to create life. One must turn to and create something else.

So I had created my garden. . . .

How beautiful it all was! My soul went cold at the thought of giving it up. But it had to be.

A purchaser soon appeared, and in a short time we were back in London.[16]

They came to Kensington. Barrie had moved from Lancaster Gate to 3 Adelphi Terrace House, Robert Street, taking up a lease previously held by Edith Craig, Gordon Craig's sister. Sylvia Davies was dead and the care of her sons was in his hands. For many years they were to be Barrie's deepest concern; 'my boys', he called them.

Lillah McCarthy became a close friend.

I have sat with Barrie night after night in his high flat over the Thames . . . [she wrote in her autobiography]. He sits tucked up in a chair puffing at his pipe, absorbed, silent . . .[17]

The coast was clear. Luath returned happily to walks in Kensington Gardens and the canine delights of London lamp-posts. Billy chased sheep in Hyde Park. Gilbert set himself to work even harder.

5

'One of the Intellectuals'

Bernard Shaw

FOR the Cannans Kensington was first 23 Gordon Place and then Edwardes Place, where they rented Number 5, a pleasant terrace house built in 1820, at the top of Kensington High Street and close to Holland Park. The garden was not large enough to satisfy Mary and the walk to Kensington Gardens too long for her liking but from here Gilbert extended his literary and social life, and, although they both longed for the country, they seemed to have settled down well enough at first.

In February 1911 Gilbert had joined the Savage Club, proposed by Alfred Sutro, the playwright, and seconded by Mostyn Piggott and Reginald Geard. He had stopped reviewing for *The Star* at the end of October, but Bernard Shaw's animosity towards Gilbert smouldered on, and in 1911 became publicly obvious in *Fanny's First Play*. On March 16th, 1910, Shaw had made 'a disgraceful scene', as he put it in a letter to Arthur Pinero written the following day, at the Dramatists' Club. He had complained bitterly that every candidate he proposed for membership had been blackballed, although he had never blackballed anyone himself.

Wild recriminations arose on all sides: and I fomented the excitement by citing the cases of Hankin, Hall Caine and Gilbert Murray. All sorts of reasons why these candidates should not have been elected were presently hurtling through the air.

Shaw had gone on to insinuate that members of the Club simply blackballed everybody except their own friends on 'purely private personal and sentimental grounds', demanding that if sentiment was to be the rule he should have a share in it.

When the discussion was at its hottest and was turning on the point of how far members were justified in letting themselves be influenced by personal motives in blackballing, I said by way of illustration that if Gilbert Cannan were proposed by a member I should certainly blackball him unless he were proposed by Barrie himself. Having fired this off with some more soothing rhetoric of the same description, I happened to look round, and found that Barrie had just come in and heard everything. Of course it did not really matter, as Barrie and I are good friends, and he knew I had not seen him come in.[1]

Fanny's First Play was put on anonymously by Lillah McCarthy at the Little Theatre in Adelphi, above which she lived in a small flat with Granville Barker. She wrote in her biography that Shaw surrounded his play 'with all kinds of mysteries'

I have not put my name to it [he told her]. Do everything to suggest the play is by Barrie ... You can say with good conscience that the author's name begins with a capital 'B'.[2]

But Gilbert Gunn was so obviously based on Gilbert Cannan that, quite apart from the inimitable Shaw style, no one who knew the un-revengeful and shy Barrie was likely to suspect him of wishing to draw any attention to the man who had already brought too much unwanted publicity on his head. 'Before twenty lines had been cast over the foot-lights', recalled Lillah McCarthy, 'there were whispers of "It's Shaw, of course it's Shaw!"'[3]

On its simplest level *Fanny's First Play* is an attempt by Shaw to get his own back on the critics. Fanny, the daughter of a rich count, has written a play, which her father wishes to be judged by experts, and the impresario, Savoyard, is summoned to gather together a bunch of critics to give their opinion. The sniping at Gilbert starts when Savoyard describes the men he has invited for the task.

'Then I thought you'd like one of the latest sort: the chaps that go for the newest things and swear they are old fashioned. So I nailed Gilbert Gunn.'
The Count: 'What is Mr. Gunn's speciality, if I may ask?'
Savoyard: 'Gunn is one of the intellectuals.'
The Count: 'But aren't they all Intellectuals?'
Savoyard: 'Lord! No: heaven forbid! You must be careful what you say about that: I shouldn't like anyone to call me an Intellectual. I don't think any Englishman would! They don't count really you know; but still it's rather the thing to have them. Gunn is one of the young Intellectuals: he writes plays himself. He's useful because he pitches into the older Intellectuals who are standing in his way. But you may take it from me that none of these chaps really matter.'

After the play they comment:

Gunn: (with studied weariness) 'It seems to me the most ordinary sort of old-fashioned Ibsenite drivel.' ...
Another critic: 'Who would you say it's by, Gunn?'

Gunn guesses the play is by Granville-Barker. 'Why, Old Gilbey is straight out of the Madras House.' On being accused of being decadent Gunn retorts: 'Decādent! How I love that early Victorian word!'

When these experts find that the play is after all by a young woman their attitudes change. They become charmingly smooth-tongued and a little patronising. Chivalry, which Shaw sees as hypocrisy, comes to the fore, before the curtain falls.

Fanny's First Play quickly becomes a talking point among those who knew the people on whom the critics were based, but there appears to be no record of Gilbert's own reaction. In fact the intellectual whom Shaw thought he knew had travelled a long way since the days when Kathleen Bruce had told herself, 'He's nothing much except tall and strong and very vital and moving, with the minimum of inhibitions.'[4] Now others found him lacking vitality.

It became our habit to refer to him in real sympathy as 'Poor Gilbert' [Swinnerton relates], so much did we feel his loneliness even cloudiness of spirit . . . his conversation while never in the least superior or contemptuous, seemed to come pleasantly from a great distance; yet he was always lost in a realm of meditation. It was unwise to accept his communications about other people.[5]

Meanwhile Gilbert had made little progress as a novelist, for *Devious Ways*, an undistinguished book which he later disliked, had not been well received. *The Times Literary Supplement* reviewer found in it 'fertility of thought' but 'not enough of the sincerity that seeks the simple truths'. The book is not very convincing and not, as Swinnerton was later to suggest, autobiographical. It is probably based on the life story of one of the several young men who had shared Gilbert's lodgings from time to time.

Now, however, he felt the need to turn back to himself. He began his third novel, *Little Brother*, which was to alienate still further the Charles Cannan family in Oxford, for here Gilbert depicts Edwin as a dried-up, disagreeable eccentric. In it he tells us also a little about his own life at Cambridge, indicating that he was perhaps very much lonelier than Charles Mendel Kohan suspected. The Stephen in *Little Brother* is seen through the eyes of his elder brother Mordaunt Lawrie (an amalgam of Angus and a Cambridge don), with whom he has left an autobiographical manuscript, before disappearing with a girl of humble birth once a servant in his parents' house. Mordaunt, restrained a little by his more perceptive wife (shades of Mary here), bowdlerizes the story. This is how it was in the book during that first term at Cambridge.

1b Henry, Gilbert's father

1a Violet, Gilbert's mother

2a Angus, Gilbert and Margaret Cannan

2b Edwin Cannan

Stephen rushed from set to set, but nowhere could he gain admittance; and yet, strange to say, he was not 'barred' . . . He was respected but, like Peter Bell, he was also feared. Why, heaven alone knows. I am sure he meant no harm and asked for no more than companionship; but the callow minds of the men of his year seem to have shuddered away from him . . .

Having failed to make any lasting friendships at Manchester Grammar School, Gilbert had come to Cambridge in high hope, and finally had been 'allowed the ordinary degree' in modern and mediaeval languages and finished with a breakdown in health severe enough for the kind Edwin to decide to send him on a cruise to South Africa. Later he was to feel that he had been handicapped by lack of connections, that he had arrived unheralded and unknown (a point he makes forcibly in *Little Brother*) whereas others came with reputations already made, mentioning without bitterness to Swinnerton that:

when he was at Cambridge University he heard reports of a wonderful youth who was at Rugby and who was coming to Cambridge later. When Cannan had left Cambridge, and was in London, he heard of a wonderful young man who had arrived at Cambridge and was shortly expected to reach London. The young man—in each case it was the same young man— was Rupert Brooke. He finally reached London with a reputation already made.[6]

Little Brother is important in any study of Gilbert because it demonstrates how as a young married man he viewed his childhood and youth, and it describes several traumatic events which he was incapable of discussing with his friends. Had he been able to talk about the treatment he suffered at the hands of Angus and their grandmother, he might not have needed to write about it. Clearly there is much in this novel, and other books about Stephen, which tells us that Gilbert was not a normal child. There is also an element of wish-fulfilment, a chance taken to show up Mordaunt (Angus) as an idiot in not recognising earlier the strength of Stephen's imagination and philosophy of life. Indeed, while reading the manuscript Mordaunt falls under the spell of the younger brother he once despised:

It has unsettled me. It has set me wondering about things which are better not thought of; it has interfered with my world; it has haunted me, obtruded itself upon my conversation with my male friends. Nothing has happened to me since I read it, but I have found myself wondering what my brother would have thought of it. My tastes have adapted themselves to his; I have found myself laughing at things which I had hitherto always regarded with respect. A spirit of levity and jocularity has crept into my lectures, and I have shocked more than one of my pupils from Newnham and Girton.

And then Mordaunt (Angus) remembering Stephen (Gilbert):

He always had a white face, and strange heavy eyes, and the sight of it used
sometimes to drive me into a frenzy, and then I would lunge out at it with
my fists. Sometimes he would fall flat on the ground and lie without a sound,
until I was nearly sick with fear that I had killed him; other times he would
stand still gasping for breath until the sensation of pain had penetrated the
thick crust that I really believe was over his brain and then he would fly at
me in what we used to call one of his besearck (*sic*) rages, and whirl his arms
and gnash his teeth and look so horrible that I used to turn tail and fly before
him.

An exaggeration perhaps, but Angus's daughter, Elizabeth Cannan,
confirmed that her father considered Gilbert to be a 'cry baby' and took
it upon himself to turn him into a 'real boy'.

Some of Gilbert's whiteness, feebleness and weeping, so despised by
Angus, was probably partly due to hunger, as well as psychological
problems. Much taller and thinner than his elder brother, he was a poor
eater and, to make matters worse, food was sometimes in short supply
in the Cannan household owing to straitened circumstances and
inefficiency during the early years of their marriage. Each morning,
before leaving for work, Henry would give his wife two shillings on
which to feed the family for the day, which was just enough if there
were no other calls on Violet Cannan's purse. But frequently there
were—and then lunch would be only hot thick gravy poured over
boiled potatoes eaten (ironically) from a well laid table complete with
high quality china and silver napkin rings.

Gilbert also experienced at times a heightened sense of feeling and
vision, perhaps suggesting some hyper-electrical action in the brain:

I can remember shying away from the appearance of things because I could
visualise them so sharply that they hurt. A room into which I had been was
recorded for ever, but what I wanted out of it was more than visual detail.
I wanted its contribution to my knowledge, that it should be distilled, as it
were, and dropped into my store in essence and all the time I was aware that
I was waiting and that whatever was going on around me was not basically
my affair.[7]

A lost, strange child, beating against bars to find a path into the
world, is another way in which Gilbert sees himself in *Little Brother*.
But his sense of detachment and difference may also have been partly
the result of a mild form of epilepsy, as the following episode described
in that novel, and confirmed to me as fact by his sister Margaret,
suggests. Here the incident is seen through Mordaunt's eyes. Both boys
are staying with their widowed grandmother, Mrs. Lawrie (Agnes
Cannan).

One other memory I have of Stephen is in that spot under Jean Paul; lying on the floor of the passage and clutching hold of the bannisters, he could just reach the wainscoting with his feet. He lay so, stiff and with hard staring eyes, while my grandmother stood over him and lammed into him with a cane. He had refused to go to a school (kept by my aunt Phoebe) because they had put him in a pair of boots cast off by a richer cousin, a parcel of whose old clothes had been sent for our use . . . He did not stir under the blows of the cane, and did not stir for nearly an hour afterwards. He lay in a sort of cataleptic condition and then presently there resounded through the house the most tremendous and appalling hiccoughs . . . I have never seen my grandmother in such a state of alarm. She sent for a doctor, an imbecile who knew nothing of Stephen and saw only a child who had been beaten into a state of hysteria.

I happened to know that Stephen could hiccough at will. He had displayed the accomplishment to me with some pride when he discovered it.

Catalepsy or epilepsy or symptoms of schizophrenia? Margaret writing to me about the event some seventy years later, believed that he suffered occasionally from the *petit mal*. She had some experience of the disease because the youngest Cannan child, Gertrude Sheila, who was born in 1900, was badly afflicted with epilepsy and eventually died in her early thirties in an institution for epileptics. Margaret wrote that she was present on the occasion of the beating, and that the boots were girls'; hence Gilbert's obduracy. Her description of the event differs little from that in *Little Brother*:

He lay silent however hard she thrashed him; it was I who cried. Martha, my father's nurse, at last *frightened* my grandmother into calling a doctor. He came and didn't know what to do. After he had gone, Gilbert, still without moving started to hiccough.

Since Gilbert was supposedly unconscious for much of the time, it seems likely that he heard the full story from his sister. The setting is based on fact. The picture of Jean Paul, a present from Gilbert's great-aunt Mary to his grandfather, James Cannan, was of special significance to him, as those two people were undoubtedly the most important members of his 'company of souls'.

Writing *Little Brother* was catharsis as well as creation but the book does not lack humour. Subtly, Gilbert derides himself as well as Angus. It is almost as though he is saying 'How green I was!' His break with George (Edwin) is treated wryly, his sycophantic behaviour towards those he considers great, with irony; his shallow love affairs with three young women (all of whom seem to have preceded Kathleen Bruce, if indeed they existed in reality), with a hint of ridicule. It is also at times a bitter book which marks the end of the naïve Gilbert so youthfully eager to meet Meredith and Conrad. The young man of the novel is finally disillusioned by a Mrs. Gerrans who asks him to dinner to tell him of the shabby love affairs of those he admires—a job probably taken on in real life by Sylvia Davies or Mary Barrie.

Here is how the elder brother puts it.

> It seems incredible that a woman of experience should talk so to a young man in his early twenties. But all things are possible and I cannot believe that Stephen invented it; he was too much affected by it. What she told him made his morals stand up on end. He tried hard to cling to the remains of his old bourgeois morality and crude conception of marriage as a sacrament; but against her facts he was powerless. She gave no names but she sketched her life and the life of her friends cruelly, brutally, cynically—intrigue piled upon intrigue: the right use of studios, the trips to Paris, the partie carrée, a whole underworld of illicit affection which fills drawing rooms and clubs with gossip . . . she was bitter.

> 'What a life!' she said: and she mimicked certain of her friends, archly smiling and twittering.

Most of all, this Mrs. Gerrans disillusions her young friend about the man he admired, Professor Wherry, who is the centrepiece of the book, the king of hypocrites, considered by many to be a moral force for good. If such disillusionment did come about in such a way, it is easy to see how much simpler it became to slide between the sheets with Mary Barrie, to turn consummation into a fashionable adventure, an act which supposedly took place after *Peter Homunculus* was finished and youthful romantic notions had been jolted. The young man in *Little Brother* has lost his footing. He wants to please, to care, to behave decently (which does not mean conventionally); above all, to love. He turns at last to a poor but pretty girl, an older version of the maid to whom Gilbert was innocently attracted as a boy.

The title *Little Brother* refers to Stephen, Mordaunt's younger brother, and perhaps, as one reviewer coyly suggested, to the little brother of the soul in all of us that is struggling to get out. It also in its way stood for George, guardian to Stephen, because that was the pet name Charles Cannan gave to Edwin and still used when they were both adults. The title therefore drew the Oxford Cannans' attention to the fact that Edwin was in the book. The man who had been kind to Gilbert, seen him through Cambridge and paid him an allowance in London, was now derided. It was, Charles Cannan felt, too much. Edwin, deeply involved with his beloved son, was able to dismiss the insult as youthful folly. Charles, less vulnerable and less damaged by bereavement, and long Edwin's protector, did not forgive: his fraternal feelings would not allow it. His second daughter, May Wedderburn

Cannan, in her memoirs, *Grey Ghosts and Voices*, wrote that he considered the book to be a breach of confidence.[8]

Little Brother was published in February 1912 and was reviewed briefly in *The Times Literary Supplement* on the 22nd. The anonymous critic considered Stephen's character and career had in them the makings of a good novel,

but they are not worth the elaborate machinery invented for them — the 'Prefatory matter,' the 'Introduction', the manuscript left by Stephen, the working it up by his brother Mordaunt, with interjections by Mordaunt's wife. One has the feeling of Stephen being continually pushed on the stage and being told to 'play up', which, with Mr. Cannan's staccato manner, too often becomes fatiguing.

But perhaps predictably, the critic in *The English Review* of March was more enthusiastic:

This is one of those books which are more curious than beautiful [he began], but, by the arresting quality of the matter, and occasionally flashing sentences it triumphs over a clumsiness of construction so obvious, that it seems it must be wilfully contrived. It is as though the author said, in effect, 'Here is my company of ideas, I present them without any allurements of dress or greasepaint. Such as they are, let them stand or fall by themselves.' And they stand, for here is that rare thing, a novel of thought.

Some time in the previous year Gilbert had also written three short plays: *Wedding Presents*, *Mary's Wedding* and *The Perfect Wedding*. He had also been working on translations of the last volume of *Jean Christophe* and *L'Ordination (The Yoke of Pity)* by Julian Benda, which was published by Fisher Unwin in 1912. As usual, he sent a copy of each of his books to his mother, to whom he was also regularly sending sums of money to assist in the bringing up his younger brothers and sisters.

Miss Horniman's production of *Mary's Wedding*, a one-act play, at the Coronet Theatre on May 6th, 1912, received appreciative notices. The critic in the *Daily Telegraph* was especially complimentary:

A bit of stern and saddening realism this, but pictured with a fine feeling of constraint. It is the great virtue of Mr. Cannan's work that, dealing with a horrible and repugnant theme, he does not attempt to harass us unnecessarily. The pity of it all remains, however, and sinks deep.

The theme was alcoholism. Mary has loved one man for years and has promised to marry him if he can keep away from liquor for six months. He succeeds until the wedding day when he reels in drunk to 'show himself'. The play is delicately perceptive the dialogue moving and sometimes eloquent. The enforced brevity of such curtain-raisers assured that every word was chosen with care. Irene Rooke played Mary and Charles Bibby took the male lead.

The Yoke of Pity was also well reviewed. The critic in *The Times Literary Supplement* of August 21st found the translation sensitive and understanding and remarked that:

> ... Mr. Cannan has realised what Mr. Benda is 'at', has caught his queer and remote point of view, and followed him faithfully through his minute analysis of the agonies of the hero, who had to give up being a philosopher because he learned to love his wife and invalid child.

By now Gilbert had started work on his fourth novel *Round the Corner*, which was to be without contrivances; a book in which Stephen plays only a small part in a minor key.

While living at Edwardes Place Gilbert met John Middleton Murry and Katherine Mansfield and, soon after financial responsibility for their magazine *Rhythm* was taken over by Stephen Swift, he became a regular contributor, his first story 'The Midwife' appearing in the July number. This was followed by the publication of *Miles Dixon* in two parts, a column called 'Observations and Opinions', some drama criticism and several beautifully written short stories. In this last medium Gilbert's style, although sometimes a little mannered, was usually at its best, brevity again forcing on him a self-discipline which might have improved some of his novels. His criticism and philosophical articles in *Rhythm* were less skilfully presented, lacking the stringency and tautness of his stories. Although not on the staff, Gilbert rapidly became an enthusiastic member of the group which was to make it so distinguished a magazine.

In October 1912, when the plausible but unreliable Stephen Swift absconded, leaving Middleton Murry with debts of £400 to settle, Gilbert was among those who put up money to help out. Swinnerton recalls a meeting between five young people to discuss the crisis. It was held in 'an extremely dark, chilly room' in Chancery Lane, this being the home of Middleton Murry and Katherine Mansfield as well as the *Rhythm* office.

Besides Murry and Katherine Mansfield, who between them had published only one book, a volume of stories by Katherine, afterwards suppressed, entitled *In a German Pension*, were three men with rather more to their credit. The first, Richard Curle, a friend of Conrad, and a young traveller, was as much immersed in exotism as the younger generation of forty years later. The second, Gilbert Cannan, besides savaging 'old-fashioned Ibsenite drivel', in *The Star*, reviewing for the *Manchester Guardian* (he went to school in Manchester) and writing his first precocious autobiographical novels, *Peter Homunculus* and *Devious Ways*, had begun to translate with superlative copiousness Romain Rolland's already copious *Jean Christophe*. He was the star of the party. The third was myself.[9]

The five young people decided that *Rhythm* should carry on. It was a venture which had begun with the Murrys life together (an important facet in their love affair) and, with its very modern outlook and European correspondents on the arts, was unique at the time. The first English magazine to publish drawings by Picasso, it had started beautifully with many decorative headings and tailpieces; other artist contributors were Vladimir Polunin, Othon Friesz, Jessie Dismorr, Peploe, Anne Estelle Rice, Gaudier-Brzeska and the first art editor, J. D. Fergusson.

Commenting on Gilbert's friendship at this time in his biography, *Between Two Worlds*, Middleton Murry wrote:

Gilbert and Mary Cannan had become good friends of ours. Gilbert had been attracted to *Rhythm*, and had come to visit Katherine and me at the very beginning of our life together. Not only had he worked hard to help us with the magazine, but he had adopted a kindly protective attitude towards me in particular. Perhaps we struck him as oddly *farouche*, for it was he who gave us the nickname of the Two Tigers, which—hardened first into Tig, then softened into Wig—was the origin of my name for Katherine till the end of her life. With his stick, his pipe and his shaggy dog, Gilbert would stride over from Kensington to Gray's Inn Road, sit silent in a corner and smile an inscrutable smile.

We liked him and we trusted him, though we found him hard to understand. The centre of him seemed to be totally withdrawn and impenetrable, but by no conscious effort of his own. And I was far too timid to make any direct inquisition into that in him which baffled me. I was far too conscious, besides, of his kindness to me to risk disturbing a relation which struck me as curiously though beneficently one-sided.

Now in the winter of 1912 the brilliant young publisher Martin Secker, who was to become one of Gilbert's staunchest friends and greatest admirers, volunteered to publish the magazine in place of Swift. Edward Marsh, patron of the arts (and private secretary to Winston Churchill), offered a guarantee of up to £150. Wilfred Gibson, the poet, became assistant editor. The old format was kept, but the decorative head and tailpieces were cut to save money.

Through *Rhythm*, Gilbert was to make many new friends. Edward Marsh he had, however, met earlier. Indeed he may well have been instrumental in bringing him in as a guarantor. Twelve years senior to Gilbert, an inveterate diner-out and first-nighter, Eddie Marsh was quick to recognise and encourage talent when the opportunity arose. In September of that year Gilbert had accepted an invitation to dine with him at the Moulin d'Or, only to cancel it on the day (the 24th) because 'my wife is too depressed with a cold to let me go out tonight'. Was Mary piqued that she was not also asked? The next sentence in Gilbert's letter suggests she wanted to be included in any further meeting: 'She hopes—as I do—that you will dine here with us some night soon.' An invitation eventually shared by the Middleton Murrys, who were surprised to find their sophisticated new friend somewhat apprehensive:

I remember Eddie was very worried, or perhaps pretended to be. He had met, in our room, some evenings before, Gilbert Cannan, who was a friend of ours. We did not realise he had known Cannan before; but now we had all been invited to dinner with Gilbert and Mary Cannan at their house in Edwardes Square (sic). Eddie had known Mary Cannan much better than he did Gilbert; but that was when she was J. M. Barrie's wife; 'I really don't know how I ought to behave,' he said, lifting his eyebrow. We laughed outright. Eddie not knowing how to behave struck us as a really comic notion.[10]

In the autumn of 1912 Gilbert also joined the Georgian Group to help Rupert Brooke and Edward Marsh with *Georgian Poetry 1*, packing copies to be sent to bookshops, for although his own poetry was never to be included he had many friends among the contributors.[11] In his idealistic world friendship meant wherever possible throwing oneself whole-heartedly into the efforts of one's friends.

Now he increasingly needed the companionship and affection of these younger people, for many of the old guard disliked him, partly because he had threatened them with his own success and partly, perhaps, because he had turned his back on them. For him they belonged to the old life when youthful hopes had been shattered, the time before the trauma of the divorce.

We spoke a little of Gilbert Cannan [Marie Belloc-Lowndes wrote in her Diary on June 10th, 1912]. It is sad to see how much he is now disliked. Ross told me that he was once hailed as the most marvellous genius of his age, and that he, Ross, possessed a letter from St. John Hankin in which ran the phrase: 'Shaw, Barker and Galsworthy all believe Cannan is going to wipe them out.'[12]

So in 1912 Gilbert was courageously building a new life among *real* people, the helper rather than the helped. His plays and criticism showed no sign of wiping out any established playwrights, but his novels were beginning to make their mark. Among these new friends was Gordon Campbell, who had married Beatrice Moss in August, and at Christmas the Cannans, the Murrys, and the Campbells went to Paris to be at a party given by Anne Estelle Rice, who was soon to marry O. Raymond Drey, *Rhythm's* recently appointed art critic.[13]

For Mary it was not an entirely happy time. She was becoming increasingly conscious of belonging to a different generation from most of Gilbert's friends, and she did not like Katherine Mansfield whom she found 'remote and reserved, unapproachable and impossible', a woman who 'always gives everyone what they want', meaning that Katherine Mansfield changed her personality or response to fit in with what she imagined was wanted from her.[14]

Amateur dramatics were now a feature of many of the parties to which the Cannans were invited. Beatrice Campbell, in her autobiography, tells of an evening at the St. John Hutchinsons'[15] house in Hammersmith:

They gave wonderful parties in which charades were a speciality. I remember one which included a scene in the Russian Court. 'Hutch' (St. John Hutchinson, often called Jack) was a splendid Greek Church Archbishop, Gilbert Cannan the Czar, Viola Tree the Czarina, Gertler the Czarevitch and Molly MacCarthy (Desmond MacCarthy's wife) was an English governess to the Czarevitch. Boris Anrep played Rasputin. The actors used anything they could dress up in, as well as things supplied by Mary Hutchinson, I felt honoured when I recognised that a rather shabby fur stole of mine had been turned into a hat for the Czar.[16]

On these occasions Gilbert was at his best. He loved acting. As a child he had avoided being himself by becoming a buffoon, the clown in his family, and he had been in the annual play every year at school.

Another writer with whom Gilbert became friendly while at Edwardes Place was Compton Mackenzie, then working on *Carnival*, who had previously written the songs and sketches for H. G. Pélissier and the Follies for their *Revue* at the Alhambra, Leicester Square. Both his parents and grandparents had been on the stage and he possessed that streak of exhibitionism so often found among actors. Writing of Compton Mackenzie in 'Publisher's Progress' in *The Cornhill Magazine* Spring 1974, Martin Secker tells how:

Like others, I had fallen an easy victim to the charm of his personality, his good looks, his wit, his wide range of interests both in prose and poetry and the intoxication with words which expressed itself in the lyrical passages of *Sinister Street* and *Guy and Pauline*.

Otherwise conventionally dressed, Compton Mackenzie always wore outside a soft wide-brimmed hat and carried a walking stick. His actor's instinct to dress the part never left him and when I met him a year or so before his death, his dark blue pyjamas were given a certain panache by a red-spotted scarf tied, pirate-like, round his neck. This feeling for dress, for atmosphere and personal visual effect was absent from Gilbert. The two were very different in many other ways and Compton Mackenzie, known to his friends as Monty, was in fact to see Gilbert on and off for over a decade without ever caring for him as a person. Unlike Gilbert, Mackenzie could see the funny side in most aspects of life and his own conversation sparkled with jokes. Moral dilemmas, sexual problems and puzzling philosophical paradoxes did not lie heavily on his shoulders. He in turn found Gilbert's conversation irritating, 'he would turn everything into a lecture'. He was 'too fond of preaching to become a good novelist'.[17]

In a letter Mackenzie accused Gilbert of preaching in his novels '*à la* Shelley'. Constant indignation, Mackenzie thought also, could be extremely tedious. He made no allowance for the weight of Gilbert's inheritance from a line of clergymen and teachers which impelled him to expound his theories and point the way. Gilbert could not tell a story without trying to wring a great truth out of it, to show the stupid world where it had gone wrong. He found 'more beauty in indignation than in the charm of a lie'.[18]

Mackenzie was partly instrumental in bringing Gilbert's next book to Martin Secker.[19] At this time both Secker and Mackenzie were in their thirties, with like tastes. They met often, frequently in the company of John Nicholas Mavrogordato, occasionally at the Café Royal, more often at the Café de l'Europe, or in the evenings at De Hem's Oyster Bar in Macclesfield Street, just off Shaftesbury Avenue. 'Mavro' was at that time literary adviser to J. M. Dent, and later became editor of *The English Review*. It wasn't long before Gilbert was joining them for a drink or a meal. Unlike Swinnerton, they did not feel sorry for him, but accepted him as he was. Secker, for one, always found him good company and admired him as a writer, only having reservations about his philosophical books and literary and theatre criticism.

On October 22nd Gilbert announced cheerfully in a letter to Compton Mackenzie:

Round the Corner is finished and I give it to Secker tomorrow. I have the delightful feeling of a mother who has found a kind nurse at last. Heinemanns was like a workhouse crèche.

He goes on to mention that Frank Mills, the producer, was trying to persuade Broadhurst, author of *Bought and Paid For*, to like a melodrama he had written in 1911.

If you see Broadhurst tell him, as a genius, that I am a genius too. People like things in quantities and are more likely to believe in two than in one.

I'm feeling very frivolous and holidayish but can only kick up my heels for a day or two and then must get on dragging my cart.

On November 5th he wrote to Mackenzie in America,

I am living in expectation of proofs of *Round the Corner* rather excited about it and not able to settle to anything serious until I'm through. I've finished the translation of 'Jean Christophe' and feel more or less my own man again.

He mentions that his wife's *Happy Houses* is just out, 'getting good reviews though slow in coming in as the [Balkan] war is crowding everything out of the newspapers. I see "Kensington Rhymes", well displayed in Smiths and in Mudie's in the High Street, and hope it is doing nicely.' And in a postscript he tells Mackenzie that his lecture in Liverpool did well and that he is 'doing it again in Manchester on December 4th'.[20]

Round the Corner was to catch the interest of a number of leading authors of the day and lead to new friendships. The second of six novels based on the lives of Gilbert's relations, it is I think his finest book. A story he *had* to write, it came quickly with little revision and is based on his conception of the truth about those who made him what he was. In his preface to the 1923 American edition Gilbert was to write that he possessed at twenty-five a very clear conception of the history of the industrial revolution seen through the spiritual history of his family.

I have to return to the subject again and again in spite of all the efforts of publishers, critics and politicians to make me desist.

And in his little philosophical book *Love*, published by Batsford in 1914, he was to write:

To win through to a fair idea of love a man must first have a clear idea of himself. To this end he sets to and recreates himself, toils and labours until upon his mind there is graven an image which in his heart he can recognise as himself in relation to the forces which are greater than himself.

His obsession with his family was to some degree part of his obsession with himself and his own sense of isolation, another attempt to become real through others or through his analysis of, or identification with, others in his work.

With *Round the Corner* he escaped into the world of his maternal grandparents, retelling the stories he had heard from his merry, light-hearted mother in all those different Manchester houses. Information seemed to accumulate in his subconscious and then years later come out on a wave of inspiration. He seems to have checked nothing, yet all the basic facts in the novel are true; the awful death of Nicholas, the suicide of Frederick, the return of Serge, the secret wedding of Stephen's parents, the fierce parochial battles over the clergyman's High Anglican practices. The local papers of the time, the reports of inquests, relevant parish registers, all bear out the facts. The discrepancies between truth and fiction relate only to small matters. There is a charming scene, for example, when the young Bennett (Henry Cannan) sees Annette (Violet Wright) swimming naked in a pool. In reality Violet only learnt to swim in middle-age.

The Times Literary Supplement reviewer found *Round the Corner* a disappointment, considering the characters in it at least as unattractive as Gilbert found Manchester.

For while you cannot read it without admiration for its cleverness and literary skill, the general effect is one of squalor. From the jibe on the title-page at *'le siècle le plus éclairé qui fut jamais'*, through the epigrams of the little preface down to the touching death of the Rev. Francis Folyat, there is a claim to set forth a serious criticism of life as it is. To which the only comment is that life, seen wholly, is not like this, for all the vivid presentiment that seeks to persuade that these stereoscopic figures are human beings.

The reviewer, surely, had no experience of poverty-stricken life in the provinces. And sadly there were people who did not *want* to know that such people as those depicted actually existed, got young women pregnant and committed suicide on trains.

The theme, the problems, the views expressed on marriage were too much for the large lending libraries, who banned the book. Martin Secker countered with an advertisement:

Not an Immoral Book.
Those who have already read and enjoyed Mr. Gilbert Cannan's new novel, 'Round the Corner', will be surprised to learn that in the opinion of the large circulating libraries it is not a fit book for them to send to their subscribers. Where the offence comes in, no one can discover, and it now lies with the public either to insist on being supplied with it freely, or to allow the author to suffer under the cruel, unjustifiable and damaging stigma of having written an immoral book. 'Round the Corner' is a novel which, for his part, the publisher is proud to have issued, and he appeals for support to those of the public who refuse to be dictated to by a self-appointed committee of literary censors. The 'Westminster Gazette' says: ' "Round the Corner" is a notable book . . . informed by a high seriousness of purpose which sets it apart from the thousands of books sans vue ensemble' . . . In 'Round the Corner' the author has striven for and achieved something truer and more profound than any young novelist of today.

Other reviewers and people of note were more encouraging. In an undated letter from 17 Church Row, Hampstead, H. G. Wells wrote:

My dear Cannan,
I've been reading *Round the Corner* with the keenest interest, nay great admiration. You handle a parson as well as Samuel Butler (you know his

Way of All Flesh) but with more sympathy and humanity, and you steer your family one among the others as skilfully as that delightful and all too little praised Charlotte M. Yonge. And I like the large intentions behind your large design. They are after my own heart. The book is a great tale of just things well done, an immense advance in power on your previous fiction, and a novel that is fit to rank with any novel that matters. What the asses found to censor in it, I can't imagine. Apparently we aren't even to hint at masturbation and the troubles of youth. For fear the young should hear of them. You commit one grave artistic crime, but a noble one, and one in which I too have dabbled. You run an impossible 'exponent' character. His very name is out of drawing. Why should Francis call his eldest son *Serge*! Have you ever known any man get Serge's kind of wisdom knocking about the world? Seek out and study Bart Kennedy and Manly Roberts. Serge would really have come back with a rancid imperialism & some Chinese variety of venereal disease. You & I must form a secret society of two for the elimination of 'Serge' & Serge-ism from our work. It won't do. It eases us much but it puts the reader's back up & spoils the book altogether.

Hugh Walpole was also quick to put forward his views, to which letter Gilbert replied from Edwardes Place on January 15th, 1913.

I was delighted to have your appreciation of my book. One artist sees the work of another from the inside as well as the outside. He gets nearer to whatever truth there is in it, but also he is a thousand times harder to please. Thank you.

I'm distressed at Smith's morals being shocked because it necessitates a not altogether desirable sort of advertisement & makes a number of people approach the book in the wrong spirit, and look in it for an intention which was never mine. However, as they do that with the Bible, Fielding, Burns and Shakespeare one is in tolerable company.

I hope you'll come and see us here.

H. G. Wells was of course unaware that Serge was based on Gilbert's uncle, the daring and independent Henry Charles Seppings Wright, who came back after an unconventional life in South Africa, without the venereal disease forecast by Wells. There had been a line of successful naval men in the Wright family and Seppings had been sent to sea at thirteen to follow the tradition, but had jumped ship to go diamond hunting, and later became an artist. After failing to establish himself in the Manchester area, Seppings eventually distinguished himself as a war artist, working for the *Illustrated London News* in the Russo-Japanese War, the only reporter to sail in Admiral Togo's ships. Afterwards he wrote the story of these adventures in a book, *With Togo*, published by Hurst and Blackett in 1905.

Short, bearded, straight-nosed, strong-jawed, he was not surprisingly Gilbert's favourite uncle, a man of many parts and experiences, but high principled. In *Round the Corner* Gilbert appears occasionally to use Seppings (Serge) as his own mouthpiece, finding it easy to identify with the artist, adventurer, sailor and journalist in the man, perhaps turning him into more of a philosopher than he may have been. Gilbert's answer to H. G. Wells does not seem to have survived and we are left to wonder whether he was amused or irritated by the older man's criticism of the unreality of a character based almost entirely on fact.

There are several passages in the novel which indicate that now Gilbert's disillusionment with marriage as generally accepted, was almost complete.

Superstition will have it that marriage is a good thing and, being one of the most powerful agents in human affairs, forbids discussion of its pseudo-axiom. Superstition uses marriage as a club with which to lay men and women low . . .

It is one of the most disconcerting phenomena of existence that, when passionate love has answered its purpose it simply disappears, leaving its instruments wedded by such truth as they have discovered in each other or divorced by the lies they have forged for each other's delight. Very rarely, however, is the issue so simple. The bone-and-shadow business comes into play here also, and most people marry with very little passionate love and a great deal of careful imitation of it, so that most marriages are strangled in their birth with a very tangled web of lies.

The eccentric and arresting Lady Ottoline Morrell, then in her fortieth year, was another who wrote to Gilbert and Mary after the publication of *Round the Corner*, inviting them both to visit her at 44 Bedford Square. Here they fell quickly under the spell of her sympathetic interest, and were to become for a time captivated by her generous if idiosyncratic personality. She cared for Gilbert rather than Mary, and was obviously touched by their fondness and admiration for her. They took gladly all she had to give and tried to give back something of themselves. Gilbert, of course, always delighted in an unconventional and courageous woman and in 1912 Lady Ottoline was not as overwhelming as in later years.

In her *Early Memoirs* she wrote:

I cannot trace in the dark tunnels of my memory how I first knew Gilbert Cannan and his wife. That rather charming and gifted, but conceited novelist of whom we saw a great deal, and who was the forerunner and introducer of other people who played important parts in our lives.

I believe I must have written to him about one of his first books, *Round the*

Corner, which I thought original and interesting. He had recently run off with Sir James Barrie's wife, and perhaps I felt that people would be preju-diced against him on this account, and certainly on the outside it did not appear very honourable, as he had been one of Barrie's protégés. I believe Mary Cannan, however, had not found Barrie very satisfactory as a husband and she became entranced with this young man, who had indeed the appear-ance of a rather vacant Sir Galahad, and whose mind was prolific, poetic and romantic. I never understood how he could have been tempted to run away with this lady, for she was double his age, and devoid of any atmosphere of romance, and certainly unable to run very far or fast. But how can one divine the reasons for such foolish acts? It was probably prompted by quixotic pity on Gilbert's part, but it was doomed to be a failure, and this doom ahead already cast its shadow backward. She was, poor woman, so deter-mined to keep herself young and sprightly when they came together to see us—she so solid with thin lips and a carefully preserved complexion, like a very competent lady house-decorator and upholsteress (this was, in fact, her chief interest), he, thin and tall, towering above her always looking with his pale, romantic eyes into space, and shaking his fair hair and tilting his large thin nose in the air, while she vigorously chatted in a loud harsh voice about what she and Gillie had done. It made one raise one's hands like Henry James, in horror.[21]

Lytton Strachey saw few if any redeeming features: 'The poor fellow must have a dim time of it with his wife who's years older than him and very distressing'. And he didn't like *Round the Corner* at all:

It would be difficult to conceive anything duller and more completely lacking in the joie de vivre. I stuck to it and read every word of the blasted thing, but while I was doing so I felt a cloud over my life. The poor fellow is so modern and broad minded too, but, oh! the taste!—and the pointlessness![22]

A meeting over tea only confirmed Strachey's generally poor opinion of Gilbert.

Pathetically pleased at being taken up by Lady Ottoline, it was Mary who corresponded with her at first, her careless writing sprawling across the page. Replying to the letter praising *Round the Corner*, on April 6th, she wrote:

It was very kind of you to write to us about my husband's book and your appreciation has given me—and him—the keenest gratification.

If you will let us know a day when you are to be at home we will come to tea with great pleasure.

They passed the test of tea. Lady Ottoline was interested in them. 'We are so glad you liked us and want to ask us again,' wrote Mary humbly on April 21st, accepting an invitation to dine. This was followed by a meal with Ottoline, probably at Peppard, with a difficult journey home. 'The lamps went out one by one, until we were left with a small side light, and your coat kept me beautifully warm and I was most grateful for it.'

A few days later Ottoline took the Cannans to the Russian Ballet at Covent Garden. Michael Holroyd believes that Lytton Strachey resented Lady Ottoline's friendship with Gilbert, and so many invitations within a few weeks does suggest that she found him especially attractive, a fact she admits although she suggests it was his mind that attracted her rather than his physical charm:

They both came fairly often to tea and to our Thursday evenings, obviously enjoying being 'received'. Sometimes he would come and stay a night or two in our spare room and I would immensely enjoy his talk, which was a mixture of the ideas of Blake, and Plato and Goethe. Indeed I still believe it was good—he was quite impersonal and seemed as if he were talking his thoughts aloud, but as the thoughts were sympathetic and stimulating to me I enjoyed it. He consumed a vast number of cigarettes while he mused and held forth.[23]

By now Mary and Gilbert's longing for the country had prompted them to rent a cottage at Bellingdon near Chesham in Buckinghamshire, a single storey building, a mile or so down the hill from Cholesbury Common, where they were soon to live.

Gilbert's impatience with much of the drama being produced in London at that time appeared to be growing. In an undated letter to Albert Rothenstein (later Rutherston) from Edwardes Place, he complains of the 'blather' being talked about the *Winter's Tale*, adding rather petulantly 'there are so many people in London, and they all talk such a lot. It is neither here nor there to drag in Craig and Reinhardt, what has been done was bound to be done'. But this time he finds praise for Granville-Barker, who 'altered the machinery—all honour to him for it'. He goes on:

Your costumes for instance are brilliant and courageous and charming, often splendidly delightful in the play. The scenery on the other hand is, while skilful enough, cold and hard and instead of absorbing your colour into the play drives it out to the audience, so that they are exhausted . . .

In fact, the talking, the lunches and the parties were beginning to pall a little; for Gilbert now suffered from the problem common to most writers: the need for both solitude and communication with other people of like mind. The trouble was how to get the right balance. But now in spring he thought he had found the answer.

My dear Walpole [he wrote in a long letter from Edwardes Place, on April 30th, 1913], I was glad to hear from you in your solitude. I'm rather suffering from London. It's beginning to ask me out to lunch—high time to clear out. We've taken a windmill to clear out to—in the Chilterns and I'm to have a round study in it looking towards the four corners of the Heavens and the Earth. I shall like that.

A third of a novel sounds industrious! I've been doing nothing for many weeks, the sort of miserable profitable nothing in which five eighths of one's work gets done. A little unfairly too in such periods I always read the classics, or at least the terrific swells, unfairly because one looks at them in the sort of warm and rather exhausted annoyance with which a pregnant woman looks at children. These things that exist for better or worse are so unenviable by the side of one's hopes. One is always yearning to get more than one's bucketful out of the ocean of thought and feeling . . .

I've only begun to work on a new book, slowly, ironically, with much disgust—as usual—and hatred both of my own clumsiness and the tiresomeness of pen, ink, printer and publishers as the vehicle in which one has to transfer one's vision (after it has been lived up to as best one can) into form that shall give it currency in human consciousness. . . .

Although he mentioned that he started books slowly and clumsily, both David Garnett and Compton Mackenzie told me that Gilbert normally wrote very quickly. Indeed his output would suggest this; *Mendel* for example was written in two months. Martin Secker confirmed that Gilbert was not a reviser and certainly some of his work would have benefited from more revision. It seems likely that in April 1913 he was drained by his proliferacy. Yet his ambition, financial problems and addiction to words (and probably also an increasing depression with the facts of his marriage) were such that he could not hold back from beginning another novel, on this occasion *Old Mole*.

1913 was to see the performance of his one-act play *A Short Way With Authors* at the Cosmopolis (London?) and in Boston, and the publication of three of his books after the appearance of *Round the Corner*: his translation of *Jean Christophe* Vol. IV, his *Four Plays* and the *Joy of the Theatre* as well as a number of articles and short stories, theatre criticism and *Opinions*. But at Cholesbury he was to work even harder in a truly Herculean effort to please Mary, to make his income meet his expenses, fulfil the promise others had seen in his work, and escape from fears of failure and inadequacy which seemed to alternate with that sense of greatness which was later to turn disastrously into a state of exaltation.

6

'A True Man'

Mark Gertler

AND SO in early summer 1913 there came to live in Cholesbury, a lanky comparatively long-haired Gilbert, his fine nose thinner and his cheeks a little hollower than in the days when he had first known Kathleen Bruce. He came with two dogs, Luath and Billy, with hundreds of books, and Mary, to whom he was about to dedicate his next novel. The villagers noticed his tallness and the fairness of his hair, and some called him 'the writer'. He talked of his work to the carpenter, and joined the local cricket club and occasionally played bowls in the little pub, The Full Moon.

The Mill House was partly tile-hung and, according to Secker, rather suburban, but more important to Gilbert was the windmill with its sails still attached, and its view to the four corners of the earth. This was the place I think Gilbert loved best. He was its first occupant, for it had been used until he came for the storage of grain. Now it had been turned into his own private haven and place of work, with a sitting-room complete with pianola, below the study. He loved the country with a passion known only to those who have been reared in an ugly heavily polluted city. As a child the highlights of every summer had been the two weeks he spent, usually with Angus, at his Great Aunt Mary's house, the Sheiling, at Grasmere, close to the hills and the river Rothay.

In earlier youth he had been equally enchanted by the home of his retired grandfather, the Reverend Francis Arbuthnot Wright, in Topsham, Devon, described in *Round the Corner* and mentioned in Gilbert's memoirs. Here his mother had sometimes taken him to recuperate after one of his many illnesses, on visits that were always too short because his father who could never last for more than a day or two without his wife, would telegraph for them to return. Now, seven hundred feet up in the Chilterns, Gilbert was to enjoy the countryside again. 'Commons and wheatfields and beechwoods, where the loveliest wildflowers grow,' wrote Mary.[1] While he loved especially the common, the blazing gorse, the wide views from his study and the glory of the roses.

The Cannans employed a maid. 'The perfect maid',[2] as Mary later called her, by which one must suppose that she was quiet, efficient, decorative and pleasant. This second woman living in the house, moving deftly and good-naturedly about her work, perhaps stirred in Gilbert memories of the maid he had innocently loved in his youth (the tender-hearted Alison in *Little Brother*).

Soon, characteristically, Gilbert wanted his younger friends to share his good fortune. There was Katherine Mansfield still in London, coughing miserably in the dark cold room in Chancery Lane, and Middleton Murry frightened by Gaudier-Brzeska (who had attacked him because he had not paid for work Gaudier-Brzeska had done for *Rhythm*, now *The Blue Review*). The canary bought to cheer up Katherine had died; the Murrys, their finances tottering, kept their precarious health going with cheap meat pies for $1\frac{1}{2}d.$ and potatoes for $\frac{1}{2}d.$ in a restaurant where the knives were chained to the tables.[3] Murry explained:

... When the Cannans, who were making ready the Mill House at Cholesbury, suggested that we should take the cottage next door to them, we responded eagerly. The cottage was, in reality, a semi-detached red brick villa; but Mary Cannan, well-practised in such transformations—indeed, a born 'interior decorator' before it became a profession—convinced us that it could be made to look beautiful inside at least. And its situation on the very edge of the Common was indeed magnificent, and the fare was cheap. So we suggested to Gordon Campbell that he should go shares in it for the summer. He agreed ...

Campbell taught the Cannans and Murrys to play poker. Nobody ever won or lost more than two shillings, even though they might play for three or four hours on end. He also invented a Rabelaisian cipher for the usual poker terms, and a few new ones, a secret known to the Murrys but not to the Cannans. His 'praeternaturally solemn and shocking remarks' would reduce the Murrys to hysterical laughter, while Gilbert, half-guessing,

would become contorted between a laugh and a frown (Murry wrote). And Mary's innocent bewilderment, and Gilbert's uneasy effort not to arouse her suspicions were so funny that we could only explode again and again. 'What is it Gilly?' Mary would say in plaintive exasperation. And that question, and Gilbert's ensuing embarrassment, would send us into final hysteria. . . .[4]

But although poker was fun, the countryside was not to be so attractive to the Murrys in winter. Before Christmas was out they had left for France, and the cottage was free for Vladimir Polunin. All this time the Cannans had been fully occupied.

We've been so busy getting the house shipshape that we've hardly been in Town at all and my friends have been neglected [Gilbert wrote on a December Sunday to Edward Marsh]. We want you to come down for a week end early in the new year—come down with Jim when you return from Italy.

S.P.E.? Yes, I'll join that and will write to Pearsall Smith.

I'm coming up for a children's party on Monday week and may want to stay the night. Will you put me up?

Old Mole comes out on Jan 1, and there's another little book, which I will send as a Christmas card . . .

In a postscript he adds:

The Tigers have shaken off the dirt of London and settled in Paris. Jack has written a book which is to come out in the spring with Sidgwick.[5]

The Mill House garden was already laid out, but the land around the windmill lay rough and untended, and soon Mary took part of a paddock to enlarge it. A courtyard was laid and later shrubs and trees were planted. Such joint activities gave the marriage some temporary stability. Indeed Mary and Gilbert were by no means entirely incompatible; they used the same idiosyncratic phrases, and still shared many interests. But increasingly they seemed to live at different levels of experience and feeling, Gilbert sinking into depths that Mary could not plumb or rising to an intensity of vision that she could not share. Probably more serious was sexual incompatibility, perhaps partly due to their difference in age, and for Gilbert, the traumatic experience of the divorce bringing about by sheer force of circumstances the state he was later to describe as 'the cloying security of marriage'.[6]

The local carpenter, alive but frail in November 1974, told me that he was soon at the windmill putting up shelves for Mr. Cannan who had spoken to him of *Round the Corner*. (The old man was proud of remembering the title.) He saw little of the Cannans afterwards and could not recall Mary at all, but Gilbert struck him as a pleasant young man, tall and friendly with remarkably fair hair. He remembered too, the 'Russian' who lived in the nearby cottage, the Gables, by whom he meant Polunin, who was indeed not the kind of person you would expect to find in an English village.

Dark-haired and bearded, Vladimir Polunin (1880–1957) was then thirty-four. He was married to the painter and stage designer, Elizabeth (Hart). In early 1914 they had a four-year old son, Nicholas, and were expecting a second child in November. Born in Moscow, Polunin had graduated in forestry at St. Petersburg before becoming an artist. His work was very Russian, much of it based on the old Byzantine tradition in fresco and icon painting, full of imagination and vitality. His drawings for *Rhythm* and *The Blue Review* were striking and original, his landscapes in general stylised and formal. He is probably best remembered today for his work as Diaghilev's scenery painter when he collaborated with Derain, Picasso and Bakst, an interest shared with his wife who designed the scenery and costumes for the first production in England of Rimsky-Korsakov's *The Snow Maiden*.[7] Lively and temperamental, with an endearing childlike pleasure in his own success, Polunin was in every way the antithesis of Gilbert; a man who could infuse the dullest spirit with enthusiasm, passionate in thought, dynamic and completely lacking in affectation.

In the round study in the windmill a tall monkish desk was installed, which aroused the scorn of David Garnett who found it affected and pretentious, and here Gilbert was to write standing up or sitting on a high stool.[8] The idea was probably Mary's, for she had planned the transformation, the colour schemes and the special environment which she hoped would encourage inspiration and possibly strengthen those fragile threads of genius which she may still have considered to be part of her husband. Perhaps like Kathleen she also asked rhetorically, 'With discipline, to what heights might he climb?'[9]

Trying still to reach that summit, Gilbert reviewed books from time to time, too harshly for the taste of his contemporaries, who were eventually to get their own back. On October 14th, 1913, he had defended himself in a letter to Compton Mackenzie:

... I've been turned out my study by a Russian painter who lives up here and has insisted on doing a frieze. As his is a tip-top design for it I don't resent giving up a fortnight and I can fill it up with mild work, reading and letters. Old Mole is finished, printed, corrected, and off and I'm now wondering what to tackle next.

Walpole's a juggins. He wants to step into the shoes of his predecessors but is afraid they'll pinch or be out of fashion, if wild persons like you and me break through the ringed fence. Oh! dear, that ringed fence and the poor beasts inside it, living for all I can see, on each other's droppings. My stomach's too strong for that fare, so I've kicked my heels in the air and upped and offed. As to being hard on my contemporaries I'm no harder on them than I am on myself. They want to have everything nice and easy and comfortable and polite. But literature isn't of either—not very legible—I'm afraid.

From the end of 1913 many of Gilbert's friends were invited to visit him in his new place. Reactions were varied. S. P. B. Mais wrote in 1930:

It must have been seventeen years ago when my friend, Mr. Gilbert Cannan, the novelist, asked me to visit him in his windmill home and I found the round walls lined with thousands of the world's most delectable books. I saw then how wise the man is who can afford to live in a mill, because he had wonderful wall space for his books, sunlight all the day and warmth in winter.[10]

L. M., Katherine Mansfield's friend, was also enthusiastic:

The big floor had been turned into a wonderful circular living room, the walls of which Mrs. Cannan had decorated with great flower patterns, cutting out and pasting up each flower and leaf and branch to her own design. It was an impressive bit of work and most ingenious, but it was not to Katherine's taste.[11]

Compton Mackenzie claimed to believe that the spiral staircase installed on Mary's advice had eventually turned Gilbert's head and driven him mad.[12]

David Garnett, who went there later, wrote:

I arrived in time for lunch on Saturday and was shown into the dining room, which was decorated with a dado of brightly coloured frescoes by Polunin, a Russian artist—very different in style from Duncan Grant's mural paintings at Adrian Stephen's house in Brunswick Square. When we sat down I noticed many artificial fruit piled up in a big majolica dish: semi-transparent glass grapes, alabaster peaches and a pottery pineapple lent their stony support to three little apples; two bananas and a gritty pear which were all that one could actually eat. Before I left on Monday it had occurred to me that the heaped profusion of uneaten fruits were perhaps symbolic of Gilbert's marriage.[13]

Meanwhile, the friendship with Lady Ottoline flourished. More letters went from the Mill House to Bedford Square in Mary's hand. Then on January 27th, 1914 (the letter is wrongly dated *1913*) Gilbert wrote himself to thank Lady Ottoline for sending her congratulations on the publication of his latest novel, *Old Mole*, which had come out that month with Secker. She had expressed a desire to see him and he proposed the following Tuesday or Thursday. Another letter dated February 3rd, arranged a second meeting, setting a pattern which was to continue for some months.

By now Gilbert had met, probably through Eddie Marsh or Albert Rothenstein, the twenty-two-year-old mercurial Jewish artist Mark Gertler, a small passionate man with bright dark eyes. An immediate liking sprang up between the two men, and before 1913 was out, Gilbert had invited Gertler to stay at the Mill House.

I am sitting by a huge fire in this very nice country house of Gilbert Cannan [Gertler wrote to his friend the Hon. Dorothy Brett in a letter dated January 1914]. Gilbert Cannan is an extremely nice man and ought to do good things. I have got on with him very well—we talked and talked last night. I told

him all about myself. They were so interested in my life. I told them all
about where I came from and all about my people. Cannan thought I was
extremely lucky to live in the East End among *real* people. He loves the
Jewish theatre and agrees with me that it is far and away more vital than the
English, in fact there is no comparison. We discussed the milk and water
attitude of Roger Fry and his followers and most of the so-called 'advanced'
people . . .[14]

It was the child-like aspect of Gertler's nature which probably
appealed most to Gilbert at the beginning of the friendship, the
younger man's naïve enthusiasm, vulnerability and lack of inhibitions.
There was nothing artificial or smooth-tongued about him. He was as
real to Gilbert as Gilbert to him. In addition Gertler needed help, and
Gilbert loved to feel needed. They shared a dislike of Shaw. Gertler
was sickened by *The Doctor's Dilemma* and described Lillah McCarthy
as that 'terrible woman' who wriggled into 'so-called beautiful and
classical attitudes'.[15] Disgusted by most homosexuals, it is probable
that the 'honest serviceableness' of Gilbert appealed to him. 'An over-
intellectual man is as dangerous as an over sexed man,'[16] he claimed, a
statement with which Mary would certainly have concurred.

In April, Gertler was again writing from the Mill House, this time to
Carrington on a Sunday night after a country drive in 'the little car'. He
was sitting in a 'very pleasant bedroom'.

But what I enjoy most is the company of Gilbert Cannan and the talks with
him. He is a *true man*. There are not many like him. I like him truly. In the
evenings we sit in the dimly lit Mill, where he plays Beethoven to me and
then we talk and talk. Last night he read some of his poems to me. They
sounded to me very good. I feel about him as if he was my greatest friend. He
tells me I can use his cottage as if it were my own! I am doing no work here
at all! . . .[17]

Gilbert loved to be with people younger than himself, to watch them
reaching out to experience as he had reached and perhaps he hoped,
too, to spare them some of the traps into which he had fallen. Gratify-
ingly several of them, including his younger brother John (known as
Felix or Binkie), Rupert Brooke and Alec Waugh, felt that they could
look to him for wisdom and advice, while he saw them as the future
perpetuators of the 'New Spirit' which, in moods of optimism, he was
sure must come to replace eventually the old dull stultifying order.

Some indication of this can be seen in the way Brooke had accepted
Gilbert's adverse opinion of his play *Lithuania* with apparent equa-
nimity: he only wanted to see more of the man he had met sometimes at
the Cheshire Cheese with the staff of *Rhythm* and at Eddie Marsh's
rooms in Raymond Buildings:

I want too many different things . . . [Brooke wrote to Cathleen Nesbitt from
Suva Fiji in November 1913]. I want to sit at the table at Eddie's, with you
there and Violet Asquith's brilliance, and Gilbert's wise silences, and Eddie's
monocular stories—and TALK . . . I'm going to get up such performances,
that'll turn old Cambridge upside down. I'm going to have Yeats and Cannan
and Craig and Barker to give a lecture each on modern drama.[18]

On April 28th, 1914, Gilbert wrote to Lady Ottoline after she had
paid her first visit to Cholesbury, enclosing 'another little book which
is to be published soon' (probably *Satire*), humbly beginning:

It was a great delight having you here the other day to see the beauty I so
undeservedly live in . . .
Mark Gertler's address is 32 Elder Street, Bishopsgate E. If you could persuade anyone to buy a drawing of his occasionally you would be helping him
both materially and spiritually. London is so absurd a place that one little
voice can raise echoes to breach the appalling silence which out of the
hubbub can descend upon an artist. A genuine artist must come to a fight
through a period of isolation, but Gertler's too young for it.

Ottoline, nothing if not generous, responded by visiting Gertler's
studio.

The Cannans saw a great deal of him—he had been sent to stay with them
to get some country air*—and they arranged that I should go down to see
him in Spitalfields. I went off to Liverpool Street Station and found my way
from there to the mean, hot, stuffy, smelly, little street where he lived. I
found the house and felt very tall and large walking up the creaky little stairs.
Gertler always says that the first sight he had of me was the crest of a purple
feather: nearer and nearer it ascended, and at last the hat itself and then me,
as if a large and odd bird had arrived. Indeed, I hardly believe that I was able
to stand upright in the room, so tall and erect was this feather, so low was his
room. I found the Cannans and Gertler showed me his pictures.[19]

And Gilbert, increasingly attracted to Ottoline as a perceptive and
ever-helpful friend with an intellect which seemed to complement his
own, wrote on May 18th:

Bless you for [being] a good fairy godmother and for extending your blessing
to Gertler. He writes rapturously and is very sure that heaven is on earth.
This is not a conversion, but a release of his own inborn certainty—though
perhaps that *is* conversion. Whatever it is, nothing for a long time has given
me so much happiness, and I thank you for it . . . I keep Mark's naïve letter
of bursting happiness [he continued on the 20th]. 'Lady Ottoline gave me a
lot of beautiful flowers. Now I am rich.' That is like the young Heine, and
indeed he reminds me greatly of Heine, though stronger.

* This is incorrect. He was invited by Gilbert.

Here we have just put out hammocks and summer chairs and coloured lanterns. Next month I have a birthday—the 25th—and if you will come I should like to have a party. If you won't or can't come then I shan't have a party, but it would be good to have you here for the day—and the night if you could stay.

On Monday evening, he told her, he had delivered an oration on the Village Green. The Liberal candidate was late in turning up

and I was implored to fill in time. I did. I talked about the land, and patriotism beginning in the love of the land, and the interdependence of towns and land and much more. The village loved it, but I don't think the Liberal Chairman and gentry liked it at all. Certainly they did nothing but abuse the Tories, which seemed to me both dull and shortsighted. What struck me about the meeting was that the peasants can believe in landowners (more or less benevolent) as human beings, but the Liberal candidates with their figures and desiccated tales of woe and hardship are impossible to believe in. They come out of a strange world very far away and say, 'We are going to do this for you', not 'You can do this for yourselves if in your minds and hearts you believe that it should be done.' This fellow talked about the masses as something entirely separate from himself and because of this all the quite sensible things he said could not penetrate, they could not carry over the ditch of his own digging . . .

It was my first political meeting, and you who live so much in politics may be interested to know how I felt about it.

On May 26th Gilbert was writing again to thank Ottoline for three happy days which included seeing *The Magic Flute*, to which Gertler was also invited. 'Philip has his share in it, too, and for both of you I have written this poem.' He enclosed thirty lines of verse, inspired by the opera (and published in *Adventurous Love*).

On June 14th, he wrote again, declining an invitation to visit her.

I've got my nose down on my novel and don't move further than the common, and I don't think I am likely to be in Town next week, though I should greatly like to see you. That hardly needed to be said. But you are coming down soon. I had a note from Mrs. Asquith to say that you had arranged for the 22nd.* That is Monday week: Tomorrow week. Is that right? I hope nothing is going to interfere with my cherished plan. The roses in the garden and other wild roses on the common are coming out at the thought of it and must not be disappointed.

It is a great happiness to me that you liked the sonnets so much. You are the first to have read them and I was left so exhausted by the impulse that brought them, so distressed by the long cold labour of revision that I cannot judge them at all except by an unusual conviction that they are 'somehow

* Mrs. Raymond Asquith.

good', and an entire absence of my usual feeling of my work that it has been useful to me in getting on to 'something'. I should immensely enjoy reading them to you. It would help me.

These last days I have been haunted and most passionately moved by the story of the girl, Laura Grey. Her unassailable spirit thrust deliberately through the worst in life has shone splendidly for me and I wrote this poem which I send to you now . . .

Laura Grey, a suffragette of good family, was imprisoned and forcibly fed while on hunger strike and eventually committed suicide when pregnant by taking an overdose of veronal to which she had become addicted. Her death aroused strong feelings against the suffragette movement, the inquest being widely reported and discussed. Here was a girl whom Gilbert would have loved to cherish and the poem he sent to Ottoline called simply *Laura Grey* was his response to a story which moved him deeply.[20]

On June 17th Gilbert wrote a happier letter to Ottoline about plans to celebrate his birthday:

The 23rd: Tuesday. It is underlined for high holiday, a private little mid-summer carnival all to ourselves.

Polunin came running in this morning to say he had met you at the Coq d'Or and you had introduced him to Barker and Barker had asked him to lunch at the Savoy Hotel and what was he to wear? And through all this excitement he then showed a very charming picture of you in your sea of silk, a fine spirit rising out of the brilliant world, so that artists turn to you and love you as they love the creatures of their imagination.

And afterwards Mary wrote in two undated letters:

It was the dearest kindest thing your coming down, and enjoying it so much. We were very happy, and only hope that you will suddenly write and say 'May I have a few hours in the country, your country? I come by the next train.' Gilbert says you stimulate him and make his brain alert and respon-sive so you see the pleasure is all on one side. But all the same he is a terrific person . . .

My dearest Ottoline we very nearly cried when we said goodbye. Gilbert was so touching that I gulped. He has the dearest way and is more like a really natural being than anyone I know. You make us so happy. I wish I could tell you how much so . . .

After sadly remarking that they could not spend the weekend with Jack Hutchinson because Gilbert's sister and brother (Felix) were coming down and must not be disappointed, she continued:

Gilbert is in the worst depression and feels the end of his capability for work has come. He is finished, he says. I propose a liver pill and shall conceal it in his food I think. He is not often down but he is just now and it is awful to see him go silently about with his joy gone. It is as though all the colour has gone out of the garden.

To feel finished, to suspect temporary lack of inspiration to be permanent, is as we know, a state of mind familiar to most authors at one time or another, but for Gilbert the depression could well have been deeper and more complicated. The failures in his marriage expressed in the sonnets published in *Adventurous Love and other Verses* and the inherited strains of instability and possibly an innate neurological abnormality together with complexities caused by his childhood environment, factors not understood by Mary, may well have contributed to Gilbert's despair. Ottoline seemed to understand him, but she could never be his: nor could anyone else, if he remained honourable, and his earlier experiences would have made him very reluctant to enter into an affair with a married woman even if she had wanted it. Ottoline's intellect was sharper, more perceptive than Mary's. She seemed to look deeper into the heart of problems, to explore them with Gilbert, so that the bizarre quality of her booming voice, the famous drawl, did not grate. Together they pursued knowledge and exchanged philosophical ideas. The friendship was closest when Ottoline's affair with Bertrand Russell was losing its magic, and she needed a stimulating intellectual and sentimental association rather than a sexual attachment.[21] So many visits, so many talks and confidences in so short a space of time do point to an attraction greater than that suggested in her *Memoirs*. Both felt themselves to be spiritual people, holding several similar beliefs.

I stretch out so instinctively towards contact with fellow creatures—loving talk, discussion, friendship, warmth and humour, endlessly interested in other people's lives, and indeed at times feeling their troubles too intensely. . . .

Understanding and wisdom are the great things, and with love one can attain them, and it is a great happiness in life to feel other personalities touching one's own, feeling one's love going out to them. This feeling is happy contact with one's fellow human beings . . .[22]

These sentiments of Ottoline's could just as well be attributed to Gilbert, for they also echo a belief that was at the very core of his being, reiterated by him even as his mind took him away from reality.

It was easy to see why Gilbert was attracted to Ottoline both for her virtues and her failings. Gathorne Hardy wrote later that her misdeeds always struck him as those of a child and that her conduct was the result of inspiration rather than judgement, and so, in her, Gilbert probably found, too, the child-like streak which somehow always made communication easier for him.[23] In turn he sometimes inspired her:

Dear Lady Ottoline [he wrote on June 28th], or dropping the Lady and its defences, my dear Ottoline the Laura Grey poem is beautiful and I am glad to have that much more of her spirit . . .

They were good days:

full of true active happiness [he wrote on July 6th], and all those splendid moments when one's mind can take in and give out 'in one action' as the cricketers say of their ideal in fielding . . . I am glad it was in your house that I met Bertie Russell and had that splendid windy passage with him. . . .

Gertler and Carrington and my little friend Birch have been here, Gertler fretting and tearing himself into bones and nerves. It is, I think, the strains of his bad time beginning to tell on him after the relaxation of his efforts. You can bear up as long as you must: but when there is no more need for resistance then there is an inrush of hungry bad ideas that have been before kept within a distance. He'll get straight. He has a good will and a practised one, though more, as yet, in his art than in his life.

Mary sends you her love and mine is from the letter M at the beginning to the letter N at the end.[24]

Since Gilbert shared some of Ottoline's aspirations to encourage writers and artists, and to provide for them a focal point and a refuge, the Mill House became for a time a poor man's Garsington; those who could not be accommodated in the house or mill were encouraged to rent cottages nearby or stay in rented rooms. Increasingly it was Gilbert's desire to heal the emotional and spiritual wounds of those in need, an urge which had once prompted his mother to say that he should have been a parson.

So we find him writing to Lady Ottoline on July 14th about Carrington's deaf friend, Dorothy Brett, who was then in love with Professor Fred Brown of the Slade School.

Dorothy seemed happy here. I took her for a long walk in the woods on Sunday and let her talk. I don't think you need worry or be disappointed in her. She seemed to me to have gained a good deal from her storms, especially in courage (I fancy she had confused that with recklessness) and tenderness. She had been living too serenely with the knowledge of her brain. The body always kicks against that sooner or later and the soul uses the body to kill the clever theoretic knowledge of life untested by experience which so many of us come by in these days when we gulp down philosophies and ideas with such an alarming rapacity . . .

On August 2nd he completed *Young Earnest* a novel about social hypocrisy and a young man who leaves an academic career after an unhappy marriage, and wrote eagerly to Lady Ottoline, asking that he might dedicate it to her.

Lytton Strachey was here on Friday and we played bowls at the pub. He wants to find a cottage and I think there will be one soon right in the middle of the common at the other end, a piece of land filched off the common. Our builder has just bought it and promises us the first offer of the tenancy.

Our great time was with Bertie Russell. He and I had tremendous walks and talks and explored each other's imaginations and had thrilling adventures in them. The theme of some of them is in the book. . . .

And then four days later with war declared, enclosing an anti-war poem:

Yes. Do come whenever you can for a night or two to get the peace of the hills. I want to hug Philip for his brave word on Monday . . . I feel the real fight comes when all the bloodshed is over and mind must exert itself. There must be men to write, speak and organise, against false government that sacrifices life to interest. No moment is too soon for honest words to seek each other out . . . We cannot stop the war now, but we can prepare to build out of its ruins. I see no other duty and with my pen shall follow it, and with any other weapon I can lay hands on . . . There should be neither excitement nor despair. We are to suffer? Very well then. Out of suffering comes life and large ideas and faith . . .[25]

With war declared, Gilbert's philanthropic work continued although it is unlikely that he would have seen it as such. Men, women, homosexuals and children, all were welcome, especially the love-sick and bereaved, with Ottoline sharing news of their welfare and steps to recovery:

Goldie Dickinson came down on Sunday and was looking ill and tortured, he stayed until late at night and we spent most of the day in the woods coming back at moonlight. Such glorious nights we have been having, as though the whole world were shaming us for the brutal ugliness we are making . . .[26]

Helen Dudley, who had crossed the Atlantic in the vain and understandable expectation of marrying Bertrand Russell, was also in need of succour:

Here is the first Bulletin. The patient slept well. I took her out for a walk in the moonlight and made her physically tired so that her nerves would no longer be able to prey on her vitality. Also we talked of the economic fallacies at the bottom of the present mess, of some philosophy and of poetry and the nature of poetry. The treatment seems so far to answer, and her eyes are becoming more human and less dog-like . . .[27]

At the same time he continued to share Gertler's problems with Ottoline. The Gertler family had been in agonies, he related, with the

Russians marching over their place in Austria. But Mark's father had been doing rather well; he supposed because people were buying only cheap furs for the winter. And in an undated letter he mentions that Gertler had been in despair, because his friends were looking askance at him because he was not in uniform.

Some of Gilbert's temporary success as an amateur psychotherapist may have been due to an inability to establish his own sense of identity, which made it easy for him to identify with others, and practise self-abnegation. He preferred to hide his true nature, playing the role of listener, lecturer or silent observer. In later life Gilbert's sisters remembered him as kind, gentle and generous: a very sweet-tempered elder brother, always ready to meet them as children off trains, help them patiently with their homework, but none could go further. They had never known him well on equal terms. Perhaps he was disliked eventually by most of his male contemporaries because they knew in the end that he had never given them part of himself: ideas, help, hospitality, almost everything that he could give was available, except his own basic humanness. There the door slammed shut. This inability to reveal his real self was probably partly due to a basic self-dislike, which was increasingly to alternate with a compensatory fantasy which took the form of a growing sense of his own importance and potential power.

It seems likely that for three years Ottoline, with her genius for drawing out the sensitive and shy, came nearer than most to finding the real Gilbert, putting a little stuffing into what she saw as a vacant Sir Galahad and providing him with some sense of identity and, more important, a feeling of worth. She seemed to care for him for what he was, enjoying his talk as much as Kathleen Bruce had enjoyed his letters and handsomeness.

But in the summer of 1914 he had also come under the influence of a man so committed to his art, so bent on discovering, understanding and experiencing the sensuous, sensual and spiritual meaning and being of life, that in comparison the more diversely gifted Gilbert was to seem lacking in depth and singleness of purpose.

Gilbert had met D. H. Lawrence in 1913, probably through the Middleton Murrys, and in that summer of the war he persuaded him to take a cottage in Bellingdon Lane, near Chesham, called The Triangle, to which Frieda and Lawrence came soon after their marriage. So began a particularly rewarding time for Gilbert, months busy with visiting friends. Among those who came were: Edward Marsh, the Campbells, Catherine Carswell, the St. John Hutchinsons, John Drinkwater, Compton Mackenzie, Russell, and, of course, Ottoline, and many of Gertler's colleagues who became automatically the Cannans' friends, too. Indomitably Mary joined in their joys and sorrows, picked blackberries with Lawrence, talked chirpily to Catherine Carswell when Gilbert was silent and gloomy, and tried to provide a civilised setting for them all.[28] Gilbert introduced Lawrence to Ottoline and took Secker over to the Triangle to meet him, so that later, when *The Rainbow* was banned, Secker was there to step in and add Lawrence's work, including eventually *The Rainbow*, to his remarkably distinguished list.

So Gilbert's protective attitude was extended to include Lawrence, whom he was to support in every way open to him for as long as he was able, a fact which Lawrence, predictably, came to resent. Mary, who had retained useful and influential friends from the days of her marriage to Barrie, was able to put in a word through Maurice Hewlett and Alfred Sutro, to persuade those who administered the Royal Literary Fund to turn their attention to him. Lawrence was at first appreciative, writing to Edward Marsh:

We have got a little furnished cottage here—quite nice though I don't love this exhausted english countryside . . . We are quite near Gilbert. I like him.[29]

And again on September 13th.

I am moved almost to tears by the letter and the money [a loan of £10] this morning. It is true we are in poor condition. Pinker, however, promises me some money somehow: I should have waited till it came or asked my sister for a little. Frieda has always got money from Germany when we have been badly reduced before. Now she can't. But Mary Cannan wrote and told Alfred Sutro and Hewlett that we were very badly off. If I had known I think I would have asked her not to do it. Then Sutro sent me [this] £10 in advance . . .[30]

Gilbert announced that he had become a policeman, Second Reserve unpaid, 'The village having gone in for that form of patriotism.'[31] According to David Garnett he was detailed to guard the waterworks, armed with a walking stick and a brassard. Indeed Garnett and Frankie Birrell were halted by him on their way to Chesham Station after they had lunched with Lawrence, the familiar voice asking 'Who goes there?'

By now the Mill House was being used by Gertler almost as a second home, to which he came and went much as he pleased, even popping in for meals when he was supposed to be housed and fed in Mrs. Gomm's rooms, a habit which was understandably beginning to irritate Mary. She appears to have been consistently kind to him, but she did not like him. In her opinion, he was too much of the back street Jew to be a wholly agreeable companion. Egotistical and unrestrained, he grated on her nerves. She resented his habit of bathing only once a week. She felt he took up too much of Gilbert's time, for, with all the self-absorption and selfishness of youth, Gertler sometimes forgot that Gilbert's writing was vital to support the Mill House and its visitors. Gilbert bore these tribulations with paternal patience and affection.

In October that year the Middleton Murrys came back to the area, renting Rose Tree Cottage, at the Lee, near Great Missenden, three miles across the fields from the Lawrences and two from the Cannans. They had been with Gilbert and Mary at the Lawrences' marriage celebration dinner at Gustave's on July 13th, and now Murry wanted to get Katherine Mansfield out into the country again.

During the next three months the three men were to meet frequently, sharing a deepening hatred for the war and a determination to create a better world to follow the bloodshed. They were, in their own estimation, the *thinkers*, three of the few who could stand back and see the folly of the conflict. They laid a tremendous responsibility on their own shoulders and their confidence in their ability to change climates of opinion, deep-rooted prejudices, capitalism, the balance of power, a country's way of life, business and art, was astonishing.

Gilbert's declaration to Ottoline four days after the outbreak of war was now supported by Lawrence and, to a lesser degree, Murry. Indeed Lawrence's absolute belief in the power of the individual undoubtedly added to Gilbert's persistence in his efforts to alter the course of history, and man's understanding of the universe. 'I profoundly believe that a single individual may prove to be of more worth than the whole generation of men in which he has lived,' Lawrence was to announce in 1916, referring, Catherine Carswell says, to himself.[32] Gilbert and Lawrence also shared a conviction that the sexual act had a spiritual meaning, a holiness which should not be degraded.

In the quiet countryside around Cholesbury the three couples must have seemed a little bizarre. Gilbert, shaggier now, his gloomy face slightly coarsened with age, striding across the fields with head high, thick fair hair falling forward, his walking stick in hand and two large hairy dogs at his heels. Middleton Murry shorter, less noticeable, with splendidly arched eyebrows, fine aquiline nose and somewhat wide mouth, a man who bicycled rather than walked and shrivelled up in the cold; and Lawrence, with his newly grown beard, 'a deep glowing red in the sun and in the shade, the colour of tea'. Lawrence, his dust-coloured hair parted on one side above his 'deep-set jewel-like eyes' in a pale tubercular face,[33] appeared like 'someone who had been under-nourished in youth making his body fragile and his mind too active'.[34]

The women were no less remarkable. Mary in her mid-forties

Gilbert aged about 12

Gilbert in his twenties

d. Mary Bowie

a. Kathleen Bruce

was desperately hanging on to the last shreds of her youth, hair dyed a reddish-brown, thin mouth and fine features beautifully made-up. A woman described by Catherine Carswell as 'exquisite' and by David Garnett, who was attracted to more exotic females, as 'wholesome, like rice pudding',[35] impulsive, charming, chirpy and a little overwrought. Katherine was in contrast, mysterious, self-contained and unconventional, her dark hair worn in a fringe above eloquent eyes, a trim girl capable of an almost Oriental stillness, deceptively demure in appearance and manner. Beside them walked the handsome, alien Frieda, the very opposite of Katherine: big, blonde, volatile and dominating, her Prussian features at times seeming stern and rather frightening, her utterances often loud and distressingly unpremeditated, for she practised none of Mary's more subtle feminine approaches.

The women did not enjoy the walks and the talks, the dinner parties, the tea-times, the deep probings into the nature of the universe, the philosophical musings and the escape fantasies, as much as the men did. Mary once again found Katherine distant, and Katherine, who was suffering from rheumatism and a longing for Francis Carco, the artist, cared little for Frieda. Both the Triangle and Rose Tree Cottage were damp and inconvenient and quite unsuited to Lawrence's and Katherine's health, although probably better for them than smoke-polluted London. Lawrence was later to declare that he was often ill while living near Chesham but at first the friendship was stimulating to all three men, to be remembered by Lawrence with nostalgia:

I can't tell you with what pain I think of that autumn at Cholesbury—the yellow leaves—and the wet nights when you came to us, and Gilbert and the dogs—and I had got pork chops—and our cottage was hot and full of the smell of sage and onions—then the times we came to you, and had your wine—those pretty wine glasses on your long table—something inside one weeps and won't be comforted. But it's no good grieving.

There was *something* in those still days, before the war had gone into us, which was beautiful and generous—a sense of flowers rich in the garden and sunny tea-times when one was at peace—when we were happy with one another, really—even if we said spiteful things afterwards. I was happy, anyway. There *was* a kindliness in us, even a certain fragrance in our meeting—something very good, and poignant to remember, now the whole world of it is lost . . .[36]

The highlight of these months was Christmas-time, the last splendid Christmas in 1914 before the true horror of the war was apparent; a time of brilliant sunshine and blue skies, with the gorse still golden on the common and the frost silver on the bare hedgerows. Gilbert, who had been lent a gramophone, played Caruso records while the Middleton

Murrys walked over to the Triangle to borrow Chinese lanterns for the Cannans' Christmas party and picked gorse on the common.

The night before, a party at the Lawrences had got off to a slow start, but finally came to life when Gertler plunged into a vigorous dance, and everybody started stamping and clapping in time.

Christmas came [Frieda wrote]; we made the cottage splendid with holly and mistletoe, we cooked and boiled and roasted and baked. Campbell and Koteliansky and the Murrys came, and Gertler and the Cannans. We had a gay geast (*sic*).

We danced on the shaky floor. Gilbert with uplifted head sang: 'I feel like an eagle in the sky.' Koteliansky sang soulfully his Hebrew song 'Ranani Sadekim Badanoi.'[37]

On the 25th the Murrys stayed with the Cannans, sleeping in a cold bedroom. Gertler was housed in Mrs. Gomm's 'wretched and uncomfortable rooms'. Katherne Mansfield, still yearning for Francis Carco, was in a strange emotional state, wanting a lover more vigorous and demanding than Middleton Murry. At the Mill House the long table was laid with the best cutlery and wine glasses, while in the kitchen a whole pig roasted, though when the time came to eat it no one knew how to dismember it. Feeling depressed, Middleton Murry, who had become inebriated on rum the night before at the Lawrences, began to drink heavily.

'The Cannans' party was very extraordinary' . . . he wrote in his Journal soon afterwards:

It divided into two parts—one in the dining-room and the second in the Mill. The first, while we were at dinner waiting for the Lawrences who were late, was dull. I was not at all drunk but profoundly melancholy—and after negativing all proposals *for toasts to King George or King Albert, and suggesting Anatole France—I got up and sang stentorian songs at the table.* I was then sitting next to Gertler, very distinctly conscious of a hostility between us and trying in a forced way to be amiable. Soon after Gertler, Gilbert and Tig acted the music hall sketch 'Humanity', for which they had prepared us. It was not at all bad—particularly the realistic fight.

This was followed by a play, 'Driven from Home', which was 'badly acted' by Gertler, Lawrence, Katherine and Frieda, and a psychological piece, suggested by Murry, with Mary, Gilbert and himself.

The fourth play was disturbingly convincing, for Gertler and Katherine, who were supposed to be temporarily in love, broke conventions by acting too realistically. The planned reconciliation between Katherine and her husband, played by Murry, never took place. An intoxicated Gertler declared a genuine love for Katherine and when a shocked Lawrence remonstrated with Katherine saying 'You don't love him', she only replied 'Yes, I do, I do.' Then the young and impulsive Gertler burst into tears saying something about 'What have I done? What will Murry say?', not realising that he had unwittingly been a stand-in for Francis Carco.

The feeling that these plays had led the actors into deeper waters than the spectators could understand, into a dream that seemed almost reality, disturbed the party. Beside herself with rage, Frieda accused Katherine of leading the young man on and threatened never to speak to her again.

In a letter to Ottoline thanking her for a paper knife, Gilbert wrote:

I am groping out of the strangest and most astonishing evening I have ever spent. We had a big party, the Lawrences, Gertler and a Russian Jew a friend of theirs, with some other friends. After a merry dinner we began to act little impromptu plays and those went on and on, growing one out of the other & absurdly & sometimes almost terribly into life. They were all people with much vitality & there came a tremendous tussle, between the dream they created and the circumstances they knew they had to sink back into. It was like a chapter out of a Dostoievesky novel. The mill is still very queer with it & I have been out in the woods all day shaking it off. It was to everybody I think a great emotional relief.[38]

In spite of his tears, Gertler on the other hand felt invigorated. 'The most exciting things that happened were the Christmas parties,' he wrote to Carrington from Elder Street at the beginning of January.

They were real fun. Katherine Mansfield was so good. Gilbert Cannan's party was most extraordinarily exciting. Katherine and myself—both very drunk—made passionate love to each other in front of everybody! And everybody was drunk too. No one knew whether to take it as a joke or scandal. Fortunately, the next day everybody decided to take it as a joke—the Lawrences were the last to come to this decision, as they were most anxious to weave a real romance out of it. Seeing that Katherine's man and myself were just as friendly afterwards, they *had* to take it as a joke. They were very disappointed to have to take it so. I like Katherine Mansfield.[39]

So the new year came, and, looking back on the old, Gilbert could legitimately suppose that 1914 had brought him nearer to financial stability and an established reputation. His almost unremitting efforts seemed at last to be repaying him some reward. Although some critics had carped and continued to label him 'clever', in March Henry James had singled him out as one of four up-and-coming authors with significant work to their credit. Gilbert, hearing in advance of the article which was to assess his standing, wrote to James, enclosing a book, which was probably *Satire*, but could have been another slender volume, entitled *The Joy of The Theatre*, which came out about the same time.

Henry James wrote back from Carlyle Mansions on March 20th, with a thick nib, a letter without paragraphs, the words bending downwards, like wind-battered trees, where they hit the right-hand margin:

I take it very kindly of you that you send me the elegant little volume on the elegant big subject. It came this morning and I haven't yet had time to master it—during a day of much preoccupation. But everything shall presently give way to it—I shld. like this to reach you soon enough to tell you not to expect much of the stuff in the Times—I mean in the way of specifications. It consists of some very general considerations; however, these may interest you as the reflections of an aged novelist upon a craft he for a good many years practised. I like the question of how or why or whither—but my paper, cut into two—isn't in the least a 'review' of anybody.

I greet Mrs. Cannan very kindly and am yours and Mrs. all (*sic*) truly.

The first half of the 'stuff' which was entitled *The Younger Generation*, came out on March 19th, on the front page and, according to Compton Mackenzie and Swinnerton, aroused much jealousy among those who had not been chosen by the 'master'.[40] The four young writers whose work Henry James considered were Hugh Walpole, Compton Mackenzie, D. H. Lawrence and Gilbert Cannan. The older ones, with whom he compared them were Joseph Conrad, Maurice Hewlett, Galsworthy, Wells and Arnold Bennett.

The author of 'Tono-Bungay' and of 'The New Machiavelli' and the author of 'The Old Wives Tale' and of 'Clayhanger' have practically launched the boat in which we admire the fresh play of oar of the author of 'The Duchess of Wrexe' and the documented aspect exhibited successively by 'Round the Corner', by 'Carnival' and 'Sinister Street', and even by 'Sons and Lovers', however much we may find Mr. Lawrence, we confess, hang in the dusty rear.

For it is interesting, in spite of its leaving itself on our hands with so consistent an indifference to any question of a charmed application springing from it all as pleases it in the forefront of its type. Again as under the effect of Mr. Bennett's major productions our sole inference is that things, the things disclosed, *go on and on, in any case,* in spite of everything—this serving as a sort of formula of the show; with Mr. Cannan's one discernible care perhaps being for how extraordinarily much, in this particular example here before him, they were able to go on in spite of.

And further on in the article:

'I answer for it, you know,' we seem at any rate to hear Mr. Cannan say with an admirably genuine young pessimism. 'I answer for it that they were really like that, odd, or unpleasant or uncontributive, and therefore tiresome, as they may strike you'; and the charm of Mr. Cannan, so far as up and down the rank we disengage a charm, is that we take him at his word. His guarantee, his straight communication of his general truth is a value . . .

To be picked out thus and discussed so seriously by one of the respected old guard was very gratifying. The American rights in *Round The Corner* were now sold, and, on the drama side also, Gilbert seemed to be advancing, for on February 18th, 1914, John Drinkwater had put on *Miles Dixon* in Birmingham with himself, Cathleen Orford and Betty Pinchard playing the leading roles. The play was taken seriously but the notices were not very encouraging. *The Birmingham Gazette* found the spirit of the play never obscure and the characters cleverly drawn. *The Birmingham Post's* critic was less happy, seeing morbid depressing elements in the play. But Gilbert and Mary enjoyed a few days' stay with John Drinkwater, and one thing seemed to be leading to another. For on February 26th, at Mary's instigation, Gilbert sent Drinkwater two more of his plays, but on March 8th he was asking for the return of *The Perfect Widow* . . . 'Marie Tempest is talking of doing it and I want to make some alterations and you have my only copy.'*

His friendship with Secker had continued to grow and he had spent several pleasant weekends with Compton Mackenzie at Secker's Queen Anne home, Bridgefoot, near Iver in Buckinghamshire, where he had enjoyed the use of a pianola and played croquet on the wide green lawn, and many hours of chess in the evenings.

Meanwhile, the majority of critics had continued to find Gilbert's work disappointing. *The Times Literary Supplement* reviewer, while feeling that *Old Mole* was probably Gilbert's most agreeable novel so far, nevertheless complained that it was bitter with 'dry mouthed railing', and labelled the writer as 'clever'.

Some day [he finished] we believe that Mr. Cannan will write a book that will begin where at present he leaves off . . . The vision is there: some day it will consume him wholly, and he will communicate to others.

By this time more of that vision had been incorporated by Gilbert in *Love*, a book less cynical than many from his pen, showing him as a man who genuinely longed to be good. His form of love derives from the New Testament rather than the Old, which he castigates, in this perhaps also expressing Gertler's disillusionment with its God.

That terrible God of the Jews, a trafficker of men's lives, a bargainer, a ruthless slayer, bored and restless as the Jews with all their power of assuming nationalities, so that He has become more English than the English, more

* I have not been able to trace this play.

German than the Germans, more Gallic—(consider the French version of the Bible)—than the French...

Now, like Middleton Murry, Gilbert was drawn towards William Blake, finding some affinity with the sentiments and ideals expressed in Blake's writing. He quotes in *Love*:

> *Seek love in the pity of another's woe,*
> *In the gentle relief in mothers' care,*
> *In the darkness of night and the cruel winter's snow*
> *In the naked and outcast, seek life there!*[41]

Certainly he tried hard through much of his life to follow that maxim, but sometimes it was as though the devil drove his pen and all the hatred, the bitterness and disappointment which festered unexpressed in his youth would come to the surface. And for one with high ideals there undoubtedly was an unacceptable level of injustice, disease, suffering and bloodshed to be seen and felt.

Earlier his particular kind of goodness found expression in his chivalry towards Mary. 'I only care about her happiness,' he had written. But sadly Ottoline's *Memoirs* and the love sonnets sent to her suggest that this gallant aspiration had wilted. Worse still, as time went on, Gilbert seems to have decided that the love had never been real but counterfeit, and that although Mary grew to care deeply for him in a maternal way, she had begun the affair in an attempt to make jealous a lover who had scorned her. Parading Gilbert, she had hoped, he thought now, to show that she could still attract young men, a realisation which seemed to Gilbert to make his own later infidelities less culpable.

> *Now there is hung a curtain between us two*
> *A curtain pieced together of strange things*
> *Done, thought, and felt, unwilled; the puppet strings*
> *Of chance directing all we strove to do.*

There were ups and downs, hills and valleys, moments of hope and despair all mirrored in the sonnets which were published in *Adventurous Love and Other Verses*. Some are bitter; the following lines were perhaps inspired by the long wait after the divorce and do not suggest a happy marriage:

> *This looking backwards turns my heart to stone*
> *Time weighs heavy with us. Failure stings*
> *To numbness. Years are marked in us as rings*
> *In trees. But they give strength. The winter's gone*
> *And we have borne its buffeting alone ...*

And from two other poems.

> *Is that enough? What if your spirit harks*
> *Back to the old hope? There is no diadem*
> *To give you there. 'Tis dead. My soul embarks*
> *Upon another quest though you contemn. . . .*

> *In all unworldly things I sought to find*
> *The beauty of my vision, not their own,*
> *And wrinkled pleasures bit into my mind.*
> *Their disappointment turned my heart to stone*
> *And made me live too much in hope. Behind*
> *My hope of love were shapeless shadows thrown. . . .*

A reviewer writing in *The Times Literary Supplement* described the sonnets as 'following, analysing and discussing the changing relations of the poet and his love'. Whether his judgement was correct we are unlikely now to know. To me many of the verses seem to speak of a growing sense of sexual impotence, an increasing apartness which no doubt prompted Middleton Murry to suppose there had never been any sex between Gilbert and Mary. Perhaps the following quotation from the verses is some indication of how his desire had waned.

> *I have a room wherein each day I sit*
> *Word-weaving. I have windows south, east, west,*
> *And with the changing sky my eyes are blest*
> *Over this wide Heaven I let my wit*
> *And fancy roam. My thoughts like birds do flit*
> *Against the clouds in happy, happy quest*
> *Of straws and twigs and moss to build their nest.*
> *This is the spring when days with love are lit.*
> *My thoughts are happy, but my envious heart*
> *Watches them mate, and knows himself alone,*
> *Wedded to nothing but the writer's art.*
> *A kind of savage pride to be apart*
> *Possesses me, and I am cold as stone,*
> *Wanting the will to make my love my own.*

Yet, if these sonnets tell a tale, there also seems to have been a re-flowering of love, which may of course have been concerned with someone other than Mary. Clearly at this time Gilbert's marital life no longer give him the mental and sexual satisfaction that he felt he needed to mature and find lasting happiness. It is likely that by the end of 1914 his thoughts and interest were beginning to wander, or had wandered, towards other women. Mary should not have been surprised for he had now made clear in his writings that he believed in free love.

7

'A Power for Good'

D. H. Lawrence

ONE view of Gilbert's initial and rather naïve attitude to the war has been recorded by Compton Mackenzie who put Lawrence and Gilbert and their respective wives as minor characters into his novel, *The South Wind of Love*. John Ogilvie's (Mackenzie's) visit to Daniel Rayner (Lawrence) and Frederick Rodney (Gilbert) is based on fact and is as accurate as Mackenzie could make it with only the names changed. Mackenzie, who wrongly believed that Mary supported her young husband financially, described Gilbert (Rodney) as 'tall and slim with a Wellingtonian nose and a deliberately portentous manner'.

Here are a few extracts in which I have given Rayner and the Rodneys the names of their originals. It must be remembered that Mackenzie ('John') was inclined to show himself in the best possible light.

'Gilbert is writing in the windmill', Mrs. Cannan told John when he arrived. He felt that to announce Gilbert was breathing would hardly have been a more superfluous statement.

The Cannans did not live in the windmill, but in an agreeable small modern house . . .

John chuckled to himself as he entered the windmill and by a spiral iron flight of stairs corkscrewed his way up the room at the top, where at a very large table Gilbert was seated writing away on his octave sheets, and as John could observe in a quick glance without a single erasure or correction on any sheet in sight.

'Look here, Gilbert, what are you doing about the war?'

'The war?' echoed the novelist. 'Oh well, I suppose unless one does something . . . I'm a special constable. I watch the gasworks at Colchester two nights a week.'

'But you can't go on doing that indefinitely,' John protested.

'Why not?'

'Don't you want to get out on active service?'

'I don't feel active service would be a particularly valuable experience for an artist.'

'Why not?'

'It's too unusual and too violent. What transmutation value has an attack of scarlet fever or a street accident?'

'Transmutation value?'

'Into art,' said Gilbert severely.

'In certain circumstances both might have considerable value.'

'That's because you regard life as a dramatist, and rather an old fashioned romantic dramatist, John, I'm afraid.'

John Ogilvie then picked up a copy of the magazine *Blast*, of which he clearly disapproved.

'Surely these bold lads won't have become special constables? I know Marinetti has already declared for Italy entering the war on our side.'

'The people who run *Blast* disassociate themselves from Marinetti . . .'

'You take this stuff seriously?' John asked, turning over the pages of *Blast*.

'On the whole, yes. It's a bit noisy. But we have to blow up the old world.'

'The war may do that before it's finished.'

Gilbert shook his head.

'The war will be over by Christmas. We shall have forgotten about it a year from now.'

'You may be right, but suppose you are wrong?'

'That's an even stronger argument against having anything to do with it. Balzac said nothing was easier to lose than the power to create. Cease to create and atrophy sets in at once. No artist could take an active part in a war and hope to produce creative work' . . .

And after further argument

'But I disbelieve in war, I'll do nothing to help it.'

'Then why the hell are you guarding the gasworks at Colchester as a special constable?'

'That's not positively helping the war.'

'Yes, it is.'

'Not at all. It's on the same level as Red Cross work.'

John uttered a ribald ejaculation of contempt.

'I claim it is,' Gilbert insisted. 'I'm acting solely towards the end of saving human life.'

'If you saw some German Guy Fawkes creeping up to the gasworks with a bomb, wouldn't you lay him out if you could? If you wouldn't you'd be a damned rotten special. All right that's helping the war just as much as blazing away at the Germans in Belgium.'

Gilbert looked thoughtfully down his Wellingtonian nose. 'I did it really to please Mary,' he acknowledged at last. 'And I like walking about at night. But perhaps it does invalidate my moral attitude with regard to war. We'll find out what Lawrence thinks about it. He's very anti-war. You've never met him, have you, John?'

A lively description follows of Mackenzie's visit to the Lawrences with no indication that the author was aware that Lawrence found him 'breezy' and alien in spirit.[1] Here Mary throws in the odd word, disappointed that Gilbert does not shine in a conversation about trees, indeed she wants 'to prod him in the way a competitive mother prods her backward child at a party'.

Back at the Mill House John Ogilvie becomes as oppressed by a sense of unreality as David Garnett had been.

It was all so comfortable and well run by Mary Cannan; the maids were so neat. The very dogs were so well behaved. Yet for Gilbert Cannan the Mill House and all it contained, including Mary herself, was just an armchair in which he found it easy to write.

'I'm resigning my job as a special,' Gilbert announced after dinner.

'Oh Gilbert darling, why?' Mary asked. 'I thought you were enjoying it.'

'Lawrence is right. It is the duty of all artists to hate this war and do nothing which will help it in any way.'

'Well I like the Lawrences very much, but I think they're both a little mad,' said Mary pettishly. Then her annoyance of the afternoon came back to her. 'You sat saying nothing Gilbert. You let Lawrence have it all his own way, Lawrence and John. And even you didn't argue with him, John. I think it's weak to let one man dictate to everybody in the way Lawrence does ...'[2]

The armchair was not of course as comfortable as Compton Mackenzie imagined. Indeed, although he might 'command her loftily' to go to bed,[3] in many ways Gilbert was dominated maternally by Mary in a way that was likely to make him feel and perhaps become irresponsible and prevent him maturing. Unknown to her the Mill House was becoming the epitome of the setting for the 'cloying security of marriage' which he described in his little book, *Love*. More and more he needed the freer air outside, and yet as we shall see he eventually turned again to a woman whose interest in him was largely maternal.

In the meantime he continued to write, to play the pianola, talk with his friends and long from time to time for the company of Ottoline, complaining on April 23rd, 1915: 'Has Garsington swallowed you up? Are your friends neither to hear from you nor see you? That is hard.'

For him 1914 had been a year of hard work. To please Mary it was essential to establish himself as a writer at least equal to Barrie; her pride demanded that the world saw that she had exchanged one great man for another. Several of the Cannans felt, perhaps unfairly, that it was her pressure that drove Gilbert to work so hard, that having left her own career she could only find the fame she desired through her husband. The four works published in 1915 indicate how industrious Gilbert had been: *Young Earnest, Samuel Butler, a Critical Study, Windmills, Adventurous Love and Other Verses.* In addition he had continued to translate; he had also written plays and innumerable articles, some under the pseudonym 'Moulin à Vent', contributed reviews to the *Manchester Guardian* and lectured on modern drama.

On May 5, 1915, *The Right to Kill* which Gilbert and Frances Keyser had translated from the French play by Pierre Frondaté, who in turn had adapted it for the stage from Claude Farrère's novel, *L'homme qui assassina*, was staged at Her Majesty's Theatre with Herbert Tree, Arthur Bourchier and Irene Vanbrugh playing the leading roles. The play received the most damning notices and was little short of a disaster, although there was some praise for the Turkish interiors designed by Hugo Rumbold.

It wasn't easy for Gilbert to return to the London theatre:

I have taken refuge in digging [he wrote to Ottoline from the Mill House]. The strain of passing from my own work to rehearsing with Tree was too great, so I renounced the one and fled from the other and took spade in hand, with the result that I can hardly hold a pen.

But the retreat could only be temporary for the following Monday he had to return to London for a week, when he hoped to see her. Not forgetting Ottoline's interest in Lawrence, who had left the Triangle, he went on in the same letter to say that he had stayed with the Lawrences at Greatham three weeks earlier, and

had tremendous talks with him and lovely walks over the downs—12 miles one day. I wish you could be here for a day or two. Heavenly gorse, cherry trees coming out, the woods as they were that day when you came with Dorothy.

It seems that at this time he wanted, like a lover, to share everything beautiful with Ottoline, his pleasures as well as his failures and misgivings. The day following *The Right to Kill*'s disastrous first night he wrote:

My dear Ottoline, I am back here convalescing after my comic Tree experience, in its way quite wonderful, having its climax in a sort of gala opera audience, all the spurious people in London all bent on insisting that an entirely unimportant play (though not bad of its kind) was important. I had frightful struggles to keep it from being pretentious and could not altogether succeed. However it's over—I don't want to think about it any more. Mary says she will never go to London again so much did she hate her old world of snobs and celebrities—I'm very happy that you like *Windmills* so much. Bertie likes it too and wrote me a very charming letter about it: that has made me very proud and happy for I would rather have his commendation than any man's. Here is a loveliness to heal and restore and purify: the gorse is blazing on the common; the first trees in blossom; birds in full song; a summer sky . . .

His books continued to receive serious, though by no means always favourable attention in the leading papers of the day as well as the smaller more exclusive literary journals. *Satire*, which examines that subject, was given two full columns in *The Times Literary Supplement*:

He is clever throughout, but without cumulative power in his cleverness . . .
And he seems too much in love with his own style, using phrases that by their turn distrust one from his sense as if it were his taste that had found them, and not their meaning.

Young Earnest was reviewed in the same edition also at length, with one especially significant sentence:

In spite of his sincerity, therefore, in spite of the genuineness of his characters and their emotions—and this book is at least as good as any of the earlier ones that justly aroused hopes—Mr. Cannan remains still but a man of promise.

His critical study of Samuel Butler fared little better in the same paper, being 'too much a product of egotism' to please the reviewer, who complained that all the best pieces were at the beginning before the memory of the Victorian public became too much for the author,

Butler has to make room for a fitful appearance where he can: there is room for little except the surge of Mr. Cannan's opinions on Victorian art, science fiction and family life.

On the whole the anonymous reviewers in *The Times Literary Supplement* were hostile to Gilbert's work throughout his career.

Shortly after the 'Tree experience', Gilbert went to Paris, where he probably met Romain Rolland who had been run over by a car and was suffering from a broken arm and damaged leg. The trip was mentioned by Gilbert in a letter to John Drinkwater inviting him to stay and thanking him for a copy of *Rebellion*.

I've just been over to Paris and saw Copeau and his Vieux Colombier: a delicious place. It and your theatre have made me happy.[4]

Lawrence had enjoyed the Cannans' stay with him at Greatham, writing to Ottoline:

The Cannans are here, I must say I rather love them. Strangely enough, I feel a real, unalterable power for good in Gilbert. But he is very crude, very

shockingly undisciplined, and consequently inarticulate. He is not *very*
passionate. But he is a power for good nevertheless, and I like him to be with
us. Mary is rather nice, too: she *is* rather a dear, but shallow. I like Gilbert,
I am glad of his existence . . .[5]

Interestingly, Lawrence's view of Gilbert as crude was in direct
contrast with the opinion of many of their contemporaries. But
Lawrence was inclined to talk excessively of sex and the importance of
a shared climax. (Indeed Sir Compton Mackenzie told me that he
became so bored with Lawrence's obsession with the matter that he
asked him to consider the visual aspect of the act. Was it not very
comical? At which, he related, Lawrence was annoyed.) Gilbert's
reaction in similar circumstances may have been to become shockingly
and uncharacteristically crude, in an effort to outdo Lawrence. Or, on
another plane, Lawrence may have felt simply that Gilbert lacked
intellectual subtlety. Later Lawrence writing again to Ottoline from
Greatham, this time under the influence of Russell, mentions that he
was thinking of taking a hall in London where lectures would be given
on immortality and ethics: 'Murry must come in and Gilbert—and
perhaps Campbell. We can all lecture, at odd times.'[6] And he asked
that Ottoline should send on his 'philosophy' to Gilbert. The Cannans,
however, were busy with visitors, Gertler and the Jowitts, but Gilbert
gave the 'philosophy' a first reading and while writing to Ottoline on
July 9th to decline an invitation gave his initial impression of it, and of
Clive Bell's 'Art and War'.[7]

It is certainly good but at first incoherent. There is no precise statement of
motif nor are the symbols to be used set forth or expounded. It needs an
almost musical structure. I am rather baffled by some of it, the absolute
cleavage for instance, between becoming and being, which makes a discon-
tinuity, and the phrasing is often baffling. The use of the word God drags in,
against L's intention, absolute ideas of the Godhead. But one criticises it very
lovingly and tenderly . . .
  Clive Bell's pamphlet has reached me. It is sound argument but flimsy. It
is content with a world in which people have their pleasures. Such a world
there was and it has come to grief because it was content to be no more than
that. However the pamphlet has the air of being good sense and is good
sense and may therefore be read by people who will not face anything that as-
saults their habitual values. I certainly hope it will be read.

In fact Lawrence's 'philosophy' was to have a profound effect on
Gilbert, the symbols assuming an importance for him out of all
proportion to their usefulness to Lawrence himself. Lawrence and
Gertler's welfare and art continued to be a concern Gilbert shared with
Ottoline. Earlier, on May 17th he wrote:

I saw the Lawrences: they were up for the bankruptcy proceedings. He seemed ill and exhausted and I arranged for them to come here at the end of the month and to be taken over to you when they want to move on. Greatham has worn very thin and Lawrence has had enough Meynelliana. Hardly any reviews of Windmills yet, discreet and cautious and giving no hint as to what the book is really about. However with you, Lawrence and Bertie pleased with it I'm quite content to let it go at that though I'd like to see it circulating . . .

Restless and unsatisfied, he seemed much on the move. On June 2nd he wrote:

My dear Ottoline, Good! We'll come over one day next week to lunch, if we may, whichever day suits you best. We are just back from a jolly tour in the car—first to Beaulieu, then to Wittering—the Hutchinsons, where we met the lovely Clive Bell children—and then to Rottingdean, Lady Lewis's, where also was Suggia, alas, without her cello. Without it she is just gamin, though full of a splendid vitality. I bathed much in the sea and am as brown as a bun, and so full of spirit that I find it hard to settle down. We're expecting the Lawrences soon though we haven't heard from them for some time . . .

An enthusiastic letter followed his first stay at Garsington dated June 17th:

What a happy time! I think a very essential part of me took root in your world in those days when I had the little bed at the top of Bedford Square and it has a delight and a free expression that the rest of me rejoices in, and to have it transplanted to Garsington was wonderful. Because it is so happy there it must be a happiness with you too, for I know that what I have of you here is happy also . . .

By now Gilbert was attracted to Carrington, in, he was quick to reassure her, a fatherly way. He called her Daisy and sent her a letter depicting himself as the sun and her as a little flower basking in his warmth. Writing on July 30th:

My dear Daisy, I've finished my novel and taken it up to London and now hasten to write to you to inform you of your adoption into my family. Outward formalities there are none since I repudiate patria potestas, the power of the parent. Rights? I don't think there are any rights either, except your right to come to the room in the mill whenever you wish. In what then does adoption consist? I should say, in a declaration of affectionate intent:— see the book of Ruth; the assumption of the delicate relationship which is the flower of sympathy, the little daisy glowing modestly in the heat of the sun. Thus . . . [A picture followed, then:] Mark has been depressed since you went away and began to crave philosophical London as represented by Kotelinanski (*sic*). However he began to work and the craving passed off & now he is excited at the discovery that he can sit in the sun and paint trees. He does it very well and produces sketches that are solid pictures. He and I have had some tremendous walks and on one we made a song of Gertling, from the new verb to Gertle.

> *I've gertled in the West End,*
> *I've gertled by the sea.*
> *At any sort of gertling you can't beat me.*
> *From Mile End to Piccadilly*
> *I have made the knuts look silly,*
> *For they don't know how to gertle,*
> *They are slower than a turtle,*
> *You should see the way I hurtle*
> *After tea . . .*

At the same time Gilbert was working on his book about Gertler's youth, and, to a lesser extent, Gertler's love for Carrington which was to be called *Mendel* and cause much resentment. Gertler in a letter to Lytton Strachey wrote in May that the book had taken two months to write. It was 'about a young man who, I believe, is supposed to resemble me, but I don't know'.[8]

Gertler's widow wrote in a recent letter to me that she considered it the best biography yet written of Gertler, describing with splendid accuracy the way he spoke and acted, and all his mannerisms. This time the publisher was not to be Secker, to whom Gilbert had written some months earlier (May 16th, 1916):

Pinker and financial pressure have rushed me into a contract for a novel with Methuen. I held out as long as I could but it seemed to guarantee at any rate the nucleus of an income for the next year. That will mean no January novel from me.

He went on to say there would be other books from him for Secker, as there was no chance of him being cured of his only vice—work.

The first book to go to Methuen, *Three Pretty Men* (a title predictably rejected by the American publishers for their edition)[9], was Gilbert's first major attempt to understand the Cannan side of his family. The 'pretty men' are his grandfather and two of his great-uncles, the fourth having emigrated to America. Gilbert's great aunt Mary plays a large part in the book, as in life. Edwin's father, the ill-fated David, is given a countess as a second wife, instead of the head-mistress of a preparatory school. Indeed, although also biographical the book lacks the accuracy of *Round the Corner*, perhaps because Gilbert's mother was the talker, the chronicler of the past during his childhood while his father worked, and she would of course have known more about her own relations than her husband's. Nevertheless, it is mainly authentic and describes well the bewilderment of the eldest boy (James) when he arrives in Manchester straight from the beauties and moorland delights of Kirkcudbrightshire. It also faithfully conveys the family's ill-founded belief in their own extraordinary talents and each individual's peculiar vulnerability.

Three Pretty Men is dedicated to Gilbert's brother, John Felix Cannan, the dedicatory verses emphasising that they shared a common inheritance. Beginning the 'shadow-play of which this tale is made is also yours', it continues further on:

> *They dwelt*
> *Where you and I were born. Their lives are knit*
> *With yours and mine, and what they did and felt*
> *Dictates what you and I must do*
> *In our own shadow-play through which we move*
> *Hardly less ghosts than they. If they were true*
> *We have our life and love that truth to prove.*

These Cannans were related to butchers, tenant farmers, Scottish ministers, frustrated actors and writers, linguists, academics, business-men and bankers. In Felix, the actor streak clashed with the business-man, as it had with Angus, who had solved the conflict by going into shipping professionally, and acting as an amateur. Felix was soon to become the rope in a tug-of-war between Angus and Gilbert, Gilbert winning the first round when he arranged for Felix to join Fred Terry's company touring with *The Scarlet Pimpernel* and *Sweet Hell* until he was old enough to join the army. Good looking, aquiline, pleasant and mentally stable, Felix made a promising beginning on the stage, but his administrative ability and business flair, which were to make him a leading figure in the shipping world, were too strong, and Angus was eventually the winner.

Looking back thirty years later Felix wrote that he had never met anyone who had quite so much charm and personality as Gilbert.

He never talked down to anyone and was interested in everybody. I remember once writing a play for a scout concert (absolute rubbish I have no doubt) which he read and criticised exactly as he would have done with one of his contemporaries. It was an idyllic relationship and, for I was very unsophis-ticated for my age and scandals were right over my head, a period of real hero-worship.[10]

Gilbert introduced Felix, who spent most of his holidays between 1913 and 1916 at the Mill House, to many of his friends, the St. John Hutchinsons, the Jowitts, Roger Fry, George Moore, Koteliansky,

Milton Rosmer, Irene Rook, and Miles Malleson among them. He also took Felix to stay at Garsington on more than one occasion.

It was a happy arrangement for, although fourteen years separated them, and Gilbert had been informally adopted by Edwin and was therefore only at home in term-time during the first years of Felix's life, the brothers had to a large degree a common background. For both, amateur family dramatics had been an important and enjoyable part of childhood, and Felix's earliest recollection of life is of a home-made production of *A Christmas Carol* with his father playing Scrooge. They had both enjoyed being read aloud to from Dickens in the evenings, and writing for the family magazine *The Star*, to which as a young child, Gilbert had contributed

> *Of all the jams that ever were*
> *The hardest jam to spread*
> *Is blackcurrant 'cause the currants*
> *Roll off the slice of bread.*

In summer 1915 Gertler started his painting of the Mill (using the Cannans' motor shed as his studio)[11] which now belongs to the Ashmolean Museum, Oxford. The two dogs depicted either side of Gilbert are Sammy and Luath.[12] By now the Cannans had parted with Billy, because he had developed the habit of attacking other residents' dogs. Sammy, his son, was quiet and well behaved and devoted to Luath. He seemed to have assumed Gilbert's personality within canine limits, being strangely detached and lacking even as a puppy, the youthful boisterousness usually found in his breed.

There was still much pleasure for Gilbert that year, particularly in his visits to Garsington where he would join Gertler in a lively Jewish dance for the entertainment of fellow guests. In spite of Gertler's reservation, Gilbert's encouragement and hospitality meant a good deal to the artist as the following extracts from letters show. March 4th, Gertler to Carrington from Penn Studio, Hampstead:

Gilbert Cannan came here to tea the other day. He thought my studio 'simply splendid' and he loved the Heath. He wants to buy my charcoal study of 'Abraham & the Angels'. But I must keep it as yet, as sooner or later I will paint it. I promised to reserve it for him. How he does like my work. He seems to understand me more than anyone else.[13]

Undated letter to Koteliansky from the Mill House, probably written in 1915:

Although I came here very unhappy I have now recovered and am feeling comparatively happy. Gilbert is a good companion. He is soothing. I like him immensely. I shan't rest until I also have a good wife and a comfortable house. *Plainly* that is what I want, I don't care what *you* say.[14]

One Saturday in June 1915 Gertler wrote to Carrington from the Mill House:

Mary sat in the further room as usual doing some work. Of this arrangement I was glad because then she could not interrupt as she usually does by talking. Gilbert played splendidly [the pianola]. I never wanted it to end . . .

It ended and then Brett and Mary went to bed, while Gilbert and I woke up because we talked of you. I told him all. He thought our relations wonderful and worth much and he envied me for knowing you. He appreciates you very much and I love him for liking you.[15]

But, although Gilbert might appear soothing to Gertler, he did not feel calm inside. He felt frustrated and perhaps as an attempted remedy he renewed later that year his friendship with the widowed Kathleen Scott, now a well-established sculptor. This proved a disturbing experience, but typically, although torn by conflicting calls of conscience and desire, Gilbert was still mindful of the welfare of Gertler, who had recently broken with Eddie Marsh. He wrote to Ottoline on October 26th:

My struggles ended in a violent convulsion which blew me up to London, for almost a week during which I passed through various storms and came out battered but toughened. I'll come over soon and tell you as much as I can of it all.

Meanwhile will you keep in your mind that Gertler has to be kept going. He has thrown Marsh over and won his freedom back and in a month or two will be very near the rocks . . .

Then with passionate words written in November after a week-end at Garsington, his handwriting uncharacteristically shaky, Gilbert tried to pick up the old threads, to slip back into his 1908 skin and write again a letter to Kathleen Scott to be read with the relish of 'a lioness'.

Days and days of a tearing agony and no words. To live again in the life we made all those years ago, to find it grown so huge, so filled with a blinding light brings a terror to my soul that has lived confined and cramped in a bitter world which I must now slip into my waistcoat pocket. O you, good and evil you, good of my good, evil of my evil you can never go so fast but I shall catch up with you. You can never sink so deep into the unfathomable but I shall dive down to you and bring you again to the sun, to lie with me on the burning sand with the cool water breaking over you and the wind blowing in your hair . . . so that it is salt to my lips, bitter, bitter to the taste, sending the soul deeper into you for its sweetness. So deep it goes that it needs prodigious agony to come out to the body of you . . .

Heady symbolic stuff; yet although he might write in the old vein, the love was different now. The skin of 1908 no longer fitted. The world had changed and with it their bodies and their minds and, however ecstatically Gilbert might talk of freedom, blinding lights and the convenience of the waistcoat pocket, he was still rational enough to feel bound by past decisions, past mistakes and complex emotional ties. The recklessness of youth was past; no longer alone searching for new experiences, he possessed commitments from which he could not and did not want to escape. No daily love-letters from him would fall again on Kathleen Scott's mat, however much he might desire and admire her. He had been through too much to be again capable of the intensity of his first love for her. Uncertain perhaps in the beginning, he appears to have held back, possibly weighing up the situation, trying to protect himself from being racked by a love-affair which could only lead to problems, a tangle of lies, scandal and unhappiness for Mary. Certainly the next letter suggests that hesitation or lack of enthusiasm had brought a reproach.

My Freedom (for you are that. You set me free from boyhood and now again free for manhood and love). Have I been ungracious and niggardly? I can't write you words except they be (*sic*) good words and those have been denied me by the stiffest bout of thinking I've ever had. I don't know how you feel but *I have* been knocked out of time by the discovery that I had caught up with my real life which all that time ago shot ahead of me. The job has been to get rid of the imitation lives that have cropped up in the interval. I think it's done now and the New Year which began for us a couple of months ago is really open. I have bared my arms and cleaned up my brain and girded my loins for the jolly task of filling it. The bird of time? Wring his neck. I'll come up early in January and we'll do it together and then cook and eat him as a sacrifice to love sacred and profane: for I won't hear of it being either: it must be *both*. There have been blessings poured out on the wind to you. Have you had them? Of course you have for since the adventure you are open to the spirit of me as I am to the spirit of you. O! but this thing is worth fighting for. Tell them to stop the war because something really important is happening. Please, please be a fine patient woman for I'm fighting my way to you and am due to arrive on January 10th. More & better letters shall follow this but meanwhile have a happy Xmas with Peter.[16]

This time there may have been perhaps more sexual fulfilment, 'the adventure' being his word for that, but ultimately Gilbert was not to be Kathleen's man; he would never be the father of any child she bore, and there was now the obstacle of Mary who had no intention of taking second place. Kathleen Scott wrote in her unpublished diaries:

Jan. 12 1916 G.C. Mary came up with him; he's having hell and can't get off.

Feb. 3rd. 1916 G.C. came to lunch; he was very delicious with Peter. They dropped me at Vickers[17] and went back together. I asked Peter whether he liked him and he said, 'Very much, I might also say I loved him.'

Feb. 4th 1916 Dined at Queens with G.C. His attitude about the war is that it is so maniacal that he will have no share in it—His arguments are so much what I have always felt and yet—what's to be done? If you saw a man belabouring your sister you would be bound to belabour the man.

And yet I can't be intolerant of G.C.'s view. *I see it!*

He still loves me as he did years ago, he thinks more. It is a very wonderful thing. It is the jolliest thing in the world to see his grave face light up into radiance at the sight of one . . . Oh dear me if he'd been with big people always instead of the microscopic ones he might have been very wonderful. I suppose if he'd been big enough, he'd have grown thro' them, perhaps he may still—bless him.

Kathleen Scott was certainly moving with 'big people' herself, among them Asquith, with whom she was growing increasingly involved. And it seems from her unpublished diaries she was not above provoking the Prime Minister with her praise for Gilbert, pressing him to read the younger man's work, and talking of his anti-war theories. The pattern of 1908 seemed to be repeating itself, with Asquith, to whom Gilbert had been introduced by Ottoline, the 'other man' instead of Scott, but with Gilbert's own reactions more muted, less overt, his protests fewer and his understanding of the situation more complete. For Kathleen there was again a wish to help Gilbert, to care for him and promote his work, which would have been entirely laudable if it had not combined with the self-gratification of seeing Gilbert's desire again aroused with no chance of it ever being satisfied in a permanent relationship. Her instinct was right, he was not the man for her, but she underestimated the pain her decision caused him, how it drove him in the end to other women even less satisfactory.

Pathetically he turned to the maid in this time of frustration and growing division within himself. This was the girl Middleton Murry described in his Journal as 'Mary's perfect maid', a quiet, outwardly well-behaved girl, who did as she was told and worked to the high standard demanded by her mistress. Exactly when the affair started we do not know. According to Frank Swinnerton, Gilbert boasted at one point of having given a woman a baby when she needed just 'that boon to make her happy'.[18] But for Gilbert there was no *soul* in the liaison, and a loveless mating for the purpose of a baby does smack of the farmyard sex which he despised. Here perhaps we come to the very core of Gilbert's predicament: his hopes, visions, lofty idealism were incompatible with the actualities of his life. He probably wove a romance around the sad little affair to please the girl and rationalise his own actions, while at the same time satisfying the sexual needs stimulated by his continued meetings with Kathleen Scott.

The fact that the maid approached him in the first place, as he was to tell his sister, Margaret, does suggest that she knew something of his needs and desperation and was attracted by his gentleness. She saw that his marriage was floundering. Mary's maternal love was beginning to pall. A superb administrator, she had taken over the running of the house, the garden and the man and she was determined to benefit vicariously through Gilbert's successes. People would say that she had *made* Cannan in spite of his vagueness, his ill-formed ideas and crazy idealism. Before she met him he had published almost nothing and now he was famous. But Gilbert wanted to be loved for what he was, warts and all. He now convinced himself that Mary had loved him mostly for his youth and the short-lived vitality that had so nearly captivated Kathleen Bruce, while more coolly assessing his potential. And, as time went on, he began to believe that he had only loved her for loving him.

The maid was simple, different, without guile. In *Little Brother*, *Young Earnest* and *The Little Slavey* Gilbert had glamorised the servant class and revealed a special interest in poor working-girls. Indeed sex with the Cholesbury maid could have been mixed up in his mind with his tender affection for the Welsh girl, so consummating that thwarted and only half-understood love of his adolescence. Judging the affair on a different level there were, of course, examples in life and literature and in particular in *Jean Christophe*, which may have seemed to Gilbert to make the liaison acceptable within his circle of friends, many of whom had expressed their belief in free love. Lillah McCarthy for example had given her heart to this belief when she played Mrs. Crummins in St. John Hankin's play, *The Last of the de Mullins*, which Gilbert must certainly have seen soon after he became friends with Mary.[19]

In the 3rd act [wrote Bernard Shaw] Lillah appealed with extraordinary gusto to every unmarried woman of twenty-eight in the house to go straight out and procure a baby at once without the slightest regard to law and conventions. As Lillah regards this as a most obvious doctrine, she had no idea of the effect she was producing in the audience . . .[20]

On top of all this was Gilbert's desire for independence, the need to break away from Mary, to rebel against the mother-figure, a rebellion which had not come about during adolescence because his real mother had never wished to hold or to dominate him. He rented a flat in Hallam Street, wanting also to escape from the comforts of the Mill House. Others were fighting and dying or struggling in poverty to express their art while he was cosseted at home. Here in his guilty feelings he resembled his grandfather Francis Wright, who had suddenly given up a restful pastoral living in Devon to serve his Church in the gloomy slums of Salford. The disastrous progress of the war was making him miserable and undoubtedly driving him nearer to the madness which was finally to overwhelm him.

It is no good shutting ourselves up and denying that is happening. We have to accept the horror and take it down into our souls and when that is done then only can we turn upon it and demand in how ever small a voice that it shall cease. The war should not cease because it is horrible but because it is futile and it is foolish blasphemy. Let the wicked blaspheme, but not the innocent.[21]

Like others in the country the Cannans entertained Belgian refugees and, unlike the majority of the British, felt sympathy with such as Lawrence who had German partners, and in particular for a 'German with a Belgian wife, poor man'.[22] Gilbert's love for German literature and music and his interest in German philosophy, fostered in youth by his great-aunt Mary, all combined to increase his hatred of the war, which he saw as a crime against humanity and an act of lunacy. The speech Melian Stokes (Bertrand Russell) makes to the magistrate in a later anti-semitic novel *Sembal* sums up some of Gilbert's feelings.

I believe war to be in all circumstances an obscene outrage, and I do not consider myself bound by the restrictions imposed by war. In my view the guilt of those who brought on this war is long since merged in the guilt of those who have for so many years prosecuted it . . .
I believe that my country owes its first loyalty not to itself but to those nobler activities and achievements of the human mind which are not bounded by national frontiers or national egoism . . .

Gilbert wrote to Kathleen Scott from Hallam Street on the 13th:

I've been swimming in the very cold sea and sailing boats in a very cold wind and am now returned to foolish bewildered London. Tonight I go to the Mill but am up again tomorrow afternoon, possibly to stay although probably not, but I'll be back on Friday in any case. The chief thing is to get in touch with you, so, if you can be free at all tomorrow (Wed.) evening, write to me here & I'll come and find you any time after 6.30.

The highflown language had been abandoned and it is clear that Gilbert was now more concerned with practicalities than purple prose. Wednesday *was* free, for on that day Kathleen wrote in her diary

Gilbert Cannan came to dine and stayed till after midnight. Mary is in bed with nerves and he meant to go back to her but he didn't. His conscientious objector's views are hideously [?]. . . .

Meanwhile his friendship with Carrington continued, for she represented the other half of his ideal woman, the child-like element which was now less obvious in Kathleen. Her bobbed chestnut hair, young, vulnerable rather doll-like face and pale blue eyes continued to make Gilbert feel warm and paternal. She also shared with Gilbert an almost ecstatic love for the country, for gorse and trees and the sky. And, delightfully, she possessed a paradoxical mixture of shyness and impulsiveness, of inhibition and crudeness; above all, she was for Gilbert *real*, courageous, unaffected and unconventional. *Mendel* shows how well Gilbert understood much of Carrington's nature and background, and the clash of Gertler's Jewish temperament with that of an upper-middle-class girl. He also had an acute understanding of her earlier faults, describing her in *Mendel* as 'Just an English girl with all the raw feeling bred out of her ... true to type: impulsive without being sensual, kind without being affectionate.' Initially, the attention he paid to her may have been prompted by Ottoline, who felt that it was time someone persuaded her to lose her virginity.[23]

Gilbert, however, had joined the National Council Against Conscription and was too busy to see much of his women friends that spring and summer, having taken over some of the secretarial work of the organisation, a fact mentioned in a letter from James Strachey to his brother Lytton from 6 Belsize Gardens, dated April 14th.

Norton seems to be giving up and returning to Cambridge tomorrow. His place is to be taken by—Gilbert Cannan who is also to act as an understudy to me. I find him fearfully hard to deal with—gloomy speechless and *not* very clever....[24]

And Lytton, who was another of those intellectuals who seemed to make Gilbert feel inadequate, replied from Garsington the next day: 'Gilbert C. sounds a very dismal office companion. You'll never make him understand an Act of Parliament.'[25] In fact the ever-generous Gilbert was giving up a great deal more time to the campaign than either of the critical Stracheys, although he lacked their financial security. And if he was silent, he was also gathering material for three novels in which some of his colleagues in the movement were to appear, studying particularly Bertrand Russell whom he held in some affection.

But none of this helped Kathleen and Carrington who wanted his company and instead received his apologies.

My Daisy I shall have to give up making arrangements [he had written on May 11th] for I can never tell when I shan't be shipped off to a meeting. There is one on Friday now & that knocks my dinner with you on the head. On Tuesday I had to go to see Clive Bell at the Hutchies to discuss conscientious objectors & what is to be done about them.

What a nice picture of Sam!

I won't row on the Serpentine in this weather but if it is better next week I'll come, only I'm afraid you'll have to come & lug me out of bed as I can't guarantee waking up on time. I'm dining with Mark tonight.[26]

Another letter, dated May 24th, beginning 'My Darling Daisy, alas and damn!', cancels an engagement because he has to take Mary to the Mill, and is signed with a drawing of his profile with an overlarge nose and a long pointed chin.

On June 6th he was writing to Kathleen from the Mill House:

I hadn't slipped away. I've been stumping the country speechifying & almost forgetting that I have an individual life. I don't know what is going to happen to me & I'm not worrying. I shall go before a Tribunal at Chesham, and possibly an Appeal Tribunal at Aylesbury . . .

It may be significant that Asquith then wrote to Kathleen, accusing her of being a 'traitress'. No letter had come from her, he complained, and now he must go into the country without a signal of any kind. 'Last night', he finished, 'I pursued my usual routine and did not miss or desire "Windmills".'

In June Gilbert had registered as a conscientious objector, having been called up for the 28th of that month. He wrote to Pinker (June 26, 1916) 'If things go wrong and I am swept off I think it would be better if you made cheques payable to my wife Mary Cannan', which suggests that he had no suspicion that his marriage might not survive his bid for sexual freedom. In August he went before a Tribunal in Chesham and was exempted from Active service on account of a heart murmur. He was, however, ordered to find a job of national importance within six weeks, and this turned his mind to education.

He felt now that he might possess enough vision and experience to advise on a reorganisation of the British educational system. After all, he had experienced Board School as well as public school; he had been to university and read for the Bar. So he wrote naïvely to Eddie Marsh, who had become a powerful figure in the War Office, suggesting that he might like to speak useful words in the Prime Minister's ear. Marsh responded badly, being against conscientious objectors, and a rather acrimonious correspondence about the Military Service Act and the rights and wrongs of pacifism followed. It finished with Gilbert declaring that he could not agree with Marsh about the 'finality' of war. Gilbert looked further ahead and when the end came he did not want to see 'just a lazy scramble for jobs and plums,' but a real effort to lift the world out of the moral atmosphere in which war could be made possible.

Meanwhile he had been sending Kathleen derivative love poems which suggested intimacy, but probably overdramatize events if indeed they were intended to relate to that particular friendship. His poems were not always meant to be taken very seriously by those who received them. Ottoline and Mrs. Raymond Asquith for example had both received copies of one entitled 'A Lady in Bedford Square' on the same day, causing much amusement to the two women who lived a few doors away from each other. Nevertheless his verses to Kathleen do reveal genuine passion and may have expressed a hope and invitation, rather than lyrical appreciation of the full flowering of love:

> Go, count the daisies in the tufted grass
> The dewdrops in the grass where she and I
> Together brought this miracle to pass
> That thou, O Time, must evermore pass by.

> Or count the ripples in the shallow pond
> That cooled the ecstasy I brought to her,
> And filled it all with laughter for the bond
> Wherein I am her constant minister.

> O foolish Time, thy miserable hoard
> Of minutes in thy wallet cannot part
> Inseparable loves which must record
> A single impulse in a single heart.

And

> Ride through the air with me, winged horses, ride with me
> Souls leaping to the sun
> Swim in kind water, ME, in grey-green access of sea
> Learn all the spaciousness of earth's humility
> Resolving two in one.

> Sing, let your body sing, your soul chant with the earth
> Make music with the moon,
> Sun dragging life through you, create, create, give birth
> I, I the instrument, being flashings of God's mirth
> Laughter and child's boon.

The second poem suggests perhaps a thread of megalomania, signs of imbalance in the mind but no more. One is left to wonder again whether Gilbert's actions matched his words, for the faint reproaches which seem to have come from Kathleen do not suggest a great passion. It may be that he decided in the end that she was in love with love, and not actually with him. There is also some indication that he was afraid of indulging in too much sex for fear that 'greed' would in the end kill the romantic side of love, perhaps even passion itself. Certainly this time there was no infatuation and the affair, however great its depth, was able to cool on both sides into an amicable and affectionate friendship.

In the first week of August Gilbert had been alone to Stratford-on-Avon where he stayed in the Shakespeare Hotel and met by chance Galsworthy and his wife, Ada, who noticed he was looking very ill.[27] Indeed he was in great trouble; the maid was pregnant. For Mrs. Crummins it would have been a cause for rejoicing; for Mary, who was later informed, it was a bitter blow but one which the marriage would probably have survived had there not been other deeper problems. Galsworthy was the first of his friends to realise that Gilbert was sick. Gilbert's description of his inner life in his memoirs suggests an early neurological malfunction bordering on schizophrenia. Indeed a schizophrenic, describing in details his own experience of the disorder during adolescence, seems to echo precisely Gilbert's own experience:

I think I can trace here the fatal ambivalence of my emotional make-up, loving and hating the same thing, possessing and repudiating it, the need for society and the drive into solitude . . .

He writes of his longing for something which

I did not understand, but which was able to shake my soul, the partial apprehension of 'unknown modes of being'. It would come at moments outside my control, this strange experience, sometimes when I was reading a poem or listening to music, more often in the solitary contemplation of nature; wind and rain and rough seas and falling snow in particular hardly ever failed to set in notion that queer excitement, the sensation of wonder and awe, a wild exultation on the edge of revelation and ecstasy.[28]

At Cholesbury Gertler and the St. John Hutchinsons decided to make a determined effort to try to understand what was wrong with Gilbert. Trapping him in the shed where he was to spend the night having given his bed up to a guest, they demanded to hear his life story; when he became vague they ordered him to tell them *every* detail. They learned about Edwin's adoption of Gilbert, the paying for him to go to Cambridge, and much else. All three were depressed by his lack of excitement.

You see it was just as I thought, nothing ever *really* stirred him, nothing made a real impression . . . He told it all in the same bored voice and so on and on . . .[29]

They decided he was apathetic, yet had they taken the trouble to read *Little Brother* they would have found an adult Stephen weeping because his adoptive father had taken a wife, feeling that if George (Edwin) was capable of showing *that* sort of affection he should have been able to give more to the thirteen-year-old he had taken to live with him. They would have found in *Adventurous Love and Other Verses* an anguish of heart that showed not too little but perhaps too much caring.

Most likely Gilbert kept his voice expressionless because in his view his life story was one of failure within his family, with Edwin, at Cambridge, with Kathleen, and now failure within his marriage. There were few relationships, apart from those with children and dogs, which he could look upon as successful and happy. Perhaps like a small defeated boy he had to pretend indifference or else break into tears or violence. To show emotion was to allow the pryers more fuel for their amusement. His guests' questions must have made him feel again the outsider, but he was too good-hearted to object. He gave them just the bare minimum to satisfy their curiosity but not an iota of his private self. They went into the Mill House afterwards pretending that they wanted to go to bed, so that they could discuss the result of their probing, and one is left to wonder how Gilbert must have felt.[30]

Then to make matters worse the dogs, who had been so often Gilbert's companions, died. For Mary, this double death marked the beginning of the end of the days at the Windmill. Of Luath she wrote:

One morning he failed altogether, would eat no food, and could hardly move about. Not ill, only grown old, and worn out. I saw the end must be very near, and that it would be merciful to spare him the last hours of weakness.

The farmer shot Luath for her, but there is no record of whether Gilbert was consulted.

He was buried in the paddock at the end of the garden. Whilst his grave was being dug, Sammy, distracted at the sight of his old friend lying rigid on the grass, rushed despairingly between the house and the paddock, to try to make me come and do something. I never saw Luath after he was dead, and I am sorry for it . . .[31]

Sammy, the big sheepdog, was heartbroken; he had become so dependent on Luath, now he had no one to show him what to do, which way to go, where to find the rarest scents. He floundered pathetically trying to think things out for himself. He grieved and developed distemper for the second time in his life. A bed was made for him on the sofa by the fire, in the dining-room, but when Mary returned one day from buying medicine ordered by the vet, she found Sammy lying prostrate on Luath's grave in the paddock. 'God knows how he had the strength, weak as he was, to get so far.' She carried him into the house and the next day he died.

Publication of *Mendel* followed in November. Although Gertler is the hero and principal character in the novel, one important theme is the love-affair between the artist Logan (John Currie) and his mistress (Dolly Henry). This ends tragically with Currie murdering his mistress and killing himself.

What is most remarkable about the story is Gilbert's absolute understanding of Gertler revealed in its pages. Over-written it may be, purple in parts, marred for the historian by some half-truths and inaccuracies, but it is nevertheless faithful in presenting a true and moving picture of Gertler's early life. Portraits of Edward Marsh, Brett, Carrington, Augustus John, and C. R. W. Nevinson, are also to be found in the book.

The story, written before Gilbert saw Mark's diary, faithfully retells much that Mark has described of his life to Gilbert, but unfortunately too exactly, without any editing of the artist's more extravagant claims and statements. Much of Mark's attraction lay in his spontaneity and wit and this included a certain poetic licence in his assessments of situations, motives and reactions, which he might well have been the first to correct had he seen them staring at him in cold print. Like many novelists Gilbert could remember conversations word for word, and, just as Compton Mackenzie was later to record Gilbert's conversation in *The South Wind of Love*, so Gilbert recorded most vividly Gertler's revelations.

The reviews were on the whole encouraging. *The Times Literary Supplement* critic carped a little as usual, being disappointed that there was no governing purpose in *Mendel*, 'a life of episode rather than development', noticing in Gilbert's portrait of the man an absence of characterisation, a criticism not taken up by any who knew the original. He also complained of too much talk of sex, but found the book almost continuously entertaining, with Mendel delightfully entertaining if priggish, and Morrison (Carrington) the most vivid personality of the book. *Outlook*'s reviewer was more impressed by the character of Louis, Gertler's father, with 'his fierce pride and his appalling poverty, and his fanatical belief in his own faith'. He was also enthusiastic about Mendel himself:

We have always felt an artist's temperament must be an uncomfortable possession, but never has the belief been quite so irresistibly forced on us as after reading Gilbert Cannan's odd, brilliant study of a Jewish artist.

Mendel is dedicated to Carrington with three verses, which seem to suggest delicate urging to give herself, beginning

> *Shall tears be shed because the blossoms fall*
> *Because the cloudy cherry slips away*
> *And leaves its branches in a leafy thrall*
> *Till ruddy fruits do hang upon the spray?*

Predictably furious, she wrote to Gertler on November 1st, 1916

> How angry I am over Gilbert's book! Everywhere this confounded gossip, and servant-like curiosity. It's ugly, and so damned vulgar. People cannot be vulgar over a work of art, so it *is* Gilbert's fault for writing as he did . . .[32]

William Rothenstein, who did not read *Mendel* until 1918, was understandably upset not only to see himself in the book, but to find from it that Gertler appeared to despise him and his efforts to help young artists, of whom Gertler had been one. 'A charming happening' had been turned into a 'mean and ugly thing'.[33] The correspondence between them which followed has been published and discussed elsewhere. Gertler naturally blamed Gilbert for a distortion, although he may well have spoken scathingly of Rothenstein.

> Gilbert Cannan's version is, I assure you, *entirely false* and I am not responsible for it. PLEASE UNDERSTAND THIS. Nor could I ever be responsible for such an agglomeration of cheap trash as is contained in that awful novel . . .[34]

But although obviously upset and embarrassed, Gertler continued to be friendly towards Gilbert and visited him in a nursing home soon after the publication.

Frieda, who borrowed a copy of *Mendel* from Koteliansky, thought she recognised some of Lawrence's 'speeches' coming from the artist Logan (Currie); then, after a prompting from Catherine Carswell, she wrongly supposed herself to be Oliver, Logan's mistress: 'I was sorry that Gilbert made me quite so horrid, so *vulgar*. But there!'[35] Montague Shearman, obviously intrigued by the book and attracted to Gertler, also thought he saw Lawrence in it, and it may be that Logan is made to speak more like Lawrence than his original, Currie, but there the resemblance ends.[36]

Meanwhile, Gilbert was past caring about the book. His confession to Mary about the maid's pregnancy had brought about an unbearable hostility in the Mill House. He was clearly no longer a 'terrific person'. Some of his friends were astounded when the news broke:

> How utter was our amazement when we learned that G . . . Mary's perfect maid was having a baby by him. Poor Gilbert! He was very kind—de haut en bas—to Katherine and me [wrote Middleton Murry in his Journal].

Gertler had earlier noticed a change in the atmosphere between Gilbert and Mary but had not, it seems, suspected Gilbert's mental instability. Indeed, right up to the publication of *Mendel* he had continued to admire Gilbert and seek his advice. No one seems to have realised that Gilbert's long silences now usually indicated a retreat into a fantasy world nor how radically his character had changed; the gentle Gilbert felt a growing need for violence; the responsible Gilbert had become irresponsible. Many of the normal emotions of boyhood which he had repressed so drastically were now about to come to the fore. He turned his back on the Mill he loved, experiencing at times a spiritual euphoria which alternated with melancholy and despair.

8

'All is Lovely Save My Health'

Gilbert Cannan

So, in autumn 1916, in a state of some mental confusion, Gilbert fled not only from his angry wife and the pregnant maid but also from the old life, from the war and his friends.

He retreated quietly to his shabby rooms at 31 Hallam Street, between Portland Place and Portland Street, which looked out on a mews teeming with Jewish life and on a synagogue, but, although there was much to see, only the dogs and children interested him. He thought he had finished with grown people, who had so often put him on a pedestal and then been angry to find he was no god. He shut himself up to think about life, to find truth in silence and isolation.

He could not escape entirely however, for two friends sought him out, visiting him in his rooms and sometimes dragging him to concerts or restaurants. They were not old friends; the one he had met through Lawrence, the other probably through anti-conscription campaigning or through Bertrand Russell. Without him realising it, they probably saw that he was verging on a nervous breakdown and were perturbed by his haggard, empty face, his staring eyes and thin body. They wanted to draw him out again into the life of the living.

Samuel Solomovitch Koteliansky, a Russian Jew of striking appearance and volatile temperament, had been at the Cannans' Christmas party in 1914 and quickly became an inspiring if somewhat unpredictable friend. He had come to England in 1910 on a research scholarship from Kiev University and stayed on. His head was large, with masses of thick dark hair above a pale rather sensitive face with thick lips and dark eloquent eyes. Gilbert likened him to a black bear and others saw in him their idea of an ancient Hebrew prophet. In England he worked for the Law Bureau in High Holborn and translated Russian novels, collaborating with Gilbert, Lawrence, Katherine Mansfield and Leonard Woolf among others.

Miles Malleson, dramatist, film and stage actor, was a very different character. Conventionally educated at an English Public School and university, where he read history, he was married to the beautiful and impulsive actress Constance O'Neill, born Lady Constance Annesley.

She was having an affair with Bertrand Russell, unopposed by her husband, himself a true advocate of free love and something of a womaniser. Gilbert depicts Malleson in *Time and Eternity*, where he is caricatured as Chinnery, a rather absurd character wishing to make his way in films, and on the look-out for future stars. Chinless and spectacled himself, Malleson admired a good profile and believed Gilbert could make his name on the screen, and also, Gilbert suggests, lead a revolt against the establishment.

Probably neither friend realised quite how seriously ill Gilbert was or how strange and mentally active he felt. Of course it wasn't a new experience for him to feel so much at odds with adults, a stranger in their midst. In 1914 after a sudden and delightful sharing of experience with Ottoline, he had written:

I had begun to think that I was so strangely made that I could only be light hearted with children & dogs but now I want to laugh with everybody, and most of all, affectionately, with you.[1]

But now that friendship, too, seemed on the wane, and although Ottoline was later to speak of Gilbert quite affectionately, the allegation in her memoirs that he was conceited suggests how little she understood his deeper problems.[2]

Gilbert's marvellous memory for conversation, much of which he quoted verbatim in his novels, suggests that the following extracts from *Time and Eternity* may truthfully record his own nonsensical remarks to Koteliansky (Mr. Perekatov) when he visited Gilbert (Stephen) in Hallam Street, and give some indication of his muddled state of thinking at the time:

'I haven't read a word for years,' said Stephen. 'Not since the war. Please sit down. I'm not used to seeing people. I don't like them. They don't like me. They make me silent, but the more devastating the silence grows, the more eloquent my eyes become'. . . .

'You know', he said, 'nothing has ever happened to me. Everything I touched turned into a joke until I could stand it no more. And now I touch nothing: not because I'm afraid, but because I know beforehand how it is going to turn out. I am happier—just thinking . . .'

'I am not used to saying what I think. It is so much clearer unexpressed and so much more communicable. Speech is to silence as time is to eternity.'

Of Stephen's marriage Gilbert wrote that he had

simply let himself be cozened and cajoled and taken by a woman simply to show another lover that she was still attractive with the result that he had taken to ideas as another might take to drink.

How much of this was fact we shall probably never know, but it seems likely that if the statement was true of Gilbert's life the lover was Granville-Barker, in front of whom Mary had flirted with Gilbert at Black Lake Cottage and in the chauffeur-driven car on the way home. Further on in *Time and Eternity*, we find this confession about the women in Stephen's life:

Many whom he had known had loved love, more had loved themselves, but hardly any had surrendered, and he had wasted himself trying to surrender to a wife who had regarded it as a dangerous weakness, one that would interfere with his success.

Now searching for truth and revelation alone and strangely dis-orientated, Gilbert was unknowingly influenced, I suspect, by Lawrence, who also possessed a deep belief in the soul's power and consciousness, in the potency of silence and the power of solitary meditation. Gilbert's thoughts were now simply too much and too many for him to bear. He could not stand life as it was any longer. He wanted to enter into a condition of mindlessness so that the truth could come into his soul, and then perhaps all the paradoxes and the ironies would be explained. Obediently his mind entered a strange state, which he tried to describe calmly three years later in a philosophical book, *The Release of the Soul:*

In the year 1916, at the very crisis of the war, its intense strain reduced or raised me to a condition in which I could think with an extraordinary clarity but without words. The English Language, as up to that point I had used it, became entirely inadequate even if I had wished to express myself, which I did not. It was sufficient to be possessed by this clarity, for it was a posses-sion which estimated to the nicest degree the elements of which my life was composed and discarded most of them, everything, in fact, except the power to think and to understand what was going on in the world around me, which was singularly uninteresting, a swift reduction of superficial existence to its crudest and meanest ingredients. Soon this clear perception was broken by a strange activity of mind, increasingly intense, which rejected words as instru-ments, though to be sure I maintained the habit of writing, as I did that of eating, sleeping and talking. But my habits had nothing whatever to do with my increasing activity, which absorbed every emotion and every thought, and at last began to express itself in symbols of which, having no mathe-matical training, I could make nothing, until at last there came a symbol that burned itself into my brain in whirling fire. At first it looked like a wheel, and, being by this time sufficiently recovered from the stress of it all to consider the matter humourously, I told myself that it was the Indian wheel of life and that I was suffering from an attack of symbolism from which I should presently recover, as indeed I seemed to do; for shortly the symbol ceased its whirling and took this shape, and as such I accepted it and set it down [There follows a drawing of a circle]. I could never see it without an intense and terrible emotion, but could make no application of it, except that I found in myself an entirely new appreciation of beauty in every form, a comprehension which I had formerly divined more than felt. I attempted to explain to one or two chance-comers, but in vain. The intense activity subsided, but the clarity endured, and with it a patience altogether new; and whether in myself or not I knew with an indomitable conviction that something had been born into the world, something of such tremendous importance that the disasters then overtaking my country and mankind were in comparison trivial.

Afterwards it became clear to Gilbert 'in that strange clarity' that the symbol expressed some kind of perfection and contained in it a message which he must understand if the world was ever to be worth living in. In this absolute conviction he shows signs of a Messiah complex. At the same time a different life moved before his eyes of which he became the fascinated and puzzled spectator, a life more absorbing and important to him for a while than the world outside which had become so horrible, so full of bloodshed, slaughter and misery as to be unbearable. The symbol remained fiery, but began, after a time to project

an endless succession of elusive characters—all kinds of men, women and children, dogs, horses, houses, cats, trees, churches, all marching round and round the circle and along the diameters, in and out and round about, a regular inferno like Dante's, except that they were all jolly people, even the miserable and the suffering, and they were having tremendous fun, as I was too in watching them, though the whole thing became more and more unintelligible and exasperating because I could do nothing with it, since I could not connect it with the life going on around me in which I took less and less interest. I knew clearly what was going to happen in the world around me and could only wait for it to happen, as it always did . . .

In contemporary language Gilbert was now, of course, experiencing a nervous breakdown, although in other times he might well have successfully claimed to be a hermit, a visionary or a prophet, and in *Time and Eternity* he suggests that the Frenchwoman who lived in the same building considered him to be a saint. The symbol, the sense of heightened vision, which could be what he meant by clarity, suggest that he may have experienced also a series of epileptic fits and some chemical changes in his metabolism, not entirely unlike those induced by the drug L.S.D. He had suffered a slightly similar breakdown as a child, after an accident when he had been hit in the ribs by the shaft of a baker boy's handcart on the way back from Board School. Then he had made his way home by rolling himself along a wall. Diagnosing a bruised liver, the doctor had wound him up in yards and yards of sticky yellow bandage. The young Gilbert was nursed through that traumatic experience by his mother. Spoiled, fed on grapes, the centre of attention, he had come through strengthened, more normal, less self-absorbed than hitherto and ready to face the world again.[3]

Now, as 1916 moved towards its end, he was once more deeply in want of sympathy, love and devotion. He needed another woman to whom he could attach himself, someone who would take charge and make life seem worth living, somebody stronger than the visions; a person who could drag him back into the reality of life. Unwittingly Miles Malleson provided just such a person when on October 26th in Henderson's Bookshop in the Charing Cross Road he introduced Gwen to Gilbert. A South African of nineteen, this delicate, pale yet animated girl had come over to England to study art, help with the war effort and escape the stifling parochialism of South African Society, which seemed to her to offer only money and marriage. Gilbert and Gwen looked at one another and knew instantaneously that they were in love. There was no way out, this was *it*. The great *she* was here before a speechless Gilbert. He did not need to look; he felt and heard and knew. To many this might seem a cliché, to him it was little less than a miracle. In *Time and Eternity* he wrote:

He could only hear her voice, and that he heard rather with the recesses of his being than with his ears. It did not please him, it possessed him. Its low gentle tones released by perfect articulation sank into him and became a warm, golden flood that crept below his skin, and so overmastered him with delicious pain that at times he could hardly breathe. And so overpowering was her voice that he could hardly see her, knew not whether her hair was dark or fair, whether she was young or old: but he was certain that she was beautiful and that she was somehow golden, as a pomegranate is, or a nectarine or pineapple or a lioness, or an ostrich egg or desert sand, or any bird, beast or thing that is steeped in the hot sun.

Few are given such moments that transcend all else, and when these are mutual the effect is overpowering. Gwen, too, was possessed. She saw at once a genius, a gentle-looking man with a haunted face, a Hamlet.

According to Gilbert's account in *Time and Eternity*, this first meeting was followed by a meal in a tea-shop and, a few days later, tea in Gwen's flat. (In fact it was Gwen who went to tea with him.) Certainly there were hours of happiness while Gilbert showed Gwen the places he loved in London. He took her to the Temple and the parks, and walked with her along the Embankment. Superficially she resembled the very first love of his life; he had been taken to the pantomime by his grandfather and fallen in love with the principal girl, and it is possible that in a dreamlike way he was reliving and giving expression to those first unrecognised sexual desires. At the same time his mental illness continued to develop. He withdrew again, ate less, grew thinner, awaiting a deafening click of knowledge, a sign, a vision, a beginning or an end. His cheeks hollowed, his temperature rose, while outside the Jewish children still played their noisy games, dogs barked and people filed into the synagogue. Soon he was too weak to care about life, too ill to try to regain the clarity of vision which had brought him so near to the meaning of existence. He emptied himself as Lawrence later advised in *Fantasia*. Lawrence was an influence he could not escape; the dusty tea-coloured beard, the fervent eyes, the Nottinghamshire accent had made an ineradicable impression. In Lawrence he had seen genius, and Lawrence believed:

When at last, in all my storms, my whole speaks, then there is a pause. The soul collects itself into pure silence and isolation—perhaps after much pain. The mind suspends its knowledge and waits. And psyche becomes strangely still. And then after a pause, there is a fresh beginning, a new life and adjustment.[4]

Mary came then and brought him back to the Mill House and persuaded him a few weeks later to go to work on a farm in accordance with the Tribunal's verdict. It appears that at first he was glad to be away from the women in his life, to toil in the day and write in the evenings. But he could not escape entirely. In late November a love-letter and poem from Gwen addressed to him at the Mill House was intercepted by Mary. Matters were now coming to a head but Gilbert wanted no part in them. He could not face complications while he was struggling to regain his own stability and he found it hard to believe that so young and beautiful a girl as Gwen could find him attractive. His own strange and irrational state of mind made his actions unpredictable. He started to draw obsessionally as he was so often to do in moments of stress and anxiety. He was neither sane nor yet insane but in that mysterious vivid borderland between the two; aware of his strangeness and yet unable to overcome it.

He drew 'circular shapes and vortexes rather like those appearing in a life of Nijinsky [Gertler was later to tell his wife], and Van Gogh's vortex, suns and stars in his later landscapes'.[5] The maid he apparently missed not at all. She seems to have meant little to him. She had wanted sex from him and in hunger and perhaps delusion he had obliged, yet deep down he had remained untouched. But the war preyed terribly on his nerves.

That was a bitter winter [he wrote later], bitter to the senses but more bitter to the soul: 1916, when the shouting and the eager idealism had withered away and all meaning had gone out of the words of war. So bitter was the agony that physical discomfort had become a small thing and men and women were like ghosts pathetically trying to remember the sensations of their life in the Flesh.[6]

By now the Battle of the Somme had been fought, the casualty lists in *The Times* were horrifyingly long, the massacre of Britain's youth horrific beyond words. Gilbert, still in this highly nervous state, yet had time to consider his young friends. Gertler, for one, hoped to borrow the Mill House for a romantic week with Carrington, and in this connection Gilbert wrote on December 6th from the farm at Bromley Hall, Standon, Hertfordshire that Mary was away but Mrs. Gomm had the key to the house.

I'm here toiling in the fields and enjoying it though it's a muddy game, but I'm beginning to feel so fit and well that I don't propose to return to London properly for some time. However one never knows these days where one is going to be.

I write my new novel all evening and enjoy the solitude & the quiet. I should like it to go on for at least half a year and to see no one but you occasionally, because I do find with you a satisfaction that I get with neither the intellectuals on the one hand nor the sentimentalists on the other; I'm always baffled by the constant demand that one should be one or the other when one can be neither. You do believe in your job and that is all I ask of any man because there is nothing else.

Carrington, who loved the mill, was keen to share it with Gertler, but with a different seduction in mind, for she had now fallen in love with Lytton Strachey and perhaps only accepted Gertler's invitation on the condition that Lytton was a fellow guest. Writing on the 10th she made it clear that he would not suffer from the cold, as Middleton Murry had done:

Next week I am going to stay with the Jew [Gertler] at Cholesbury. Gilbert has lent him his castle for a week. He is going to ask you to come down on Wednesday or Thursday for a day or so. Will you come? I promise you vast quantities of food and drink, and raiment for the night season. A fire in your bedroom and our love shall out-heat the very fires and be hotter than the very soups and curries, as Ottoline would write no doubt.[7]

But the balm of the countryside brought neither sexual success to Gertler nor a cure to Gilbert, who had not succeeded in overcoming his love for Gwen. By January both were miserable. Mary Cannan was bitter and ready to talk of Gilbert's strangeness and infidelities. Going first it seems to the person who had felt the greatest confidence in him, she told Gertler 'amazing things' about Gilbert, which [the artist wrote to Carrington] I will tell you when I see you, but it is a secret and please don't mention that there is a secret or people will worry me. Anyhow in the meantime Gilbert is worse and Mary is terribly upset and I am sorry for both of them.[8]

Gilbert was at war within himself. He wanted to be honourable and decent, yet to have Gwen without losing Mary. He had been willing to share Mary with Barrie. Could she not now share him with Gwen? He suggested that he continued to live with his wife while enjoying an amorous friendship with Gwen. Mary refused, leaving Gilbert to choose between the two women. It was too much. He retreated entirely into fantasy and madness and in January Mary installed him in a nursing home after what he described as 'an explosion'.

One of the saddest aspects of this gentle and kindly man's illness was a tendency to violence. The tight hold he had learned to keep on himself as a child, shown in his refusal to quarrel or argue with Mary, was possibly a contributory factor.

These frightening and emotionally exhausting experiences inspired Gilbert's three act play, *Inquest on Pierrot*, which is part fantasy, with Gilbert as Pierrot the sad clown and Gwen the enchanting Columbine.[9] The first scene gives us a picture of a moonstruck, unbalanced Gilbert, lovable and irritating, slightly ridiculous to the friends with whom he is finishing a birthday dinner. It is set in a café with the band playing ragtime music, where he meets the dancing Columbine for the first time. Scene 2 is in Hallam Street: the maid from Cholesbury, known in the play simply as 'Mother' has come to show Pierrot the baby. There has been trouble before, so a policeman is outside. The angry wife (Mary) is waiting Pierrot's return.

Near home Pierrot is stopped. After some conversation the policeman introduces the maid to him:

Policeman: This is the party, sir.

Pierrot: A party? I've just come from one.

Policeman: A young person, sir—with a little bill.

Pierrot: Bill?—I've just paid one. There is always a bill to pay.

(He doesn't recognise the girl.)

Pierrot: Did you want to speak to me just now? I'm afraid the policeman has gone if you want to ask the way.

Mother: Way? Way?—Don't you use that trick of pretending not to know me! Don't you tell me you've forgotten the cherry orchard in blossom in the moonlight or the church meadow where the grass is tall.

Pierrot: Oh yes. I borrowed your heart from you and lent a dream or two in return . . . Cheap little dreams they were but you didn't like the best . . . You were very happy and pleasant for a time and quite pretty in the moonlight. Your teeth were very white as your lips parted . . . When the moon shone full it always seemed as though I should see things as I used to see them . . . But you don't know anything about that. There was no music in your soul and you could never dance. You could never chase the shadow of a dream in and out of your heart.

Mother: Talk! Talk! Talk!—I told you what could come of it. I've been waiting to show you.

(She holds out a child).

Pierrot: Yes. That's a child. Does it cry?

Mother: Don't you want to hold it?

Pierrot: No. Why?

Mother: It's yours.

(At last Pierrot takes the baby. With 'exquisite tenderness' he hugs and kisses her).

Pierrot: Let her have everything she wants, let her be everything she wants, let her grow into a Columbine.

The maid bursts into tears, and gives him her address.

Oh, you poor thing [she cries]. You didn't know. You didn't know what you were doing. I only want her not to want for anything.

In the house Pierrot behaves strangely and his wife's welcome gives us yet another picture of Mary trying to deal with Gilbert's eccentricities.

Pierrot: Good morning. Do I live here?

Wife: Of course you live here. What do you mean coming in at this time in the morning with such a stupid question on your lips?

Pierrot: I felt doubtful. Please don't nag.

Wife: I never nag. I asked you a perfectly civil question and I expect a civil answer.

Pierrot: The moon is shining. Won't you come for a walk through the streets, they look quite beautiful by moonlight.

Wife: I think you might have spent your birthday at home.

Pierrot: (taking off his hat and coat) You said you hated birthdays. Or was it tomatoes? You hate so many things that I get rather mixed . . . It has been a strange evening.

Wife: You look ghastly. Have you been eating oysters? You know oysters never agree with you.

Pierrot: On birthdays people may eat what they choose.

Wife: You look so ill you must let me take you back to the country.

Pierrot: But I must go on . . . I must go on. The world is dying. Bodies die and it does not matter, but if souls die there is an end to everything. . . .

[A moment later Pierrot muses, half to himself].

You were unhappy. I remember that you wanted to be free. You said you would be free if I loved you. So I loved you . . . I borrowed your heart and loved you exactly as you wanted to be loved. Then you were happy . . . until I came to town to lose myself. How I longed to lose myself among all the people . . . But you found me and made me comfortable again. Did you never think I might want to be uncomfortable? . . . The horrible monotony of life when there is no love . . .

Wife: You are more terrible tonight than I have ever known you.

Pierrot: I have given you the address . . . I am terribly ill. You must do what you can for her.

Wife: For whom?

Pierrot: The woman in the street. She had a child in her arms. She said it is mine too.

Wife: Who is this woman?

Pierrot: You must send her some money tomorrow.

Wife: Who is it? Do I know her?

Pierrot: Yes, you know her.

Wife: I knew it, but I refused to believe it.

Pierrot: She was unhappy . . . Why are women so unhappy? It makes things very complicated.

Wife: She!! Every tooth in her head is false.

[After a further exchange Pierrot asks]: Have I any money?

Wife: You gave it all to me.

Pierrot: You must send her some tomorrow.

[A moment later Pierrot cries in agony to his wife]:

O God! Your heart has left me and I have my desire. [He collapses, to be saved later from madness and a nursing home by Columbine.]

There is poignancy in Pierrot's attempt to explain himself to his friends:

Listen. I am haunted. Certain flowers, certain scents, certain notes of music, certain lights and shadows on a moony night cast a spell over me and I am then entirely abstracted from this bourgeois civilisation in which every man is a cock crowing on a dung heap, and every woman a hen scratching for pearls in the litter.

And again:

Myself. I tell you when my real self comes to light you will run away from me as those two did just now. Even you will not be able to bear it. I warn you. I warn you.

Mary's tragedy is expressed when Pierrot lies as though dead on the divan, and the wife cries, 'Can you hear me? You were so happy and full of joy. So young you were, the youngest thing that ever lived. I thought I should be young and happy and full of joy with you . . .'

In the play Pierrot is visited in the nursing home by the Politician, the Old Woman and the Advanced Man. In reality Gilbert turned to Gertler as a confidant, appealing for a visit from the artist in two undated letters written from 25 Ferncroft Avenue, Platt's Lane, Hampstead.

I wish you would come and see me and don't be worried over the bursting of the cloud of insanity that has been growing and growing in me until now when I have emerged sane and in my right mind. The facts are appalling but they are simply not open to moral judgment. I have been right through the whole Hell of it and the story is more mysterious and terrible than anyone can guess, and I want to tell it you, for I am only just now in possession of the facts of my life.

And:

I'm picking up now. Do come and see me. I'm to stay here until Thursday week and then I don't know what—I have exploded and don't know what the world is going to look like when I come in contact with it again. I find it very hard to discuss things with anybody as even Mary doesn't seem to understand the nature of the explosion, but only to be appalled at the results. I suppose that is only natural. But it needs patience to handle the situation. Come along soon. Give my love to everybody.

A third letter followed, which suggests that Gertler had described to Gilbert his sexual failure with Carrington, and that the visions which were connected with the symbol may have returned to take Gilbert away again from reality.

My dear old Mark. We do seem to be going through things together in this awful mess called life, and I wish I had your toughness. I'm not fit to go out on Thursday and I shan't be fit, I'm afraid, for some time, but I am to go out by degrees. I am to see Gwen tomorrow and will hobble over to tea with you on Friday. I'm in a very queer condition, terribly weak physically, but with such a mental and spiritual clarity as I never had, and the terrible increasing effort to get it has the growing indifference to anything else which looks to outsiders like sheer madness. However we can talk on Friday. I'll come about 3.00. Poor little Mary has lost her head in her turn, but it will work out in time.

I have found nothing appalling or horrible about the facts of Gilbert's life, but it may be that he learned in the nursing home that he was mildly epileptic and suffering from a bout of madness which, in the social and medical climate of 1917, would have been a deeply shocking revelation. As for acts of insanity, it is hard to separate legend from reality. It was, for example, rumoured later that despair over the war had driven Gilbert to throw a brick through the window of a London department store.

Whatever the truth, his life was now full of problems and as he recovered from his illness he had to decide where to go to convalesce. London, it seems, could not be contemplated, and his first thought appears to have been Leeds, where his sister Margaret lived with her banking husband, James Broughton Rideout. Margaret had always cared more deeply for Gilbert than for her other brothers and sisters. She had stayed with him on many occasions in the Temple, Black Lake Lake Cottage and the Mill House, so he was only asking for a return in hospitality and could reasonably expect a welcome, and loving attention. She agreed initially that he should come, but she had recently become pregnant a second time and Henry Cannan, perturbed lest a mentally unstable brother might put too much of a strain on her, wrote advising her to change her mind. As a result she wrote again to Gilbert asking him to postpone the visit until after the baby was born, and so he was thrown back again on the generosity of his friends. Like his paternal grandfather when marital problems arose, he started to feel that his greatest love was now for the theatre; among stage people he could perhaps be free from the talk of war, and from the intellectuals whose questioning minds taxed him too much. He could lose himself in acting. He picked up his pen and wrote in a sprawling hand, without dating the letter.

My dear John, I'm in a nursing home recovering from an explosion of insanity—suppressed drama, suppressed sex, suppressed love, but most of all suppressed drama and poetry. The details are horrible, and ought not to be for public consumption, but I'm afraid they have become so; the human misery, including my own, is terrible; the preservation of my sanity is miraculous. For the moment, perhaps for a long time, people think and perhaps will think that I am responsible, but no power on earth could stop the explosion or any single step that had led up to it . . . Will you when I am well enough let me come and live with you and potter about the theatre, for without the theatre I shall die. Just take charge of me and let me find my feet again.

So he went to Birmingham to work with John Drinkwater, who was married to Kathleen Walpole (the actress Cathleen Orford) and working with Barry Jackson at the Birmingham Repertory Theatre. Poet, playwright and biographer, Drinkwater was probably a good companion for Gilbert at this time, although there are signs that his wife was less understanding of the younger man's problems.[10] The Drinkwaters had also stayed at the Mill House on a number of occasions. John, the son of an actor, had worked in insurance for some years before joining the Pilgrim Players in Birmingham and finally throwing over insurance to become Barry Jackson's Manager at the Repertory Theatre in 1913. Born in 1882, dark-haired, strong-featured, with remarkably arched eyebrows and a chin notably short in proportion to the rest of his face, Drinkwater was pleasant in appearance and manner. He had spent some of the most melancholy days of his life as an insurance inspector in Manchester, had known poverty and failure, and sprang from comparatively humble beginnings. He had, therefore, a good deal in common with Gilbert, as well as shared interests which included cricket and a love of the country.

How long Gilbert stayed in rooms in Birmingham and worked with Drinkwater is not clear; undoubtedly as he grew stronger he visited London from time to time. Certainly, Drinkwater put on two of Gilbert's plays while he was in Birmingham, which must have done much to raise their author's morale and pull him back from the intense experiences of his insanity into the realities of life and work in a repertory theatre. He also acted, sharing a dressing room with Felix Aylmer.[11] Some indication of his recovery is given in three letters he wrote to Koteliansky from the Theatre. The first is undated, a sure sign that he was under stress, and all concern a manuscript, probably Koteliansky's unpublished translation of stories by Kuprin:

Your MS is at the Mill and I don't know what has been done with anything there, also I can't do much writing as I'm still rather jumpy & have to go very slowly. Do you mind waiting a little until I'm better and can take things in hand again?[12]

Then on April 6th Gilbert wrote that he was sure the Kuprin MS was at the Mill on the table in his room; his things were to be sent up to London soon and some of his books and papers were already at the Mallesons'. He couldn't go up himself at the week-end (as presumably suggested by Koteliansky) because there were productions on Saturday evenings, which made it impossible except in the small hours of Sunday morning. In the third letter, dated April 22nd, Gilbert was able to announce that the Kuprin MS had been found among his books:

I'm just beginning to feel well and ordinary again. The change of work and and surroundings has agreed with me. Next Sunday I shall be in town if you would like to come and see me.

So the worse seems to be over. This letter certainly followed an encouraging success, for *Everybody's Husband*, Gilbert's sardonic but lightly sketched one-act play about marriage, had just been well received in Birmingham on its first performance. In May Gilbert returned to London for a while, coming back to Birmingham for rehearsals for a second run of *Everybody's Husband* with himself as producer. A triple bill which ran for a week and rounded off the season included *James and John*. A revived Gilbert then left with Gwen for sea air, and peace. From Caerleon, Ruan Minor, Cornwall, where he had been lent a cottage, through the efforts of Martin Secker, he wrote to Drinkwater.

We're having a marvellous time here: a superb place, an isolated cottage on huge cliffs, a cove all to ourselves—and ourselves. I'm working and the play is going ahead & should easily be ready by the autumn.

I enjoyed immensely my time in Birmingham. Bless you, it gave me the very nourishment for my delicate condition & I can't tell you my feelings about it all . . .

Everybody's Husband was to be published, and on July 18th Gilbert wrote again to Drinkwater for there had been some muddle about a map which he had lost and he wanted to say that Gwen would buy a new one when in London. The play was progressing; he wrote in the intervals between bathing and walking, and when it was finished he proposed to move with Gwen to London to look for 'a habitation'.

He was sure now that Gwen had saved his sanity and perhaps also his life, and, looking back, he could see clearly that he had been battling not against a hostile world but against and within himself. Perhaps partly because of this new understanding, he became increasingly interested in his own character and emotions, finding in them little to please him. He tried to explain how he saw it in two poems. The first, from which I quote an extract, is called 'October 26, 1916' and the second simply 'Why?'

> *I saw her and let fall*
> *My life & all that it contained*
> *Becoming clay to wait*
> *The shaping of her hand,*
> *Strong hands.*

In 'Why?' he tells how he was humbled by her belief and devotion:

> *Better than I she seems to know*
> *The thing I am*
> *While I go on toiling to show*
> *A diagram*
> *On paper of the battlefield whereon*
> *An honest rage*
> *Fights the unnumbered foes*
> *Though God knows why.*
> *The fight, the fight is I*
> *And this she loves, although*
> *There nothing is to show,*
> *There's neither sense nor end*
> *That I can see to lend*

Me charm or force or strength
To let her go the length
of loving me
Of loving me,
This torn and blasted battlefield, this storm
Which is myself and has no other form.
Ah! she would like this wildness in a cage
The wild beast crouching, fawning at her toes
And all this fury stilled
Into the love she willed
In loving me
In loving me.

Cornwall was an idyll, spoilt only by the intrusion of too many friends and Gwen falling ill. The holiday strengthened their love, filling Gilbert with wonder that Gwen should care for him so deeply. But it could not last for ever for there was work to be done, people to see. By September Gilbert was back in London writing letters from 5 Pembroke Terrace, St. John's Wood; then on September 17th he was able to announce to John Drinkwater:

I'm in the thick of establishing myself in a studio & move in next week—7B Elm Tree Road, St. John's Wood, N.W.8. Note the address.

Things appeared to be looking up and on October 3rd he wrote again:

I'm delighted to hear you're pulling along so well. The Bournville Dramatic Society have asked me to lecture to them on Nov. 30 and I've said Yes. Shall I put in a week with you about then? I'm still working at my long play, but I'm going to put it away to stew for a little as Act 2 won't march.

Our abode is delicious & Gwen very much on the move.

He was back in the stream but with different friends, those who liked Gwen, and did not blame him for leaving Mary. Kathleen Scott continued to be close and helpful. He saw Gertler from time to time but the old intimacy had gone, Felix was in the army in France. Angus, who had come over from the East as a volunteer, despised conscientious objectors, seeing Gilbert's behaviour as typical of the young brother he had tried to toughen up. Koteliansky and Miles Malleson, the Jowitts, and the Hutchinsons, Galsworthy and, of course, Drinkwater, remained friends, but Gilbert's letters to Lady Ottoline appear to have gradually stopped. In letting the friendship die Gilbert may have been influenced by Gwen or by Kathleen who predictably disliked Ottoline.

In fact, to many, Gilbert now appeared less likeable than before his breakdown. In the late autumn of 1917 for example, he went to stay in Leeds with his sister Margaret, whose daughter had been born in

August, and told her of his love for Gwen, asking whether it would be possible to borrow £200 to help out. His illness had been expensive, bringing in large bills from the nursing home and medical men. The Rideouts, feeling hard up themselves, were dismayed by the change they saw in Gilbert. Margaret was embarrassed by his boastfulness and James Rideout, fearing lies, asked to see the girl before committing the money. Gilbert telegraphed and Gwen came at once, golden-haired, frail and beautiful, looking little more than a child. The conventional Rideouts were shocked by her youth and disgusted when she and Gilbert moved into the same bedroom. James took Gilbert aside the next morning and lectured him on cradle-snatching. Margaret, who had never kissed a man other than her husband, could not understand Gilbert's behaviour. All the same the Rideouts agreed to lend the money and received a signed I.O.U. from Gilbert in exchange, and were then hurt when their guests could hardly wait to leave. Margaret's dismay increased when she heard that Gilbert and Gwen had thrown a large party at their studio flat soon afterwards. She would never have done such a thing herself and she was saddened to see her once gentle and selfless brother now thoughtless, extravagant and loud in self-praise.

In February 1918 Gertler told Koteliansky of Mary's decision to finish with Gilbert, since he would not give up Gwen, and Carrington wrote to her brother in March:

Gilbert Cannan has just committed a gross misdemeanour in the eyes of the world by leaving his wife, Mary, and going off with a young female of S. African origin, also a murky past has been disclosed for the first time, everyone finds far from being the high up-lifted pacifist, with noble sentiments, too pure to live. He was a dirtee liar, a raper of young females. So another of my tin gods comes off his pedestal. True I had suspected him sometimes. But not so bad as all that. So poor Mary has sold her house and the mill & has to start life again. . . .[13]

Lawrence who had described the news about Gilbert as 'something sordid and putrid'[14] wrote to Mary later, when he wanted her help:

I heard all about Gilbert—*very* wretched for you. Frieda wanted to write to you—but I said no don't rush in: we can only upset Mary more. I must say, you have my sympathy entirely—not Gilbert. But it was most miserable. We had some jolly times at Cholesbury which I shall never forget. But I could never think of the Mill now, without pain—just pain. . . .

Do you remember that autumn afternoon, on Cholesbury Common, when we were picking blackberries—only you and I—it was before lunch really —you told me about Sutro, and how he would get me £50 from the Fund— which he did. Could you speak to him again, do you think, Mary?—or any other member of the Fund—to vote or speak for me when the occasion of a grant on my behalf comes up. . . .

Perhaps we shall be happy again. I *do* think Gilbert let you down unpardonably. But perhaps we can get right—though differently. I am terribly weary in my soul of all things, in the world of man . . .[15]

On September 29th Gilbert dined with Kathleen:

Oh, such a funny dinner party! [she wrote in her diary] . . . There was a bad air raid. The parlour maid came in hysterical and collapsed on the drawing-room sofa. The cook panted behind, and the nurse arrived with her hair down. We brought Peter down in his pyjamas. Gilbert never uttered a word.

And an entry in October tells us that Gilbert went to Kathleen for money. His problem was a familiar one for authors, then and now:

His publisher won't publish his new book until January, and it should be out now. I have therefore to subsidise him for a time. I hate him to borrow money but if he borrows it from anyone it had better be from me. How I would like to pull him through! He has so much to him.

Gilbert was already entering into legal expenses for a divorce, for at this stage he had thrown over notions of free love and he was determined to legitimise his affair with Gwen.[16] Wishing to protect her he supplied evidence of adultery before 1917, but there was nothing amicable about the proceedings. Mary had returned for legal advice to Sir George Lewis, whose wife was quick to spread damaging rumours about Gwen. Gilbert wrote (in an undated letter) thanking Kathleen for her generosity:

Bless you again for that. It isn't the bit of paper that counts but the quick understanding & the pure generosity pumping life into me, after the years of starvation of those very things. My lovely Gwen knows of my tussle but not where the puff of friendship came from. She is so fine and splendid through it all. You must love her as if she were me for she is my Second Chance, and I've fought like a tiger for it—Alas! There are things that I can't tell yet for my lawyer man has forbidden me absolutely to open my lips to a soul, but I'll tell you first.

Money? I'm rather good at it, spend little and make more, but this year with doctors, nursing homes, no place of my own, travelling, Gwen being ill, etc., has been awful—O! Bless you. I'm rather tired, but enjoying every moment of the tussle, *and* working as always.

In fact, Gilbert was becoming increasingly self-absorbed, and more of his friends were avoiding him or mocking him behind his back.

Some suggested that he had dropped Mary only when he had found another woman to support him. This was a lie, for Gwen had expensive tastes and, if Gilbert's characterisation of her is correct, liked to do things in style, and her allowance was far too small to support them both.

No match for the Lewises, Gilbert sent Kathleen Scott an S.O.S. on November 3rd and then arrived in her office in an 'awful fuss'.[17] The distinguished lawyer was looking for evidence to impugn Gwen's morals and allegedly suggested that she was actually a German. It seemed that her name could not now be kept out of divorce proceedings and she might even be called to give evidence. So Gilbert had countered by saying he would return to Mary who then as expected refused to see him. 'So,' wrote Kathleen, 'he wants a Deed of Separation. She will probably have a Judicial Separation and great advertisement.'[18]

Two days later Gilbert took Gwen to lunch with Kathleen whose comment was surprisingly favourable from one who was inclined to dislike other women: 'a nice flat-faced quite ordinary little girl rather like Una Trowbridge only 19. Nothing to her particularly, but quite a nice little thing.'[19] But some of Gwen's friends felt apprehensive about the looseness of his association with her, and on November 17th we find him writing again to Kathleen, this time under the influence of one of the 'heaviest colds that ever laid a poor poet low':

Galsworthy came to see me the other night and has taken over the job of trying to blow some sense through the female hysteria & Jewish fussiness which have made things so impossible. He is going to see J. M. B.

The house is nearly finished, & all is lovely save my health but once this cold is over I fancy that will be all right, for the strain has gone & I am so rich in love and friendship.

In fact James Barrie had already been helpful. Hearing of Mary's broken marriage and reduced circumstances, he had approached her with an offer of financial aid early in 1917 and, finding her reluctant to accept help, had written urging her to lunch with him.

If you are feeling well enough I wish you were doing war work. There must be posts you are practically fitted for. We could have some talk about that. All personal troubles outside the war seem so small nowadays. But just one thing I should like to say, because no one else can know it as well as I, that never in this world would a young literary man have started with better chances than Mr. Cannan when he had you at the helm.[20]

In April Barrie had written to Kathleen thanking her for sending him some of Gilbert's letters to show that the younger man had been 'a lad of high ideals.'

I shall always esteem you the more for the generous impulse that made you send them to me. I always held that he had many fine qualities, and I hope they will yet bring him to port.[21]

In the autumn of 1917 it seems likely that the altruistic Galsworthy went to see Barrie to ease the way to a divorce or Deed of Separation and perhaps to urge that Barrie should use his influence to stop Lady Lewis and Mary spreading slanderous rumours about Gwen, pointing out how well Gilbert had behaved during Barrie's divorce. Margaret, also anxious to help her ill-fated brother, came to London and lunched with Mary, pleading for a divorce rather than a separation, and an incongruous pair they must have been: Mary, actressy, well made-up, smart, a little faded; Margaret, stern-faced with the strong-boned, slightly curved, Cannan nose and large, unwavering, blue-grey eyes. But the lunch was a failure, for Mary was adamant in her refusal to divorce, inconsequentially claiming that Gilbert had not been her only lover, just the one Barrie could prove. 'But I've finished with all that now,' she said.

The New Year came in. *The Stucco House*, partly written at the farm, which examines in detail James Cannan's life and the awfulness of his marriage, was published at last in January by Fisher Unwin and received encouraging reviews, but Kathleen wrote of it in her diary:

. . . A deathly thing, struggling, struggling. Poor G. C. He'll pick himself to bits—self control I think is an attribute with points—I will write and tell him so. Poor lad he is greatly altered in these five years.

Yet a new Gilbert fortified by love could not see anything wrong in himself:

My dearest K, Why all the fuss and fretting about me [he wrote]. The kink blown in my life is straightened out and there's nothing more to fuss about.

I'm taking a room to work in so as not to be shut up in one place—the curse of the literary life & I want a desk. Gwen tells me that when you were here you mentioned you had one to dispose of. I'd be glad to take it over if you still want to unload.

The Stucco House is being very well reviewed. The Nation has one today which comes right out about it—but I'm working away & am beginning all kinds of new thoughts & new plans.[22]

Come & dance on Friday Feb. 1. any time after 8.15

Dances and parties, so much part of the Wright inheritance, continued to be part of Gilbert's life. The February dance had been preceded by the Christmas party (financed perhaps partly by the Rideouts and Kathleen) of which Carrington had written half-mockingly to Gertler:

Was it fun? Do write me a long description of it. And how you behaved?
Was Monty depraved? Did Jack let off air? Was Gwennie half-bare?[23]

And Alec Waugh, one of Gilbert's younger friends and admirers,
described his arrival at another the next year and his admiration for
Gwen, 'radiant as a bird of paradise':

I shall never forget my first sight of her, standing at the stairway's head; she
was fragile and pale-cheeked and small with blonde hair, cut below the ears,
so that it swung loosely like a bell; she was wearing a tight bodice and a
terraced skirt, three-layered in pink and mauve and white; her legs were very
slim and she wore pink shoes. I shall never forget the timbre in her voice, as
she waltzed past Cannan, who was in a group of talkers. 'Dance, darling,
dance.'[24]

Waugh was indeed one of Gilbert's champions. And even during the
war, the fact that Gilbert was a conscientious objector did not prevent
him being Waugh's 'hero of the moment'. Indeed Waugh had sent
Gilbert a copy of his first novel *The Loom of Youth* and was cheered by
the older man's reply which he received at Passchendaele, in the midst
of battle. Gilbert wrote:

I have read it with an eager pleasure for it is exactly what I have been hoping
from the younger people—the flat and simply sincere declaration that they
cannot stomach the world as the nineteenth century made it. Passionate sincerity brings with it a skill that no plodding or study can achieve and so the
book is well done.

'I had anxiously awaited a letter from him', writes Waugh,[25] 'receiving it as I did I might have been expected to shrug. "It doesn't mean
much at a time like this." But I did not. I was delighted.' Waugh,
unlike Ottoline, Middleton Murry and others, remained an admirer of
Gilbert for life, describing him recently as 'companionably promiscu-
ous', and mentioning earlier, in his memoirs, that Cannan was well
liked by those who knew him.

I do not see how he could have failed to be. There was nothing to dislike
about him; he was well mannered and well-bred; he was never ill-tempered
or impatient; he was temperate in drink; he never made scenes; he did not
boast about his successes with women; he rarely discussed sex, as is often the
case with men who lead full lives; he was single-minded in his devotion to
the causes that he championed. As a writer he did nothing cheap.[26]

Waugh stood of course for the younger generation, for free love and
tolerance, unshadowed by the last remnants of Victorian moral
hypocrisy. Yet his view of Gilbert was shared by Secker, an older man.
Mindful of the established author's duty to look after younger

literary men, and perhaps flattered, Gilbert lunched Waugh when he was home on leave and, after the war, was one of a cricket eleven raised by Waugh, to play Clayesmore School, along with Siegfried Sassoon. Waugh tells how Gilbert divided the party of ten into two lots, in a third-class carriage. 'Cannan and Sassoon sat opposite each other, in the centre. They did not speak a word the whole way to Winchester.' Yet, he reflected, both could be very good company when they were in the mood. Both had the same type of good looks: 'tall, thin blondish with Roman noses'; a description which suggests that although Gilbert's hair had started to recede a little and the lines of his face had deepened, he was still attractive in his mid-thirties, without the coarseness given to him by Gertler in his picture 'The Mill'. It was a handsomeness which continued to appeal to women and turn heads when he entered a room, and yet it was an attribute in which he still would not and could not believe. So clearly had the ugly duckling image been stamped on his consciousness as a child that the idea of a transformation into a swan could not even now take root. Indeed it may be that without realising it Gilbert always wanted to escape from what he perceived to be his character, nature and appearance; his infrequent delusions of greatness, even genius, being still the protective fantasies of childhood, the escape from the horrible reality of his real uncomfortable self.

1918 marked the end of Gertler's friendship with Gilbert whom he found changed for the worse. He was simply not the same man that Gertler had known at the Mill House in 1914. 'So Gilbert is really, after all, a blown out eggshell,' he wrote to Koteliansky on July 19th. 'I am not surprised . . .' And by the end of the year he was even more certain, writing to Carrington on December 22nd:

Gilbert and Pluck [Gwen] gave a party last Wednesday. Much dancing and drink, but depressing. It finally decided me against Gilbert and Pluck. It is good to feel so definite and final about anything as I feel about them—that is—that they are not worth seeing . . .

Gwen later supposed that some of the hostility felt towards Gilbert by several of his previous friends might have been caused by her youth. They were jealous because he had found happiness with a young girl. But the break almost certainly came because of the change in his personality, his new misleading boastfulness, which had to do with his approaching insanity, his basic sense of inferiority, and also with the failure of his marriage and subsequent loss of stature in the eyes of his friends.

His financial condition continued to be shaky. On July 24th he wrote to Pinker . . . 'funds have run low and I can't pay my rent. I'll be glad if you can let me have £50 to meet that and carry on'. Now, as always, he continued to work hard. He finished his book *Mummery*, which Pinker placed with Collins. The heroine in this novel has something of Gwen about her, and, more important, the scene designer in it is clearly based on Gordon Craig, whom Gilbert had met before the war. Indeed, it was Gilbert who had persuaded Craig to patent his hinged screen idea, for Craig saw in Gilbert not an aloof intellectual but a practical man who got things done. Gilbert had also supported Craig's idea of a School, which would 'conduct researches into every aspect of the theatre—Sound, Light and Movement', and helped to write its prospectus, becoming a member of the English Advisory Committee under the chairmanship of William Rothenstein.[27] These experiences Gilbert puts to good use in *Mummery*, in which portraits of a number of the leading figures of the theatre appear, including Rothenstein, loosely disguised.

The book gives us some wonderful pictures of London before the war. Here is Charles Mann (Craig) arriving after a long absence with the girl Clara, whom he has bigamously married:

On a day in August, in one of those swiftly-moving years which hurried Europe towards the catastrophe awaiting it, there arrived in London a couple of unusual appearance, striking, charming, and amusing. The man was tall, big, and queerly compounded of sensitive beauty and stodgy awkwardness. He entered London with an air of hostility; sniffed distastefully the smells of the station, peered in distress through the murky light, and clearly by his personality and his exploitation of it in his dress challenged the uniformity of the great city which was his home.

His dress was peculiar: an enormous black hat above a shock of wispy fair hair, an ill-cut black coat, a cloak flung back over his shoulders, a very high starched collar, abominable trousers, and long pointed French boots.

'But they have rebuilt the station!' he said, in a loud voice of almost peevish disapproval.

I doubt that anyone has given us a better picture of Gordon Craig, and certainly the liveliness and clarity of *Mummery* is proof of Gilbert's almost complete recovery, and perhaps, too, of his happiness with Gwen, who obviously helped to inspire the book, especially the happy ending, when Rodd (Gilbert) marries Clare (Gwen). Naturally they met, as in reality, in Henderson's book shop:

'This is Rodd,' said the bookseller. 'Adnor Rodd, a great friend of mine.'

'Rodd,' repeated Clara.

'I was just looking at Charles Mann's new book . . . Will you let me give it to you?'

He moved away to pick up the book and came back clutching it, took out his fountain pen and wrote in it in a small precise hand—'To my friend, from Adnor Rodd.'

'My name is Clara Day,' said she.

'You can't have a name yet. You are just you.'

She understood him. He meant that externals were of no account in the shock of their meeting. As they stood gazing at each other the bookshop vanished. London disappeared, there was nothing but they two on earth. Neither could move. The beginning and the end were in this moment. Nothing that they could do could alter it or make the world again as it had been for them . . . Consciously neither admitted it, both suddenly clung to what they had made of their lives.

He still held the book in his hand. She had not put out hers for it. He wrote 'Clara Day', and he wanted to write it down several times as he did with the names of the persons in his plays, to make certain that they were rightly called.[28]

9

'Poor Gilbert, a Soup Frill'

D. H. Lawrence

On April 11th, 1918, Mary was given a judicial separation from
Gilbert, the cause of the breakdown of the marriage being given as
adultery. Mary, who had told Margaret at that ill-fated luncheon that
she would not make things easy for Gilbert, was true to her word.
Although the case rested on Gilbert's affair with the maid at the Mill
House, Gwen's name was brought in quite unnecessarily when the
letter and poems from her to Gilbert, intercepted by Mary, were
mentioned.[1] So Gilbert got the worst of both worlds. No divorce and
bad publicity for his beloved and bohemian Gwen. The only con-
cession to his feeling in the matter was the omission of evidence
collected by Sir George Lewis's investigators at Ruan Minor, where
they had been much resented. Gwen and Gilbert were still unable to
marry, but it may be that Gilbert's abrupt switch from the idea of a
divorce to one of separation indicates that he had been, without realising it, a little frightened of entering again into the marital state as well
as anxious to shield Gwen. Although Barrie had given Mary a divorce
so that she could marry Gilbert, Mary had felt unable to stand aside
with dignity when her time came to do the same, despite the assurances
she had given Ottoline that she would do so should Gilbert ever fall in
love with a younger woman.[2]

By August Gwen and Gilbert were exhausted and only wanted to get
away from it all, and also perhaps a little from each other. So Gilbert
packed Gwen off to Ireland and retired to Trehemborn, St. Mervyn,
Cornwall, where, just as his spirits were beginning to rise, he received
an upsetting letter from the man who had lent him the cottage at Ruan
Minor, complaining that the place had been left in a mess and the
villagers upset by the inquiries made about Gilbert's relationship with
Gwen. He replied on August 20th:

My dear Richards,
Secker has sent me on your blowing off steam letter & I feel scalded by it.
With regard to the condition of the place I know we put in two days hard
work at it, although Gwen was at that time very ill & I had to bring her

back to London. The 'ten people' was a calamity. I asked a friend of mine in the Admiralty to come & spend his leave & he arrived, without notice other than that he was bringing a friend & the friend brought friends. We did what we could and suffered tortures. They were terrible people—two children & a slut of a nurse among them. I cleared them out as soon as I could, but Gwen being taken ill, I had to leave a great deal to them. I'm terribly sorry.

With regard to the divorce business: that is the hand of George Lewis, & I knew nothing about them having been here until I got the Bill of Costs. When I agreed to the divorce I stipulated that Gwen was not to be brought in & it was not until after I returned to London that I heard that Lewis had broken his undertaking. There was no earthly reason for him to go to Cornwall except to pile up costs & that he did without any consideration for anybody . . .

I am very sorry that the malignant fury of these people should so unpleasantly have reacted on you . . .

I'm here alone, simply resting and sweating out the exhaustion of all that business which shakes me to bits in so far as it touches outsiders and people like yourself who have been kind.

For Gilbert it was a horrible situation. Grant Richards, the publisher and writer, was not only a friend, but a reasonable, broad-minded man, and not easily rattled. He had been publishing *Noel*, Gilbert's book of sardonic and dextrous verse, in paperback instalments since 1916. A cynical tale of a South African's education, career and life in Britain, *Noel*, an epic in seven cantos, was not a work which could be expected to sell in large numbers and Richard showed some courage and idealism in sinking money in such a venture. He was, therefore, one of the last men Gilbert would have wished to offend. And that he had done so, was perhaps just another prick to send him nearer mental collapse.

In a happier frame of mind Gilbert wrote to Koteliansky on August 29th and 30th:

Gwen has just joined me here and we are so enamoured by the place that we are taking a furnished bungalow in which to spend a good deal of the winter. There will be a spare room for you and we'll bring you down by force if you don't come willingly.

I've been resting and will begin work again in a day or two. How are you? What are you up to? And when—after the end of September—will you come?

He wanted Gwen to lie back and rest after the last year's grilling and hoped the place would revive him, too.

It is glorious here & I love it & don't want to leave until it is well soaked into me . . . Your letter made us both gurgle with joy and of course we are intrigued about the Lawrences and Mary, who I feel is no longer [?] Miles Malleson will give her a job in the concubinage . . .

Gwen too was writing, her work being handled by Pinker. In Cornwall Gilbert corrected the second proofs of *Mummery*, finding in Collins a sense of 'competence most rare among publishers'.[3] Money was short again, with Gilbert asking Pinker to pay £100 into the Law Courts' branch of his bank so that 'I needn't think about money ever again.'[4] A suggestion that his love for Gwen had lost its first rapture (which does not mean it would not deepen and grow), comes in a letter to Pinker about a collection of poems, then with Heinemann:

They're rather good: written when I was extremely lyrical & thought—as one does sometimes—that the New Jerusalem had come.[5]

Although some of his letters to his agent at this time seem a little unbalanced, they are mostly proof of Gilbert's good business sense and show that he was clearly quite capable of dealing with contracts and keeping an eye on his agent, whom he did not entirely trust. Pinker was indeed not the most attractive of men. A trifle brash, he possessed the somewhat bulbous, well-fed face that intellectuals are inclined to associate with grasping businessmen. Something of an exhibitionist, his activities included fox-hunting and driving a four-in-hand. Raised from humble beginnings, Pinker had first worked as a clerk in the London Docks, then for a spell as a journalist in Constantinople before becoming the assistant editor of a magazine called *Black and White*. Swinnerton described him as 'Short, compact, a rosy, round-faced clean-shaven grey-haired sphinx with a protrusive under lip.'[6]

Once in the literary agency business Pinker's astute business sense brought him quickly to the top; he was one of the first agents to forge useful links abroad and at one time or another he handled the work of most of the leading authors of the day, including Conrad, Wells, Bennett, Galsworthy, Walpole, Swinnerton and D. H. Lawrence. As a man, Pinker lacked the idealism which Gilbert looked for in his friends, and their association was very much a business one without affection on either side. His son, who joined the firm, was however even less congenial to Gilbert and his association with them was not an easy one.

On August 28th Gilbert wrote to Pinker from Trehemborn that he proposed to stay in Cornwall for some months, probably until the New Year.

In that time I'm going to write one more short light book called *The Free Lady* & after that the end of the *Stucco House*, *Three Pretty Men* series. This will be a long book to be called *Annette & Bennett* & I'd like that to be the first book for Hutchinson. Meanwhile I'd like *The Free Lady* to go to Collins to follow *Mummery* which I suppose will be out next month or October.[7]

He went on to ask whether Pinker had done anything with Gwen's book.

She is here with me now & full of stories which she wants to write and will write all the better as soon as you open the market for her.

By the end of next week I shall be cleaned out of cash so you must pay in £100 for me or send a cheque here.

This was how it was to be for the rest of Gilbert's free life, and his letters to Pinker abound with sad little requests for payment to be made, most of it overdue; all the time he was helping his mother by contributing to the rent of the house which the Cannans had taken some years back in Newbury.

The War was coming to an end and Gilbert back in London wrote to Drinkwater, whose *Abraham Lincoln* had been enthusiastically received:

Shabby fellow you are to enjoy a triumph without letting me know. I've been down in Cornwall writing a new 100 best books but that's no excuse for you.

Send me your *Lincoln* at once. Peace is coming. We must all foregather in London to decide what is to be done about the theatre.[8]

But the terms of the armistice cheered him little, for he could not see that they would lead to a better world or lasting international peace. Carrington has described how Gilbert and Gwen sat in the Café Royal on November 11th, growing increasingly gloomier as their friends' spirits rose. Undoubtedly he saw no cause for great celebration. The massacre and the folly of that ignoble war (as he felt it to be) was to haunt him for the rest of his sane life.

Now in the winter of 1918 he could only work harder, attempting to communicate his message and pay his bills. *The Anatomy of Society* came into the first category, a philosophical book, which shows that much of his thinking was muddled towards the end of the war, yet like so much of Gilbert's writing it contains flashes of acute insight and perception. In January 1919 he turned his attention again to his parents' lives, their love-affair and marriage, when he started *Annette and Bennett.*

His fondness for young people was unabated and although he had lost the friendship of Gertler, who was soon to enter a sanatorium for tuberculosis, and of Carrington, there was still Alec Waugh needing encouragement. Waugh's father was Managing Director of Chapman and Hall, the firm which had recently agreed to take on *Time and Eternity*. Now Alec Waugh's marriage had been held up because the army would not release him, and he feared an overseas posting, so Gilbert wrote sympathetically, if a trifle egotistically:

India or Siberia sound too alarming, because I want you younger people to begin to get together before the old ones close up the ranks again and leave nothing to go on with—

I'm very happy that your father is to do *Time and Eternity*. The atmosphere of the office pleased me. I could enter it without the shrinkage that a publisher generally creates in me & I hope we'll go on . . .

Come and see us when you get your leave & don't *ever* hesitate to write.[9]

In February one of Gwen's sisters died of the post-war 'flu epidemic 'and 7000 miles separation increases sorrow', Gilbert wrote to Drinkwater. Nevertheless he and Gwen had seen *Abraham Lincoln* as soon as possible.

I'm writing about it for MacDermott's magazine, so need not say much here, except that it is important for at least three reasons and opens up possibilities as nothing in the theatre has done for ten years. I'm very glad for you and hope success will grow.[10]

In a second letter Gilbert wrote that MacDermott was arranging a series of lectures at the Hampstead Garden Suburb Institute '& wants you, me, Masefield, Barker, Shaw in that order at intervals of a fortnight—will you do it?'[11] He added that there was a good audience up there and the series was to help the theatre scheme. There was no mention of payment, but when it came to what Gilbert saw as a worthy cause, he never bothered about fees, being always willing to give his time and enthusiasm for nothing.

Everybody's Husband was put on in America, where Gilbert's books were appearing in increasing numbers, but, typically he hated publicising himself.

What the blazes can I say for Doran [he wrote to Pinker]. I don't remember being born & my work has been so interesting that I have only sat up and taken notice of my life in the last year or two. The same post brought a request that I should be filmed as one of the 'notable people who are doing the world's work'. If this is publicity give me a private life. I enclose, miserably, the best I can do for Doran upon whom—but enough.[12]

By now it was rumoured that there were three people living in the Elm Tree Road Studio, for recently a young man of wealthy titled parents had been involved in an accident with his motor-bicycle near Elm Tree Gardens. Gwen, to whom he had been introduced much earlier, was one of those on the scene and soon had him installed in the Studio. A doctor was called and recommended that the injured man should not be moved, so Gwen nursed him, and some time afterwards, according to Compton Mackenzie, there came about a *ménage à trois*, and later a change of address to Number 9.[13] Henry, an artist and writer with a good brain for business and politics, was a pleasant companion and Gilbert, who had never believed in allowing jealousy to spoil a friendship, acquiesced in this arrangement and probably received much needed help in meeting the rent. But underneath a calm and agreeable exterior another battle was raging and the acquiescence probably cost Gilbert more psychologically than he ever realised. Henry was indeed kind and generous with his money and he was also very much attracted to the slender, strong-minded girl who had nursed him with such devotion.

The trio began to be seen together, and cared nothing for gossip.[14] Henry was simply to be accepted as a brilliant young man who had made his home with Gilbert and Gwen. He was now twenty-one, Gwen twenty-two and Gilbert thirty-five. In the summer they invited Koteliansky to join them on a motoring tour, and soon afterwards Gilbert prepared to go to North America where it appears he had been invited to lecture with Hugh Walpole, John Drinkwater and Lord Dunsany.

During the summer Gilbert had become dissatisfied with the way Pinker was handling his American rights, for the agent seemed to be causing unnecessary delays and then making unconvincing excuses when trouble arose over the American negotiations. Gilbert's letters showed that he was not to be misled and that he could be hard, but although threatening a break he continued to use Pinker as an agent.

In September Gilbert sailed for America and according to Hugh Walpole 'did for himself right off by giving some lectures in a Bolshevik stronghold called the Rand'. But Walpole went on to say that his interviews (presumably with the Press) had been very 'wise and decent—much better than my own'. He added however that Gilbert's books were 'very little read, except by cranks'.[15]

Gilbert could not, of course, simply promote himself and his work. He had to have a cause in America and he made one of Lawrence, now suffering from tuberculosis. On October 16th, that philanthropic author and lecturer, Amy Lowell, was writing to Gilbert c/o Albert de Silver, at 98 Joralemon Street, Brooklyn, that she had heard through Waldo Frank of Gilbert's distress about 'the condition of our mutual friend D. H. Lawrence'.

. . . I am terribly grieved to hear (what, however, I knew already) of Lawrence's financial difficulties and bad health. I know that he wants to come to America, he has already written me several letters on the subject; but I have discouraged it to my utmost, believing that he will come here merely to die . . .

I do not suppose that you have the slightest idea of the prejudice against his work in this country. Lawrence made an excellent name for himself in England by the publication of 'Sons and Lovers', but, for some reason, probably because it is so local a tale, the book has never had the success it deserves in this country; and the excitement about 'The Rainbow', which was commented upon in all the American papers, has served to blacken, and most unjustly blacken his reputation in the eyes of the philistines . . .

But here is the state of things: It would be impossible for him to lecture, because he will have no audiences except possibly in New York. I have made several inquiries and have been told that it is a ridiculous thing to expect any lectures such as his to be a success . . .

Under the circumstances, I feel that to bring him here would be cruel, bringing him to die in a foreign country, utterly broken-hearted at his lack of success, and without his wife, who at present, cannot get into America on account of being a German . . . The thing to do with Lawrence would be to raise a fund to send him to a sanatorium, either here or in England, where he would have proper food, plenty of fresh air, and all care removed from him, etc. A man so far gone in consumption as he is cannot hope to benefit by a change of climate. . . . I should be more than willing to contribute to any fund that anyone might raise for this purpose, but I could not undertake to bear all the expense alone . . .

Such a letter was the very spur Gilbert needed. He arranged to meet Amy Lowell and took it upon himself to do all he could to change the Americans' opinion of the man, and also to raise money for him.

On January 10th, 1920 *The New York Tribune* published a short article by Gilbert entitled *A Defense of Lawrence*, which he had written in response to a newspaper's report of an interview with Sir Ernest Hodder. This well known British publisher had appeared to Gilbert to discredit Lawrence when he said that Lawrence's work was unknown to the great mass of the reading public in his country. Thereupon Gilbert, describing Lawrence as a mystic and poet, had taken it upon himself to explain the banning of *The Rainbow* in which he said 'sex is symbolised and raised clear out of the region of actuality',

Lawrence has been blocked and denied access to the public by the publishers, who, in the person of Sir Ernest, express surprise that there should be persons to speak of Lawrence as a man of genius and a person of vital importance to the intellectual and imaginative life of our time.

No senior writer has underlined his importance. No distinguished name appears on the cover of a New Lawrence Book, praising it and telling the public and the publisher that they will not be wasting their money, possibly because Lawrence has not sought any man's good opinion. He has certainly never sought mine, which makes it easier for me to take up the cudgels on his behalf and inform the American public that D. H. Lawrence has a book called

Women in Love which has been withheld from them by the confusion of mind of the puritanical section of the public and the publishers who are unreasonably afraid of that section . . .

In this article Gilbert described Lawrence as:

A man of genius who has been dogged by the ill luck of his kind, which is not the kind of Frank Swinnerton and J. C. Squire, both of them very capable, industrious talented men of letters . . .

He thought of Lawrence wasting his time, of days, weeks, years slipping by, and knowing his time was to be shorter than people realised, tried to create a sense of urgency:

The creative period of an artist's life is never too long, never surely quite long enough; and here are four or five years of Lawrence's creative life laid waste not by any malevolence or deliberate suppression, but simply by a confusion of mind aggravated possibly by the hysteria due to war conditions . . .

Lawrence was angry and perhaps particularly irritated by some tactlessness on Gilbert's side as well as the article. Naturally, he did not want charity; he wanted proper reward for his work, which he knew to be of major importance. In February he wrote to Amy Lowell thanking her for thirteen-hundred lire, which he admitted he did not mind accepting from her because she was an artist.

. . . But when Cannan writes and tells me he has collected a few dollars— which, of course, I have not received—he wrote me to tell me he was collecting a few, but never wrote again. Cannan annoys me, with his sort of penny-a-time attempt at benevolence, and the ridiculous things he says about me— and everybody else—in the American press. I am a sort of charity-boy of literature, apparently. One is denied one's just rights, and then insulted with charity . . .[16]

Gilbert seemed to have a knack of meeting the most interesting people in any country he visited and it wasn't long before he was seeing the photographer, Alfred Stieglitz, founder and editor of *Camera News*, and his talented friend, the mural and landscape painter whom he was to marry in 1924, Georgia O'Keeffe. At the same time he managed to offend John Drinkwater's wife, so that we find him writing in Philadelphia:

My dear John,
Let's have done with being at loggerheads, probably my fault—Life's much too good fun for waste of friendship & besides there is so much work to be done that both you and I can do the better for not being estranged . . . Please ask Kathleen to stop hating me—she can't go on with it if I don't hate her —and to write to me an affectionate letter appointing a day: any day next week for dinner.[17]

The Drinkwaters gave way and the friendship was patched up for the time being, but it appears their own marriage was soon to flounder, and this may have been a factor in their quarrel with Gilbert. He lunched with them on January 29th, having moved downtown to 'talk theatre' with R. E. Jones, before going off to Chicago.[18]

Meanwhile, with Gilbert away, Gwen and Henry as might be expected found themselves in love and on January 28th, 1920, they married at Chelsea Register Office, both describing themselves as 'artist and author', with Henry adding 'painter' for good measure. They appear to have agreed beforehand that the ménage should continue as before. Gwen still cared deeply for Gilbert and she wished to aid and protect him in every way possible, realising that he would always find life tortuous.

In February a trusting Gilbert wrote to Margaret Rideout that he would soon be home and was so looking forward to seeing his beloved Gwen.

In March Lawrence wrote to the American publisher, Ben (F. B. W.) Huebsch from Fonta Vecchia:

Cannan writes that Scott & Seltzer are bound to go bankrupt. Cannan wrote me a departure letter from New York. Said he was handing to you four hundred dollars to send to me. Don't suppose he ever did it. If he had an egg in his hand he'd have to suck it—I hear now, indirectly, that he is in Paris.

If you ever should have the money to send, please send it in American dollars. One negotiates such a lot better exchange over here.[19]

Meanwhile Henry and Gwen had written a shattering letter to Gilbert telling him of their marriage and then, hearing disturbing stories of his behaviour in North America, wired that they would meet the ship at Cherbourg and take him with them on their journey to Africa, an event which caused a great deal of gossip and talk among those who knew any or all of the three. On their way, Henry, Gwen and a deeply hurt Gilbert motored through France, stopping in Paris then to Italy, with Gilbert hiding his bitterness towards Henry and still championing and loving Gwen with whom he could find no fault. Her money problems were now over; as a married woman she could not be pressed by her family to return home. She was also in a position to support Gilbert financially should he need it.

Very soon an embittered and impoverished Lawrence, with Mary Cannan now a neighbour, wrote to Gilbert about the dollars collected, in which he also made unkind remarks about Gwen imagining, one supposes, that Gilbert saw her marriage to Henry as unforgivable treachery. Gilbert's reaction was immediate:

Yesterday I heard a fumbling on the terrace and there Gilbert at the foot of the stairs [Lawrence wrote to Compton Mackenzie on April 9th], in a brown hat rather like yours; gave me quite a turn! thought it was somehow you—not you. He came express from Rome in one of his tantrums because of the nasty letter I'd written him—fume! But—nay, I'll say nothing. The main upshot is that in his indignation he disgorged a cheque for £75 SEVENTY FIVE POUNDS STERLING—as the equivalent of $300 which he had collected from Americans for me. Benone! (*sic*). Fortune had it that *for once* Mary wasn't here to tea; and that he had taken a room at Domenico, as being a *little grander* than Timeo. He is tout Americain— L'Americanisato! Pocket book thick, fat bulging with 1,000 lire notes— 'these beastly hotels'—'Oh yes, picked up quite a lot of money over there'— 'Oh yes, they seemed to take to me quite a lot'—'Yes, have promised a quantity of people I'll go back this Fall.'

Oh what a Fall was there!

However we parted as friends who will *never* speak to each other again.

> *And life is thorny, & Youth is vain*
> *And to be wroth with one we love*
> *Doth work like madness in the brain.*

Poor Gilbert—a soup frill. However, I've sent my check like lightning to the bank, to see if it'll be cashed safe and sound. Aspettiamo. And today the filbert returns to Rome, to his deux monds. 'Gwen is a wonderful and beautiful character'. this to my nose.[20]

Lawrence relates in the same letter that Gilbert said that the marriage had made no difference to him. But of course Gilbert *did* care, very deeply, only he was not going to let anyone see that. He had lost his second chance, and from the ship he had written to Margaret Rideout that the news had made him unable to write, see or think.

While in America he had planned a return visit and from now on he was to be a wanderer, searching for peace of mind, for a new philosophy, an odd-man-out, without ties or lasting commitments; above all a lonely man with the threat of insanity hanging over his head. He wanted to forgive what he saw as Henry's treachery, for that was surely in keeping with his philosophy of love; he wanted not even to see it as treachery. Men must not fight over women; in such circumstances the civilized ones were gentle and kind. They turned the other cheek, and love overcame all things. For, although he was not conventionally religious, part of the Christian message and a sense of the spiritual had always been strong in Gilbert's life and thought, an influence from which, for all his cynicism, he had never been able to escape. Some time after the marriage he wrote this prayer:

> *Give me to know, O Lord,*
> *The silence of the soul*
> *That I may go O Lord*
> *As one made sweetly whole*

And let my being smile
Its song the while
Life, love and death enthrall me
Through all that may befall me.
Give me thy silent strength, O Lord
That when I fail at length, O Lord
Some deep essential grace
From my remembered face
May shine upon the passers-by
Like stars unnoticed in the sky
Give me to be the unforgotten lover
Of her in whom thy witness I discover.[21]

Undoubtedly the last plea was granted, and for Gwen, Gilbert remained a unique and unforgettable person, so that in old age she remembered him only as she had known him first. A *saint* and *genius* were the exact words she used.

But in spite of good intentions, Gwen's marriage meant the end of the *ménage à trois* at Elm Tree Road. And Gilbert's return to England was brief, for on October 30th, we find him writing to Pinker from The Hotel Great Central, London N. W.

For various reasons Annette & Bennett will have to be held up, I enclose a paragraph relating to a light novel written on various journeys—called Pugs & Peacocks. I shall finish it on my next voyage—which begins next week—and a typescript should reach you about mid-December. Please take Brown Shipley, 123, Pall Mall as my address. I'll be in London again with a stack of work about August or September 1921. . . .

This time he was to pay some or all of his expenses by sending regular despatches to the *New York Freeman*,[22] but first he made arrangements for Pinker to pay a £5 monthly allowance to Violet Cannan. He was now her only son in the country for Felix had joined Angus in the East. There was nothing now to keep Gilbert in London, and soon he set out on his travels, beginning his first despatch.

I am wandering, dear Eusebius, in the hope of discovering an answer to the question: 'What on earth are we all up to?' I have wondered now for over a year without saying a word about it, a single display of virtue in one whose past is so notoriously garrulous—America, France, Italy, England, Africa and again England and again France. This time I am to sail from Marseilles, for countries and places from which you shall hear from me, though it is more than likely that I shall write only of London and New York.

From France he went to Port Said, 'in Africa which, with all due respect to America, is the continent of the future', and then to Magadicio in the Italian Somaliland. 'A hot, tawny hill, torn by the wind and the rain, a few white houses, a large dusty brown native village, a lighthouse, a wireless station (in direct communication with Rome), furious jutting rocks and an ever-swelling sea, blue and white; that is Magadicio.' Whence in February, to Zanzibar which he found proposterous, 'too like the illustrations in boys' adventure stories', then on to Dar-Es-Salaam and Beira by which time he noted that he had been in seven ships in fifteen months.

He decided that he would hire a wagon and a tent, and forget the entertainment of the nineteenth century which did not entertain me because it wished so desperately to improve my morals. Three generations of lecturing! I have been a lecturer and I know what a bore it is, and I hereby counsel all men and women bitten with the disease of platform speaking to take themselves at once to a country where their language is not understood.

And further on in the same despatch from Beira he writes:

All this sounds very like weeping over Zion and hanging my harp in the willows of Babylon, but indeed there is not a tear hovering anywhere near my eyes. Were I to weep over humanity I would weep blood. Rather will I buy me a parcel of earth and sow it with fancies and see what a fine crop of thought I shall reap . . . I want a place where I can be quiet in my premature old age, which I hope will be over before I am seventy, so that I can have a few years to enjoy the youth of which I, in common with millions of others, have been cheated.

He reached Mashonaland in February and Lomagundi in March; in Mgutu he hesitated. Which way? East or West? Return to London via New York or to New York via London? To 'relieve his hesitation' he bought two horses, which he named Mr. Jones and Ariel,*23

And my feelings are so deeply engaged that I do not see how I can return to London or New York without Jones. It would be rather fun to ride him up Fifth Avenue in my present costume—breeches, shirt and sunburn, saluting and being cut by my elegant friends—and to take him to Lunch at the Plaza.

He began to acquire and accumulate things, people, animals, habits, 'without any particular desire for any of them', dogs, oxen, the two horses, three black men to drive the wagon and four to look after him. In Makalannga he made a garden, a place of beauty, and wrote love poems for Gwen. For a time he was busily content:

* Possibly after R. E. Jones and Gwen whom he called Ariel in his dedication in *Mummery*.

With the horses and my oranges (I forgot to mention the dogs who have adopted me) . . .

But (he asks, more typically, further on) do Americans know what America stood for in the minds of William Blake and John Donne? Do they even know what America stood for in the mind of Walt Whitman? Or do they accept their States as a land of doughnuts and dough boys?

So his writing continued, his questioning and so much else as he journeyed. And, on the whole, most of his published despatches appear to have been lucid and remarkably sane, his comments pertinent, original and to the point. In Umvukwe he began to rant a little about the folly of Europe and the British system of government and life. In contrast when writing about the black people he was calm except when outraged by the ill-bred white men's treatment of them. Victoria Falls produced an outburst: 'Shameful, shameful, shameful! I could write that word all down the page.' But often he was happy with:

Jones, the best of horses, Malekebu and I, and a wagon with tents and provisions; all day in the saddle, all night until sleep comes dreaming and sinking into the African evening, frogs, cicadas, owls, nightjars, the wind in the trees and the long grass.

He particularly loved to ride in wild places, and wondered whether he could return happily to Europe or America:

In a rare fit of Scots caution, for ordinarily, I make no provision for emergencies, I have bought a piece of this earth and built a house on it, a very little one, to which to repair should it so transpire that when I attempt to return to civilisation there should be no civilisation to return to . . . Will industrialised men want to read books? I don't know.

He met Gwen in Africa, named a cat after Stieglitz, went on trek, spent three months looking after a farm for a farmer and went his way richer for the experience of having laboured on the land. In October 1921 he was back in Beira from which he wrote that he was leaving something of himself:

my lodge in the wilderness, my garden and God knows what myth of the strange inkoos who cared nothing for money or drink or gold; and made friends with horses and dogs and had no woman and yet, using horrible language upon occasions, could not possibly be a missionary.

He sold Ariel and Jones, and sailed from Cape Town for England at the end of 1921. In August he had written to Pinker:

Please make no offers and consider none on my behalf. After the completion of the Hutchinson contract the whole business of my books will have to be gone into very carefully. I have written to Doran to cancel my previous agreement with him after P & P. That clears the ground & we can look into things when I 'hit' London again as the Americans say [And in a P.S.] Keep on the £5 a month to my mother. If you let her down I'll kill you. Sembal is ready, but I like him and want his company for a little.[24]

His remaining books and furniture were in store, and once in England Gilbert was again homeless. He went first, it appears, to Newbury, hopefully taking his mother a monkey, which she did not appreciate, but his parents' deep and lasting absorption with each other always made him feel an intruder, and no doubt Sheila's increasingly frequent fits were disturbing for him in his highly nervous state. He could not stay and he was not really wanted.

Then he wrote to his old friend, the author Francis Lyall Birch, whom he affectionately called 'Little Frankie'. A once frequent visitor to Mill House, he agreed to Gilbert's proposed stay and very soon Gilbert took the train to Cambridge where Birch had a lectureship in History at King's.

Birch, who had just recovered from a nervous breakdown himself, seeing to his horror that Gilbert's mind was affected, took refuge in King's, leaving his wife to look after their guest. The Hon. Vera Benedicta, a delightful woman of only twenty-one, found Gilbert a gentle and pleasant, if eccentric companion. She noticed that he disliked open discussion of sex and soon found that if anyone raised the topic of Jews or war he became so vehement and angry in his denunciation as to be incoherent. His attempt at what he saw as forgiveness had failed and he told Vera Birch that he felt considerable bitterness towards Henry for making love to Gwen while he was away. He also felt very angrily towards certain people in his family, for now, like many a disturbed person, he looked back to his childhood to allot the blame, laying it, I suspect at the door of his weak but highly moral father and his brother, Angus, along with other Manchester relations. For some time he had suspected that they were plotting with Gwen's husband against him, a feeling which may have been in part a reaction induced by his own guilt at hating them.

He had asked the Birches to put him up for a week, but he stayed on and on as though he was a permanent guest. Frank Birch's nerves worsened the longer Gilbert stayed. Vera, afraid of a relapse, eventually realised that Gilbert must be asked to leave, consoling herself with the thought that he was better mentally than on his arrival.[25] So, saner, but restless and lonely, Gilbert took a flat at 38 Bury Street, St. James's, S.W.1, and started to play a more direct part in the managing of his literary affairs, instructing his agent to act rather than seeking his advice:

. .'. Cable Brandt. Refuse Seltzer. Their offer is nothing like what I want.

Brandt tells me he has not yet received the abridged Pugs and Peacocks I sent you weeks and weeks ago. Please see to this at once.[26]

In late spring Gilbert went to Germany and 'slid into Switzerland' on his way home via Paris, only to plan almost at once a trip to America. Now Doran had cold feet about publishing more of his books and it had been suggested that Gilbert might like to buy back *Pugs and Peacocks* and the *Stucco House*, warning signs which must have added to his sense of insecurity. To make matters worse the young Pinkers seemed to be paying him less than he had earned. He sorted this out eventually and wrote:

That's all right then & I take it you have £45 to go on with which covers the allowance over into next year. We'll waive the subject of interest though you wouldn't if it were on the other side.

The mistake was annoying though not nearly so much as your not answering or acknowledging my letters.[27]

His own letters were sane enough but he was slipping more often into a state of unreality and developing stronger paranoiac feeling towards Henry, some of which he directed against the Jews he portrayed in his novels. His restlessness and loneliness caused him to pay ever close attention to his own affairs. In July he wrote to the Pinkers:

I'll be in town now until late August. Has the Seltzer agreement turned up yet? Has the cheap edition of Round the Corner come out? Where's the cheque? And doesn't the agreement want my signature?[28]

In August he decided to take on the payment of his mother's allowance himself.[29] In September, sensing (one suspects) further mismanagement, he decided to rearrange his affairs and hand his further business over to Mr. Tilden Smith at A. M. Heath, the respected firm of literary agents.[30] Only the change in his handwriting suggests that he was again near complete breakdown.

10

'A Genius that Never Developed'

The Times

ON October 18th, 1922 Gwen gave birth to a son who was destined for a brilliant career at Eton and a premature death in the Second World War. In Gilbert's eyes Gwen with a baby was beautiful, almost divine, but the fact that the baby belonged to Henry and not to himself may have been more than he could bear.[1] Once he had longed so much for a legitimate child, and later, when he was locked away, he visualised Gwen's son for twenty years always as a baby, as though the clock had stopped at his birth.

His chance had gone; his hopes had turned to vapour. Now much of the time he appeared to be in a dream but awake, carrying out like a zombie the automatic actions necessary for survival. His eyes had turned inwards to visions far more intense and exciting than the world could offer. Sadly, people were frightened by his insanity. Much earlier he had remarked in an unpublished novel how in 1916 people had turned away from his eyes, and Middleton Murry was later to write of meeting Gilbert at the Adelphi in 1920:

He had just returned from America and he talked strangely of the magnitude of his own exploits there. The encounter was disquieting. It was not that Gilbert had *changed*; he was merely more intensely what he had been three years before. But now, I felt, he had finally lost contact with reality . . . I fled miserably from the stare of that wild unseeing eye, with the certainty that I should never encounter it again.[2]

And Lawrence had written to Mary: 'As for Gilbert he has lapsed into the land of ghosts in my soul[3]'. Most of the rest who had come so frequently to the Mill to see the naturally generous and kindly Gilbert Cannan, had turned away, one by one.[4]

The only answer seemed to be to keep moving, to run away from the visions and the voices that other men could neither see nor hear. 'My dear Stieglitz,' (he wrote on November 30th), 'I really am sailing this time on the 6th, Majestic, and I hope to find you in New York.' Had he been delayed by another nervous breakdown brought on by increased emotional stress? There seems to be a gap in his letters to Pinker in

181

October and November, and the handwriting in the one to Stieglitz, quoted above, is a disturbing scrawl. Another written in January and wrongly dated 1922 is uncharacteristically manic:

My dear Stieglitz, Yes. The urge started six months ago, to come over and get physically and tangibly what we had then unseizably and overpoweringly —a great day!

Full steam ahead now!

On January 30th, there was a complete change in Gilbert's attitude to the photographer. He was hellishly busy but would surely see him before leaving. A claim that he was busy usually meant now that Gilbert had withdrawn into his inner self, but could have indicated this time that he had started with Mme Strindberg on their translation of *The Savage* by Artsybashev. Other letters to Stieglitz seem unnecessary and misplaced:

I am prompted to write this (although I shall see you soon) by the receipt of a letter from S. Africa sending news of the marvellous cat I named after you. He bristles with knowledge just like you.[5]

He was muddled now, despondent, often incoherent, and yet there were two certainties in his mind: the world was heading for disaster through the sheer stupidity and greed of men; it was his duty to use his vision and intelligence to turn the tides of history in the right direction. Alone in the Hotel Gotham in New York, he appears to have come to the conclusion that he must write an open letter to the President of the United States of America which he sent for publication to the *New York Times*. Clearly it was an unbalanced and strange communication but the editor of that paper took it seriously enough to make it the subject of his third leader, which is perhaps some indication of the opinion in which Gilbert was held in that country at that time. All the same, the editor saw the need to justify his decision:

We do Mr. Cannan the courtesy to indicate the burden of his appeal to President Harding, merely premising that his course in making it is to be udged very much as would have been a letter from Mr. Sinclair Lewis in England last spring giving advice to Lloyd George.

Headed 'Romantic Radicals' and published on February 4th, the editorial puts forward the chief proposals in Gilbert's letter, the first being that the President should consider the release of all political prisoners in America on the date of Abraham Lincoln's birthday, February 12th, and the second that the Treaty of Versailles be replaced by a European Pact drawn up by lawyers of the type of General Smuts who 'alone of the public men of the British Commonwealth retains sufficient credit'. Gilbert suggested that the agreement to form such a pact should be promulgated on Washington's Birthday.

If there could be anything more romantic; more in sublime disregard of the actualities of this breathing world, we should like to be told what it is,

commented the *New York Times*.[6] In fact, Gilbert's action was only a foretaste of what was to come, and writing advisory, castigating, insulting and wild letters to heads of state was to be one of his chief occupations for the next twenty years.

The poor man was now completely demented, with solitude pushing him further into unreality. His departure date (the day following) had caught him unawares, he wrote to Stieglitz on January 24th, but he sailed finally, it seems, on February 20th. When he boarded the liner he had probably already crossed to the wrong side of the thin line which men have tried to draw between sanity and madness, entering into a strange dream-like world which allowed all his pent-up anger to be released in simple physical violence.

Alec Waugh has suggested that coming back on a liner Gilbert seized a fellow passenger, Horace Liveright, by the throat, forced him to his knees and exhorted him to prepare to meet his maker.[7] What happened on his return is not clear, but almost certainly Gwen came again to the rescue and nursed him back to some form of sanity so that he could face the world once more. On March 1st he wrote a sane post-card to Lonsdale Deighton from Bury Street, saying a reply had been delayed owing to his absence in America. On March 2nd he was in Paris where he 'lost any remnants of despondency' and for the first time he had a sense of Europe,

a lovely new infantile thing that mingled with the soft caress of spring in the Paris air to make it almost an enchantment. It made the Ruhr attempt obviously the nonsense it always was & for the first time for years there was in the people the nonchalance that was their strength.

He found London in a state of 'subdued humiliation', and joined the International P.E.N. Club. He finished writing *The House of Prophecy*, in which Bertrand Russell appears again as Melian Stokes, and continued the translation of *A. O. Barnabooth* by Valéry Larbaud. Reviews of his books had continued to be mixed, *The Times Literary Supplement* critic suggesting that if you forgot when reading *The Stucco House* the period in which the novel was set, you found in the story a 'moving, breathless, headlong and sometimes incoherent protest against the civilisation of industrialism'. He thought the tragic figure of James Lawrie 'extraordinarily real ... strong enough to suffer, but not strong enough to achieve; and so he breaks himself.' But he longed to say to Gilbert:

'Quiet, quiet! Count five and take a deep breath ... Now what is it?' He is so much in earnest and yet, for want of counting five, he seems unable to make the most of his talent and fulfil the promise that he long ago gave.

Time and Eternity fared less well, suggesting, the critic thought, that Gilbert had not yet passed the experimental stage. In contrast, *Pugs and Peacocks* received in the same paper well merited praise, the reviewer writing of Mr. Cannan's 'ruthless brilliance . . .' and his 'passages of great power'. *Sembal*, in which Gilbert's new hatred of Jews is clear, was described as a 'careful, detailed and subtle study of a social carbuncle and the inflammation it sets up', but then the reviewer added 'Mr. Cannan sees all life as a carbuncle'. As for *Annette and Bennett*, the critic considered this novel in the light of Gilbert's statement in *The Release of the Soul* 'that he could think with extraordinary clarity but without words'.

He strides through the fog resolutely as though there were no fog there. It may be that he is working towards something. But once again he has left his very sincere admirers baffled.

Some of his books were now being published in Scandinavia and France, without any royalties coming through from the Pinkers.[8]

Meanwhile Mary, who had been living mostly in France and Italy, unaware of the serious deterioration in Gilbert's health, moved to Holm Lea, Cheltenham Road, Broadway, to be near (it was said) James Barrie who had rented a house for the summer at Stanway some five miles away. Infuriated by Gilbert's undiminished love for Gwen (Lawrence described her as going on like a 'wick-wack' when she had heard how Gilbert had joined the newly married couple and travelled with them to Africa,[9] she now hoped, it was suggested, for a second chance with her first husband.[10]

More breakdowns followed Gilbert's visit to France together with a frightening intensification of his hatred of Henry. Paranoiac delusions grew, until one day in August he destroyed many of his papers and books, set fire to his furniture and then accused Henry of the deed. Only Gwen could manage him. Without her he became increasingly disorientated.

> '*Man, my man*', *she called to me*
> '*Come into the world with me.*'
> *So I laid aside my pen*
> *And went into the world of men*
> *There I found the ghosts of creatures*
> *Wearing worn out human features*
> *Neither flesh nor blood could kindle*
> *In the ghostly, ghastly swindle.*
> *So I took the pen I hurled*
> *Away and made my love a world.*[11]

And now his world had gone, the loved one had borne another man's child. Reality was too horrible to contemplate. In spite of all his writing, his lecturing, no one had listened or cared, and life remained a swindle. He had been cheated from first to last, deserted by his friends. Trying to survive, he had failed miserably, come out of his dreams to live, and found life unbearable.

Gwen, who was very soon to journey to the Cape, telegraphed his parents, bringing Violet Cannan reluctantly to London, and Gilbert found himself 'shanghai'd' to a nursing home while Violet and Henry searched, on Gwen's insistence, for a house near Newbury, where he could live in seclusion until his recovery was complete.[12] They eventually found Winding Wood House, some four miles from Lyndene, which they took on condition Gwen and her husband paid the rent, wages and the cost of any dilapidations that might occur. 'I have no money of my own,' Violet was to write to Gwen's husband at a later date when asked to pay small household expenses, while Gilbert's father appears to have remained silent.[13] They were, in fact, very hard-up, having spent all the money from their latest legacy. Henry Cannan was drawn to the bottle and whisky was an extra item of expenditure, but Violet could refuse him little. She continued as always to put his interests first, but when later in 1925 they moved to a tiny cottage in Cornwall, she was glad that there was a long hill between them and the nearest pub.

So, in October 1923, Gilbert was moved from the nursing home to the country, to be deposited in the kindly hands of a gardener and his wife, good honest people by the name of Whiting, and a Mrs. Satterley who may have been a trained nurse. Here away from irritations, the stimulation and frustrations of London, it was hoped that Gilbert's recovery would continue, and a hopeful Gwen, off to the Cape, left her dog Hector to keep him company. Few knew of Gilbert's place of refuge and the local villagers were not it appears aware of his existence for the Whitings were, above all, discreet.

Plain and Victorian, Winding Wood House stood, then as now, on the sharp bend of a road where the winds blew hard across open fields from north and west. Red brick except for a tile-hung northern wall, it was graced on two sides by a pleasant garden, mainly lawned, with a sweep of drive, leading to a well-proportioned front door, beyond which a pond caught and reflected the changing lights of day. Seclusion was provided by a brick and flint wall, yews and hollies, which shielded the garden from the road and gave welcome shelter from the wind. The fields around rolled gently into one another, broken by thin hedgerows and the winding band of woodland which curved through their fertile acres like a wide belt of dark fur. The air, here on the edge of the downs, was good: the quiet, usually broken only by the little noises of the countryside, the scratching of birds, the rustle of leaves, footsteps in the road, the louder hoofs of horses from Radley's Farm, the cackle and crowing of chickens.

The Whitings' cottage was across the road, opposite the tradesmen's entrance to the house. From some of their windows the gardener and his wife could see anyone coming round the corner from the front gate or climbing the wall where it was lowest on the northern side. Yet although well-proportioned with a wide stair and pleasant rooms looking across lawns and flower beds, Winding Wood House had the sad air of a place always leased, never occupied by an owner. The atmosphere appears to have been neither soothing nor happy.

Two miles away across the main Newbury–Hungerford Road was Kintbury, which, boasting a post office and railway station, was a link with civilisation when Gilbert wanted to escape to London and to those he still believed to be his friends.

The choice of refuge was unfortunate for, although Gilbert wished to be alone, solitude always seemed to make him worse, and almost at once his health started to deteriorate, so that when he lunched at Lyndene on Christmas Eve his mother found him quite unrecovered.

Very soon he began to talk to people who were not there. The Cannans travelled weekly from Newbury to see Gilbert, but now he seemed to dislike them almost as much as Gwen's husband, with whom he still suspected his father was in collusion to wreck his life, and he asked them not to come to his room. Fearing a violent outburst they acquiesced and went away each time after making inquiries.

Then, in January, Mrs. Satterley left and the Whitings had the care of Gilbert to themselves. It wasn't easy, especially as he had been left to pay the household bills himself, for he was by no means penniless and an allowance from Rita, Edwin's wife, was now being paid regularly into his bank account.

I heard from Mrs. Cannan [Violet] yesterday telling me I had better ask Mr. Cannan for a cheque [wrote Mrs. Whiting to Gwen's husband] but I do not think she can realise how bad Mr. Cannan has been or she would know it would hardly be fair to ask him to do such a thing, he has been worse than he was when he came here from the nursing home, and my husband has had to be about with him at all hours of the night and on Monday night did not get to bed until 4 o'clock in the morning, as Mr. C—would insist upon going out in his night attire and wanted to go to London but after a long time he succeeded in getting him to come indoors and later into bed . . . but he has been quieter since and really seems improved, and I do hope it will continue now as it is rather a strain on us but we have tried to respect his wishes in not having anyone here to see him, I shall not worry him with money affairs until he is fit again as my father will lend him some to carry on with and Mr.

Cannan will not know but what it is my own. I know Mrs. Cannan does not
wish to have anything to do with it.[14]

Earlier Mrs. Whiting had written to Gwen's husband to ask what she
should do if Mr. Cannan 'had mental trouble badly'. He referred her to
Violet Cannan who told her to call the policeman, to take Gilbert to an
asylum.[15] 'I hope something better than that will be done for him',
wrote Mrs. Whiting to Gwen's husband, on February 28th. She then
asked for money, pointing out that she had been paying for everything
herself since February 12th as Gilbert was not fit enough to write a
cheque. She mentioned that he had broken crockery and a chair which
must be replaced.

Now undoubtedly angry with the Cannans, Henry wrote sharply to
Violet, pointing out that she must try to meet the small household
expenses, for which he would pay her back. After all, had not Gilbert
been very good about helping to pay for Lyndene? He also made it
clear that he was shocked at the suggestion that Gilbert should be sent
to an asylum. 'I sincerely trust this course will not be resorted to and
that you will give him every opportunity and plenty of time to recover
before such a drastic step is contemplated.'[16]

Meanwhile Gilbert had written Henry three insulting letters on
February 6th, 8th and 11th, accusing him of invading his flat and taking
his property. He threatened to expose Henry to the Press. 'It does not
seem to have crossed your mind that I am rather an eminent person &
not a Dallas or a Hamar.' And further on '. . . as a Jew no doubt you
think you can make any base use you like of your wife, but you do *not*
involve my mother and my friends without complete disaster'. Henry
tried again to put more responsibility on the Cannans' shoulders, a
move, it seems welcomed by Violet who obviously thought it was time
that Gilbert was shut away at least for a time. In late February she had
learned that the six months' tenancy on Winding Wood was un-
renewable and would end on March 31st.

I quite agree with you that you should not be mixed up with Gilbert any
more, especially as he seems to get no better. I can never thank you enough
for all you did for him last year, but I fear it will have to end in putting him
under restraint for a time at all events.[17]

Throughout much of this breakdown Gilbert had continued to write
letters. He had asked Secker for proofs and copy of the dedication of
Letters from a Distance, which was already published, a request dealt
with by Grace, and continued to think about his contracts and books.[18]
He told his mother to bring him his papers and agreements which he
then burned. Vera Birch, who had offered him a second stay in Cambridge, was then advised that he was unfit to travel. Hector, probably

scenting disaster, ran away with the Whitings' dog. And Gilbert came to believe that he was Scott of the Antarctic, so giving an ironic twist to his story. Around that time, pressed by Gwen's husband, Henry Cannan and Grace insisted on seeing Gilbert, a truly shocking experience.

Father and I went up to Winding Wood yesterday. He was up in his room in bed, so Mrs. Whiting went up to ask him if he would see us, he sent down a message to say that he was expecting an admiral to see him. We asked her to go up again to tell him that we had such a short time to stay that we could not wait long, so he said he would see us, so up we went. When we got into his room we were both dreadfully shocked to see how ill and ghastly he looked. I don't think he knew who we were anyway. He said, 'This is just a personal matter, so you must go downstairs,' so off we had to go as he would not let us stay with him.

I don't know how we are going to get him away by 31st March, but we shall have to by some means or other. He is not at all sensible; his eyes look so dreadful.

The Whitings are pinning their faith on your wife to get him away, as they say she is the only one who has any influence at all over him, but if she is not back in time what is to be done?

Shall we consult a doctor here as to how to get him out of the house? I think he is far worse than he was when you telegraphed us to come to his flat in London. He is quite quiet at present, but simply refuses to see anyone, he certainly will not be fit to go to the Birches in April.[19]

Poor Grace was perhaps the most gentle of all Gilbert's sisters, a Wright rather than a Cannan, sweet-tempered, easy-going. It was she who had stayed at home to look after her parents and the ailing Sheila after training as a nurse, and undoubtedly she looked on the brother she had never really grown to know with much compassion and sorrow, but it was not a love that would fight for him in any way. Her parents came first and she probably thought she was doing enough for the family by caring for them, and for a time also for Sheila. The prognosis of those who had examined Gilbert earlier appears to have been poor. Gwen, in Gilbert's own words, 'liked to do things in style',[20] and it is likely that she would have consulted at least one leading specialist. Later it was said that a German expert had given an opinion: certainly it was claimed that one doctor had pronounced that Gilbert's brain was actually growing softer, a process which would continue. Gwen and her husband must have seemed very young, inexperienced and idealistic to Gilbert's parents, who, in contrast, usually took the easy way out, seeing setbacks as revealing the will of God. For them it was simplest to push Gilbert away out of sight into an asylum where he would receive good medical care, leaving them to relax into a comfort-

able old age. They hesitated only because Gwen's husband was willing
to pay every penny to keep him out and it was not in their nature to
fight such dogged determination or consciously to hurt the feelings and
sensibilities of the young.

To many, Gilbert's parents in their wish to have him put away must
appear now to have acted harshly but it must be remembered that they
had been brought up within the established church and would therefore
have seen him as the black sheep of the family. 'He has not lived at
home since he was 17,' Violet wrote in one letter to Gwen's husband,
as though this fact relieved them largely of responsibility.[21] It was now
forty years since he had come into the world, and in the last twenty
years he had decried much that was close to their hearts. He had put his
family into his novels and had seemed to turn against his patriotic and
in many ways conventional upbringing. Yet one of Violet's sisters had
gone through a divorce and remained a loved member of the family,
which suggests that the real cause of his parents' apparent coldness was
a genuine lack of sympathy with him as a person and his growing dislike of them. He was not the Gilbert they had known, and perhaps they
no longer liked nor trusted him, fearing that in a fit of madness he
might further disgrace them. Above all, they were tired. They had
brought up their eight children* in difficult circumstances and now
wished to live the last years of their life in peace. In addition they were
anxious about their younger daughter Sheila, whose fits were becoming
alarmingly frequent.

While the lease on Winding Wood House neared the end of its term,
and Gilbert became more uncontrollable, *The House of Prophecy* was
published by Thornton Butterworth; an odd, disjointed book, full of
ill-judged generalisations, it was nevertheless reviewed and widely
bought, so that it ran into a second edition in April. Gerald Gould,
writing in the *Saturday Review*, was obviously perplexed. It was
certainly, he wrote, not one of Mr. Cannan's best books 'though even
here the uncommon quality of his thinking shows in places and he has
some of the old touches of romantic beauty'. Reading the book now,
we can see that the author's brain was not functioning properly but
throwing out sentences without censorship and perhaps out of per-
verseness contradicting accepted opinions, as when he wrote: 'Being
Irish, Penrose was not in the least romantic.'

Meanwhile, before the end of March, Gilbert took matters into his
own hands by escaping and running away to London (presumably
catching a train from Kintbury) where Richard Aldington later
claimed to have encountered him looking sane and talking coherently,[22]
although soon afterwards he relapsed into melancholia, refusing to go

* Nicholas died in infancy.

back to Winding Wood House, refusing to go anywhere at all. Summoned again by telephone from Newbury, Violet Cannan appears to have set the machinery into process which would ensure he was put under restraint. The exact sequence of events is not clear nor do we know whether Gwen was yet back from the Cape, a vital question for she alone could drag him back into the real world, if only for a time.

On April 15th, he was installed as a certified patient in one of the finest sanatoria for the mentally ill that Gwen knew, partly at her husband's expense, with Violet Cannan the petitioner to the Board of Control for his restraint. He arrived in a state of excitement, suffering from delusions of persecution and diagnosed as a schizophrenic. The Priory Hospital stood, as now, in fine grounds at Roehampton, close to Richmond Park, and was run as far as was practicable on the lines of a hotel. Dr. Basil William Brown had recently become the medical superintendent, having gained experience in the field as assistant medical officer at the Holloway Sanatorium for the mentally ill. From the first he stipulated that Gilbert would be better without visitors and that his family must stay away, for much of his anger was directed against them and it was inadvisable to arouse his aggressive instincts.

On hearing of Gilbert's committal to an asylum, Vera Birch, who had offered to renew the lease on Winding Wood House in her name, hurried to see his parents. Her own husband had still not fully recovered from his nervous breakdown and she felt convinced that so drastic a step in Gilbert's case was unmerited. Although far from normal while staying at Cambridge Gilbert had once again aroused in a woman the desire to care for him. Too late, the kindly Vera Birch tried to help.

The meeting was a failure. She saw Grace, who had written to her pleasantly about Gilbert but now appeared hostile. Vera Birch's very youth and intelligence seemed to make Grace feel at a disadvantage, putting her on the defensive. She apparently suspected that Vera had been having an affair with Gilbert and immediately became shy and difficult. Vera Birch said afterwards that she felt Grace actually disliked Gilbert, which made her all the more determined to fight for his release.[23]

Her next step was to go to the Priory to ask to see him. But here her way was barred. Visitors were not allowed unless they had been granted permission to see Gilbert by an uncle in Manchester. But when Vera asked for the uncle's address she was informed that the Priory did not have it. Undeterred, a month or two later, with Frankie now better, Vera hastened with him to Gwen and Henry to see whether they could undo the ill which she was sure had been done. They told her that they had fought against committal to an asylum for as long as was possible but they had absolutely no power because they were not related to Gilbert in any way. Nevertheless Gwen was allowed to visit Gilbert and was able therefore to keep an eye on him.

In the meantime Sheila Cannan's epilepsy had worsened to such an extent that she had to be sent away to a Home for Epileptics by Robin Hood's Bay and, feeling very sorry for herself, Violet Cannan went on doctor's orders to recuperate in Devon. She had then the added humiliation of asking Gwen's husband to pay the bills she had incurred when summoned to London.[24]

It was just this sort of behaviour which had surely made Gilbert so impatient with his 'silly family'. There was Edwin, a man with many investments, expecting Gwen's husband to pay his cousin's taxi fares, even though he was just about to allot £300 a year to sharing the burden of the Priory's fees.

In May Edwin and Henry Cannan officially took over the winding up of Gilbert's affairs when they became his Trustees, handing the legal side over to Messrs. Morrell, Peel & Gamlen, who had long acted in matters of law for the Oxford Cannans. The total amount to hand was £334. 3s. 1d. but the Public Solicitor's fees had to be deducted from this. There were, of course, royalties to come and payment for Gilbert's translation of A. O. Barnabooth, with Dent clamouring for the proofs. A £5 cheque from the Sewanee Review, Tennessee, had been lost. Gwen was instructed to give Gilbert's clothes to his mother. Felix was consulted about the money remaining in Gilbert's account after all expenses had been paid and it was decided that this should be given to Rita, as much of it had originally come from the annuity she had taken out for Gilbert.[25]

So Gilbert's thirty years at the Priory began. At first only Gwen visited him, waiting in the large entrance hall while he was brought by his keeper to whom he spoke as he would to a servant. Then Gwen and Gilbert would have tea together, waited on as in any good-class hotel. The food was excellent; the patients treated as gentlemen by keepers who called them 'Sir'. Everything was made as comfortable and pleasant as possible, for it was indeed a very well-run establishment with a billiard room and a piano which Gilbert played, and so relaxed in atmosphere that sometimes Gilbert thought it was his own country house and offered newcomers whisky.

A. O. Barnabooth: His Diary came out in autumn beautifully translated, described by Dent, the publishers, as an 'acute psychological study, being the diary of a young multi-millionaire who tried to lead his life unhampered by his enormous wealth'. Gerald Gould, writing in the Saturday Review, gave Gilbert's work high praises, believing it 'singularly exact in its rendering of sense', and suggesting that such an excellent translation turned one work of art into another. Indeed the book proves that in some areas Gilbert's mind had, between bouts of insanity, remained useful and efficient.

But now there were to be no more translations from Gilbert, no travelling, no return to his lodge in Africa, no sex, no love of any kind. Dogs, horses and children were never again to be part of his life. He spent many hours writing letters to politicians and long rambling diatribes against society. Under surveillance by a nurse, he would post his letters in the asylum mailbox from which they would be removed by the staff and taken to the Superintendent's office and subsequently burned.

In November, more than six months after Gilbert's committal to the Priory, Mary learned of his insanity and wrote to Secker on the 30th:

I wonder whether you have any news of Gilbert. I heard he is in a lunatic asylum & am much distressed, but I can't find out any very definite information. If you can give me any details I shall be most grateful. It is very awful if it is true.

But Secker was as powerless as everyone else and Mary was surely the last person to be of use in such a situation. Indeed Secker, too, was distressed, being one of Gilbert's truest friends who had never for a moment turned against him.

In 1935 Edwin, in failing health, called Margaret who was staying in his house, to his bedside. Knowing that death was near he explained to her that the £300 a year annuity which he had bought for Gilbert was no longer enough to pay the Cannans' share of the Priory fees, which had risen steadily. He was therefore making arrangements for his nieces, Dorothea, May and Joanna, the beneficiaries from his will, to make up the difference. Shortly afterwards Rita insisted that Edwin should visit Bournemouth, where he died suddenly of a heart attack on April 8th.

In June 1937, Mary came back from France to see Barrie, who was mortally ill. In the nursing home she met Peter and Nicholas Davies waiting sadly for the end. The years had done little to spoil Mary's figure or sap her extraordinary resilience. She was, in spite of the awe and shadow of death, still sprightly. 'Looking so elegant and pretty and we both liked her very much' Nicholas Davies wrote.[26] She went into Barrie's room alone but she was too late. There could be no last minute reconciliation, clasping of hands or whispered words of comfort. Her first husband was apparently not conscious enough to recognise her, and she was back with his adopted sons within a few minutes. But she had not been forgotten. Barrie had bequeathed to 'my dear Mary Cannan with my affectionate regards' £1,000 and a tax free annuity of £600 during her lifetime.[27]

Several of the people close to the Cannans in the days of the Mill

House were now dead or near death. Lawrence and Katherine Mansfield had died of tuberculosis, Carrington had committed suicide in 1932. Ottoline had died in 1938 and Gertler was to gas himself in 1939. Gilbert's parents were also dead. His mother had died of cancer in Devon, after a move from the coastguard cottage, and his father died soon afterwards, having, his children felt, no will to live without his wife. Neither had seen Gilbert since his committal to Roehampton.

With the advent of the Second World War, Gilbert began to rally a little, perhaps feeling in the air the sense of urgency and impending danger which pervaded the country, or responding to a new form of treatment, possibly a drug called Lagactil, or to the hormonal changes that take place as old age approaches. For some time Joanna Cannan (Mrs. Pullein-Thompson) had been suggesting that someone must see him, for otherwise was it not possible that he might merely be kept in because the asylum needed the fees? Then Rita, in Margaret's words, broke the ice and wrote that Gilbert had been quite gentle and that Margaret should come too, next time. His eldest sister went and found him quiet. He didn't talk but simply answered shortly any questions she asked him. Whether Rita's path was made easier by the fact that she had taken out in 1943 a Deed of Covenant for Gilbert to the value of £100 annually, is not clear. If this sum was a contribution from her to the fees, it would have become harder for the authorities at the asylum to refuse her a visit. Whatever the truth of the matter, she now decided to do what she could to help Gilbert and appears to have written to him from time to time, soon making him one of several causes in her life, and presently she was approaching for help those she imagined to have been his friends.

To H. G. Wells, who had grown to dislike Gilbert during the First World War,[28] she wrote on May 31st, 1944:

I venture to write to you on behalf of my cousin, Gilbert Cannan, now in a mental home at Roehampton . . .

He is better & can now read again and concentrate. I was allowed to see him twice last year & he knew me & could talk of happy days, 20 years ago, when he and my husband Prof. Edwin Cannan were such good companions.

He writes strange rambling letters, but still has an astonishing acquaintance of French and English literature & he has asked me to send him books. His wife (ex-Mrs. J. M. Barrie) took away his fine library with her. I have sent him a Ronsard he wanted, also extracts from Racine. Friends are most kind in giving me books for him, such as Ethel Sidgwick, Sir David Ross, Gilbert Murray and Lady Beveridge—& now if you could spare any and send them to me, I should be most grateful & would repay the postage (His kind Doctor is anxious to build up his sanity by any means, but fears he can never quite recover) or any modern British plays or poetry. They are all difficult and expensive to buy at present. I expect you knew Gilbert twenty years ago and think kindly of him as Galsworthy and John Buchan did.

Forgive my troubling you . . .

Gilbert's own family have cast him off long ago. He has only myself and 'Gwen' now—I am over 70—I think I have all your writings and collected them as a girl & admired you as a brave pioneer on sex matters . . .

It is a great consolation to me to think that G. gets even a few gleams of happiness in reading these books & that even for a short time he gets respite from *The Voices.*

H. G. Wells was not co-operative and a note on the top of the letter, which presumably he returned, stated that he was very ill and was sure that Gwen was able to do all.

In 1950 Felix, over for a short stay from South Africa, visited Gilbert at the Priory and was touched when

recognition dawned on that tragic face and the familiar voice said 'My God, it's Felix!' and he became again for a moment the brother I had known.[29]

On June 30th that year Mary died in Biarritz, leaving all she possessed to Magdeleine Antoine. In the Will, dated June 10th, 1948, with her usual scant respect for official documents, Mary had described herself as the widow of Gilbert Cannan, perhaps feeling that the husband she had loved was dead, leaving only a demented shell in his place.

In 1952 Gwen announced that she no longer felt able to contribute to Gilbert's fees so, probably on the recommendation of Dr. Brown, he was moved on June 12th to the renowned Holloway Sanatorium at Virginia Water. Here, at the cost of £8 a week he resided as one of eight private patients in the Pinnel Ward under the care of Richard Kelly, a dedicated charge nurse of equable temperament. By now the more bizarre aspects of Gilbert's illness had burnt themselves out; he was no trouble, quiet, polite and grateful for all that was done for him. Richard Kelly, to whom I talked in 1976, described him as perfectly happy and so accustomed to living in an institution that he no longer missed the freedom of earlier days. Much was done at Holloway to make the patients' life as normal and enjoyable as possible. In addition to television, there were Saturday night amateur concerts or plays from September to May. Cricket matches were regularly played on the beautifully kept pitch throughout the summer, and tennis courts were available to patients. Incredibly, tea dances were still held in the 'fifties and an annual patients' ball, with programmes for the ladies, for segregation of the sexes was considerably relaxed.

Although now too old to take advantage of all the games and entertainment, Gilbert soon announced that he found Holloway preferable to the Priory, pointing out that here he was allowed to handle his own money, buy cigarettes and even go to the café outside the grounds for a cup of coffee. He was taken for a weekend at the sea under supervision and generally encouraged back into the normal world.

The Sanatorium's architectural magnificence was of a kind likely to raise strong feelings of admiration or dislike. A companion building to Holloway College, designed by W. H. Crossland, it possesses in Pevsner's words, 'a sort of Franco–Flemish brick-and-stone Gothic carried through with a verve that is entirely his (Crossland's) own'.[30] It was indeed a place of privilege, dignity and some splendour. In common with the Priory, patients (accepted only on special recommendation) were treated as members of the upper classes. Humiliations were kept to the minimum. Dinner was served with style. The patients, wearing dinner jackets, shared the frescoed dining-room with senior medical staff who sat at the High Table, menus and wine lists were consulted and waiters came at the click of a finger. Extras such as a carafe of claret or a whisky at bedtime were added to patients' accounts, the assumption being that these unfortunate gentlemen came from families of substance.

At Holloway no visitors were barred, but only the two women came to see Gilbert. Letters were uncensored, but those from Gilbert to Rita have vanished and Margaret destroyed hers, finding them too distressing to keep. Telephoning was allowed on request but who was there now to ring up? Who cared? Gilbert had lost touch with past friends, even Secker no longer knew where he was. On Sundays there were services in the church within the building, with Armistice Day a special occasion for pomp and ceremony. Did Gilbert go? 'I would have noticed if he had not,' replied Richard Kelly. 'It was the thing to do, everyone went. It was part of the ritual.' Did he write? The man could not remember, it was now so long ago.

In spite of the confines imposed by his illness, the stunting of his personality and the weakening of his body, Gilbert must have been as happy at Holloway as was possible in the circumstances and there is little doubt that Richard Kelly treated him with kindness and respect. 'All my men were gentlemen', he told me proudly. 'All were polite, however ill they might be. They never forgot to say please or thank you, and, within reason, they had everything they wanted.' For Kelly nursing was a vocation and Holloway the best mental hospital in the country.

In old age thoughts often go back to childhood and so it was perhaps fitting that now Gwen's visits were replaced by those from Margaret Rideout, who deeply regretted that she had not visited her brother many years earlier. The Rideouts had moved on James's retirement to Hindhead, so she was near enough to come twice a month and soon assumed responsibility for him. Having known Gilbert in his prime she was less sanguine about his appearance than Kelly who had never seen him really well. Although the nurse described him to me as impulsive and always ready to be up-and-going, perhaps still possessing remnants of the excitability which had been a symptom of his insanity, Margaret found him a sad figure, much changed. She was told that he was too old for shock treatment and too institutionalised to go out into the world again. The security of hospital was essential to him. 'But', a doctor added, 'we could have done much more for him had he come earlier.'

About this time a rumour went around London that Gilbert was out and setting *The Times* crossword puzzle. A few past acquaintances made inquiries of Cannan relations but no friends approached anyone in the family. So protected and to some extent privileged, living in comfort but I suspect some loneliness of spirit, Gilbert moved towards the end of his seventieth year. At the end of May he went with other patients for a supervised week-end in Brighton, to see again the sea which he had loved as a younger man. On return he fell seriously ill. He was moved to the Sanatorium hospital and Margaret was told that he must undergo an operation. Apart from mental problems it was his first serious illness since childhood, but this time there was no cure. On opening him up, Margaret said, the surgeon found inoperable cancer of the liver, which had been bruised in Manchester all those years ago. He had never complained but he was in fact near death.

Margaret's husband was now a semi-invalid in his eighties, so every other afternoon she put him to bed before driving over to see Gilbert. Her brother had now spent thirty-one years in mental institutions, and he knew his life was all but finished. Haggard and gaunt, his Roman nose standing out like a cliff between sunken cheeks, he spoke little, just a few polite words, but Margaret felt that he was pleased to see her, for the crooked mouth always managed a smile at her arrival.

Then, on June 30th, a 'nice woman doctor' told Margaret that the end was very near. 'That day', Margaret wrote to me, 'he only smiled at me, but when I left, or rather when I was leaving, he took my hand and kissed it and said "thank you for everything. Goodbye."' Meanwhile Richard Kelly, going off duty, had left instructions that the dying man was to have anything he wanted. Pneumonia had now set in; Gilbert's breathing was difficult; he was steadily sinking but modern drugs assured that he was in no great pain. Thirsty in the early watches of the night, he asked for lime juice, causing consternation, for neither Pinnel Ward nor neighbouring wards possessed a drop. Then a nurse remembered seeing a bottle across the road in the nurses' home, and ran at once to fetch it. She came back breathless, diluted a draught with water and handed it to Gilbert. He thanked her politely, drank it all and died. It was half-past ten at night, five days after Gilbert's seventy-first birthday and five years to the day after Mary's death.

Under his bed in a large cardboard box Margaret found Gilbert's barrister's wig, dusty, a little moth-eaten, but still a wig, proof of an achievement which at the time he had seemed to value little. A symbol perhaps of past sanity, a reminder in some strange fashion of the wilder, happier days of his youth, when he had lost his first love to the man he was to imagine himself to be, in part of the long-drawn-out dream of his madness, before age and drugs had brought him back into some kind of reality. Dr. Mary R. Medhurst wrote on the death certificate that death was due to (a) Hypostatic pneumonia (b) marked ascites (c) cancer head of the pancreas and multiple secondaries. Gilbert's body was taken to Woking and cremated, his ashes scattered, with Margaret his only relation at the service. On her orders a commemorative plaque was put up in the crematorium.

His obituaries recorded 'a promise unfulfilled', indications of 'a genius that never developed', but no qualities of character beyond fecundity, no capacity for friendship or generosity, none of the charm and kindliness which had been part of the man before madness overcame him.

In South Africa, feeling the beginnings of his persecution mania, he had written a collection of poems for Gwen:

> *H is Hope*
> *They will not talk so much when I am dead*
> *Those folk who know my doings more than I.*
> *They will not talk & I shall still be read*
> *For what is done with words can never die.*
> *What is more living than the uttered word*
> *The word for ever stamped into the mind*
> *Of man? The rest's a babble dimly heard*
> *A rustle away upon the wind.*

Select Bibliography

Manuscript Sources

U.S.A.

Harvard University, The Houghton Library: Amy Lowell's letter to Gilbert Cannan.

Illinois University Library, The Wells Collection: Letters from Mary Barrie, Gilbert Cannan and Rita Cannan to H. G. and Mrs. Wells. Letters from the Grant Richards papers and Martin Secker letters.

New York Public Library, the Berg Collection: Letters from Gilbert Cannan to Edward Marsh and from Gilbert Cannan to J. B. Pinker and Son.

New York University Libraries: 'Romain Rolland and Jean Christophe', article by Gilbert Cannan.

Texas University, The Humanities Research Center: Letters from Gilbert Cannan to Dora Carrington, Edward Garnett, Sir Compton Mackenzie, Lady Ottoline Morrell, Martin Secker, Hugh Walpole.

Yale, The Beinecke Rare Book and Manuscript Library: Letters from Gilbert Cannan to John and Mrs. Drinkwater, Alfred Stieglitz and H. G. Wells. Letters from Henry James, Romain Rolland and H. G. Wells to Gilbert Cannan. Letters from Mary Ansell to H. G. Wells.

GREAT BRITAIN

Birmingham University Library: The Galsworthy papers and diaries.

British Library: Koteliansky manuscripts.

Cambridge University Library: Kathleen Bruce (Scott) papers. Letters from Gilbert Cannan to Kathleen Bruce.

Cannan Family Papers.

Gertler Papers: Private collection held by Mrs. M. Kostenz. Letters from Gilbert Cannan to Mark Gertler.

PRINTED SOURCES

Aldington, Richard, *Life for Life's Sake*, London, 1968.

Alpers, Anthony, *Katherine Mansfield*, London, 1954.

Anderson, Verity, *The Last of the Eccentrics*, London, 1972.

Ansell, Mary, *Dogs and Men*, London, 1924.

GILBERT CANNAN: A BIOGRAPHY

Ansell, Mary, *Happy Houses*, London, 1912.

———, *The Happy Garden*, London, 1912.

Asquith, Cynthia, *Diaries, 1915–1918* (edited by E. M. Horsely), London, 1968.

———, *Haply I Remember*, London, 1950.

———, *Portrait of Barrie*, London, 1954.

Barrie, J. M., *Letters* (edited by Viola Meynell), London, 1942.

Cannan, May Wedderburn, *Grey Ghosts and Voices*, Warwick, 1976.

Carrington, Dora, *Carrington: Letters and Extracts from Her Diaries* (edited by David Garnett), London, 1970.

Carswell, Catherine, *The Savage Pilgrimage*, London, 1952.

Clark, Ronald W., *The Life of Bertrand Russell*, London, 1975.

Craig, Edward, *Gordon Craig, The Story of his Life*, London, 1968.

Darlington, W. A., *J. M. Barrie*, London and Glasgow, 1938.

Darroch, Sandra Jobson, *Ottoline*, London, 1976.

Delavenay, Emile, *D. H. Lawrence: The Man and his Work, 1885–1919*, London, 1972.

Dunbar, Janet, *J. M. Barrie, The Man Behind the Image*, London, 1970.

Dupré, Catherine, *John Galsworthy*, London, 1976.

Ford Madox Ford, *It Was the Nightingale*, London, 1953.

Galsworthy, John, *Letters 1900–1932* (edited by Edward Garnett), London, 1934.

Garnett, David, *The Golden Echo*, London, 1953.

Gertler, Mark, *Selected Letters* (edited by Noel Carrington with an Introduction by Quentin Bell), London, 1965.

Glenavy, Lady (Beatrice Campbell), *Today We Will Only Gossip*, London, 1964.

Goldring, Douglas, *South Lodge*, London, 1943.

Gwynn, Stephen, *Captain Scott*, London, 1929.

Hassall, Christopher, *Edward Marsh, A Biography*, London, 1959.

———, *Rupert Brooke, A Biography*, London, 1964.

Holroyd, Michael, *Lytton Strachey, A Critical Biography, Vol. II, The Years of Achievement, 1910–1932*, London, 1968.

Keeble, Lady (Lillah McCarthy), *Myself and My Friends*, London, 1933.

Kennet, Lady (Lady Scott), *Self-Portrait of an Artist*, London, 1949.

Lawrence, D. H., *Collected Letters* (edited by Harry T. Moore) 2 vols., New York, 1962.

Lawrence, Frieda, *Not I But the Wind*, London, 1935.

———, *The Memoirs and Correspondence* (edited by R. W. Tedlock), London, 1961.

Lea, F. A., *The Life of John Middleton Murry*, London, 1959.

L. M., *Katherine Mansfield, The Memoirs of L. M.*, London, 1971.

Mackail, Denis, *The Story of J. M. B.*, London, 1941.

SELECT BIBLIOGRAPHY

Mackenzie, Sir Compton, *My Life and Times, Octave Four* and *Octave Five*, London, 1965 and 1966.

——, *The South Wind of Love*, London, 1942.

Malleson, Constance (Constance O'Neill), *After Ten Years, A Personal Record*, London, 1936.

Mansfield, Katherine, *Letters to Middleton Murry*, London, 1951.
The Letters of Katherine Mansfield (edited by J. Middlteon Murry), 2 vols., London, 1928.

——, *Journal of Katherine Mansfield* (edited by J. Middleton Murry), London, 1927.

Marsh, Sir Edward, *A Number of People*, London, 1939.

Meynell, Sir Francis, *My Lives*, London, 1971.

Moore, Harry T., *The Priest of Love*, London, 1974.

Morrell, Lady Ottoline, *The Early Memoirs, 1873–1915*, London, 1963.
Ottoline at Garsington, 1915–1918, London, 1974 (both edited and with Introductions by Robert Gathorne-Hardy).

Murry, John Middleton, *Between Two Worlds*, London, 1935.

Nehls, Edward, *D. H. Lawrence: A Complete Biography*, 3 vols., University of Wisconsin Press, 1957–1959.

Nesbitt, Cathleen, *A Little Love and Good Company*, London, 1976.

Roy, J. A., *James Matthew Barrie*, London, 1957.

Russell, Bertrand, *The Autobiography, 1872–1913*, London, 1967.

Sauter, Rudolph, *Galsworthy The Man*, London, 1957.

Secker, Martin, 'Publishers' Progress' *The Cornhill*, Winter 1973, Spring 1974.

Shaw, George Bernard, *Collected Letters* (edited by Dan H. Lawrence), London, 1965.

Strachey, Lytton, *The Really Interesting Question and Other Papers* (edited by Paul Levy), London, 1974.

Swinnerton, Frank, *Background With Chorus*, London, 1956.

——, *Figures in the Foreground*, London, 1963.

——, *The Georgian Literary Scene, 1910–1935*, London, 1969.

Waugh, Alec, *The Early Days of Alec Waugh*, London, 1962.

——, *My Brother Evelyn and Other Profiles*, London, 1967.

Woodeson, John, *Mark Gertler*, London, 1972.

Wright, H. C. Seppings, *With Togo*, London, 1905.

Notes

ABBREVIATIONS

A.D.M.	Ansell, Mary	*Dogs and Men*
A.H.G.		*The Happy Garden*
C.U.M.	Cannan, Gilbert	'Unpublished Memoirs'
C.L.	Carrington, Dora	*Letters and Extracts from her Diaries* (ed. Garnett)
D.J.M.B.	Dunbar, Janet	*J. M. Barrie: The Man Behind the Image*
G.S.L.	Gertler, Mark	*Selected Letters*
L.C.L.	Lawrence, D. H.	*Collected Letters* (ed. Moore)
M.B.T.W.	Middleton Murry	*Between Two Worlds*
M.E.M.	Morrell, Ottoline	*The Early Memoirs*
S.S.A.	Scott, Kathleen	*Self-Portrait of an Artist from the Diaries and Memoirs of Lady Kennet, Kathleen, Lady Scott*
S.U.D.		'Unpublished Diaries'
S.B.C.	Swinnerton, Frank	*Background with Chorus*
S.F.F.		*Figures in the Foreground*

CHAPTER I

1. Kathleen sculpted many babies' heads.
2. Grandfather: James Cannan (1822–1892) bank clerk, journalist, and Manchester drama critic. Economist: Edwin Cannan (1860–1934).
3. S.S.A., 17. Her mother actually had *eleven* children.
4. *Ibid.*, 17.
5. *Ibid.*, 19–20.
6. C.U.M., Gilbert was eight when James Cannan died.
7. D.J.M.B., 166.
8. S.S.A., 61.
9. *Ibid.*, 76, 83.
10. *Ibid.*, 79.
11. *Captain Scott* (by Stephen Gwynn), 115–116.
12. S.S.A., 81.
13. Galsworthy's letter does not appear to have survived.
14. S.S.A., 86.

15. *Ibid.*, 89.
16. *Captain Scott*, 107–108.
17. *Ibid.*, 118–119.
18. It appears that Gilbert was attempting to write a book or play based on Kathleen's experiences in that country.
19. Letter dated May 18th, 1908.
20. *Captain Scott*, 119.
21. *Ibid.*, 123–124.

CHAPTER 2

1. *My Life and Times* (by Jerome K. Jerome), 133.
2. C.U.M.
3. Letter from Margaret Rideout to the author.
4. *Reminiscences* (by J. Comyns-Carr), 91.
5. A.D.M., 11.
6. *My Brother Evelyn and Other Profiles* (by Alec Waugh), 55.
7. *Conrad's Prefaces* (by Edward Garnett), vi-vii.
8. S.B.C., 115.
9. D.J.M.B., 169–170.
10. *Letters of J. M. Barrie* (ed. Viola Meynell), 19.
11. The bookseller was probably based on a real character, possibly from E. V. Lucas's past. The MS. may have had some connection with the untraced Clara play.
12. Peter Davies's comments on his mother's papers (D.J.M.B., 180).
13. 'The Dramatic Sense', *The English Review*, June 1910.
14. *Captain Scott*, 152. Stephen Gwynn comments in a footnote: 'The likeness was to Gilbert Cannan, then in the freshness of his youth.'
15. J. B. Pinker (1863–1922), literary agent. Lawrence described him as 'that little parvenu snob and procureur of books' (L.C.L., 516).
16. The novel was *Devious Ways*.
17. Peter Davies's comments on his mother's papers (D.J.M.B., 171).
18. D.J.M.B., 172.
19. *E. V. Lucas, a Portrait* (by Audrey Lucas), 70.
20. *The Story of J.M.B.*, 407.
21. Delivered on May 3rd, 1922 and published later that year by Hodder & Stoughton.

CHAPTER 3

1. Letter from Barrie to Sylvia Davies (D.J.M.B., 175).
2. C.U.M.

3. Letter from Margaret Rideout to the author.

4. C.U.M.

5. 'Birth' was published in *The English Review*, April 1910. Elkin Mathews was a publisher, at one time in partnership with John Lane.

6. The performance of *Dull Monotony* is briefly mentioned in *The Stage Year Book*, 1910. The cast is not named but described as 'distinguished'.

7. *George Bernard Shaw: Collected Letters* (1898–1910) (ed. Dan H. Lawrence), 1910.

8. *The Greenwood Hat*, 9.

9. *The Story of J. M. B.*, 414.

10. *Little Brother*.

11. *Return to Yesterday*, 413. The 'papers' were connected with the divorce case.

12. *Ibid.*, 413.

13. D.J.M.B., 181.

14. *Daily Telegraph*, October 13th, 1909.

15. *Barrie, the Story of a Genius*, 296 (1929).

CHAPTER 4

1. Both 'Birth' and 'Death' appeared in April, but nothing by Gilbert in the May issue.

2. *The Story of J. M. B.*, 415.

3. A.H.G., 37.

4. A.H.G., 39–40.

5. A.H.G., 3.

6. A.H.G., 42–45.

7. A.H.G., 43.

8. Possibly a relation of H. G. MacKeurton (1884–1942) who was at Cambridge at the same time as Gilbert and later became a distinguished advocate in South Africa.

9. Lytton Strachey in a letter to Henry Lamb (May 17th, 1913) quoted in *Lytton Strachey* (by Michael Holroyd) Vol. II, 89.

10. Letter to Kathleen (April 14th, 1908).

11. C.U.M.

12. A.D.M., 46–47.

13. A.H.G., 67–78.

14. *The Life and Letters of John Galsworthy* (by H. V. Marrot), 68.

15. *Letters of J. M. Barrie*, 15.

16. A.D.M., 112.

17. *Myself and My Friends* (by Lillah, Lady Keeble), 97–98.

CHAPTER 5

1. *George Bernard Shaw: Collected Letters*, 909.
2. *Myself and My Friends*, 135.
3. *Ibid.*, 135.
4. S.S.A., 82.
5. S.B.C., 150.
6. S.F.F., 200.
7. C.U.M.
8. *Grey Ghosts and Voices*, 114.
9. S.B.C., 146.
10. M.B.T.W., 243. *Edward Marsh: A Biography* (by Christopher Hassall), 218.
11. *Edward Marsh: A Biography*, 201.
12. *Diaries and Letters 1911–1947*, 37.
13. Charles Henry Gordon Campbell (1885–1963), later Lord Glenavy, 2nd Baron of Milltown, Irish banker and businessman, married Beatrice, *née* Moss.
14. *Today We Will Only Gossip*, 68.
15. St. John Hutchinson, K. C. (1884–1942), a distinguished barrister.
16. *Ibid.*, 88.
17. *My Life and Times, Octave Four*, 221.
18. Mackenzie's letter has not survived. Gilbert replied at length to the criticism on January 27th, 1913.
19. Letters from Secker to Gilbert (June 28th, 1911), (July 4th, 1912).
20. *Miles Dixon* was staged in Liverpool and Manchester that year and the lectures were almost certainly on modern drama.
21. M.E.M., 245.
22. *Lytton Strachey*, Vol. II, 88, 89.
23. M.E.M., 246.

CHAPTER 6

1. A.D.M., 127.
2. Middleton Murry's journal.
3. *Edward Marsh: A Biography* (by Christopher Hassall), 218.
4. M.B.T.W., 243, 252.
5. Marsh's friend was author James Strachey Barnes. S.P.E. is an abbreviation of the Society for Pure English. Logan Pearsall Smith (1865–1946), was a bachelor and author, brother of Bertrand Russell's first wife. Gilbert's Christmas card probably *Satire* or *Old Mole's Novel Love*.
6. In his book, *Love*.

7. Information from Igor Polunin.

8. Mentioned to me by David Garnett in conversation.

9. S.U.D.

10. *England of the Windmills* (by S. P. B. Mais), 114.

11. *Katherine Mansfield: The Memories of L. M.*, 81.

12. *My Life and Times, Octave Four*, 221.

13. *The Golden Echo*, Vol. II, 7.

14. G.S.L., 63.

15. *Ibid.*, 59. Letter to Carrington, December 1913.

16. *Ibid.*, 60.

17. *Ibid.*, 68.

18. *A Little Love and Good Company* (by Cathleen Nesbitt), 423.

19. M.E.M., 253.

20. See: *The Times*, June 10th, 12th, 13th, 16th, 1914. The poem was published in *Adventurous Love and Other Verses*, with sonnets.

21. Ronald Clark suggests in *The Life of Bertrand Russell*, 99, that the quality and intensity of the affair began to alter in 1913.

22. M.E.M., 236.

23. *Ibid.*, 64.

24. Francis Lyall Birch (1889–1956), historian, linguist, translator and author, was one of Gilbert's closest friends. In a letter to Marsh (May 19th, 1914), he wrote, in connection with a new theatre movement: 'One of my chief concerns is with Birch. My objection to the ordinary theatre—even Barker's—is that everything is exploited and nothing used. Birch is so good that I don't want to see him exploited, though if it turns out that the only way to the real theatre is through Ethiopia I'll go through it with him.' But Birch's talents seem to have lain in other directions and he never became an established playwright.

25. Philip Morrell had spoken in the House of Commons against the war on August 3rd, 1914.

26. October 5th, 1914. Lowes Dickinson was feeling bereft because a close male friend had recently left to join the army.

27. (undated).

28. *The Savage Pilgrimage* (by Catherine Carswell), 29. She was a Scottish author (1879–1946) married to Donald Carswell, barrister, journalist and author.

29. Letter dated August 25th, 1914, quoted in *A Number of People* (by Edward Marsh), 228.

30. *Ibid.*, 229.

31. Undated letter to Ottoline written as from Little Marsh, Beaulieu, Hants.

32. *The Savage Pilgrimage*, 276.

33. *Ibid.*, 17, 27. According to Catherine Carswell he had grown his beard by October 1914.

34. M.E.M., 272.

35. David Garnett described her thus to the author in 1971.

36. L.C.L., 557–558, in letter dated June 14th, 1918.

37. *Not I But The Wind* (by Frieda Lawrence), 75.

38. Undated letter but almost certainly December 26th, 1914.

39. G.S.L., 78, 79.

40. Both, quite independently, told the author that this was the reaction to the article.

41. From the poem, *William Bond*, by William Blake.

CHAPTER 7

1. Letter from Lawrence to Marsh dated August 25th, 1914 quoted in *A Number of People*, 228.

2. *The South Wind of Love*, Book I, 267–281. See also *D. H. Lawrence, A Composite Biography*, by Edward Nehls, Vol. I, 570, in which a letter from Mackenzie is published confirming that the description is taken from life and that 'most of it is factually and conversationally correct'.

3. *Ibid.*, 281–282.

4. May 16th, 1915. Jacques Copeau (1879–1949), famous French theatrical producer, and manager of the Vieux Colombier Theatre, Paris.

5. *Ottoline at Garsington*, 60, 61 (undated).

6. *Ibid.*, undated.

7. Published in *International Journal of Ethics*, October 22nd, 1915, also in *Potboilers* (by Clive Bell), 1918.

8. G.S.L., 111. John Currie (1884–1914), a portrait painter, studied at the Slade with Gertler. In a fit of jealousy he shot himself and his mistress on October 8th, 1914. It is worth noting that Gertler showed Gilbert his diary and piece on Currie's suicide after *Mendel* was completed and in proof; see *Mark Gertler* (by John Woodeson), 232; also letter from Gilbert to Pinker June 26th, 1916.

9. Published in America as *Three Sons and a Mother* (George G. Doran) New York.

10. In letter to the author, March 20th, 1969.

11. G.S.L., 99. Letter to Marsh, August 1915.

12. 'The Mill' was first shown at a London Group Exhibition in June 1916 and is now considered one of Gertler's major works; see *Modern English Painters* Vol. II (by John Rothenstein), 212.

13. G.S.L., 86. Surprisingly, Gertler never seems to have given Gilbert a drawing or picture in appreciation of the hospitality he received.

14. Koteliansky MSS, The British Library, also G.S.L., 88, 89.

NOTES

15. G.S.L., 95. Referring to *Mendel*, Mrs. Kostenz wrote to the author (April 30th, 1976): 'Mark's version was that he used to pour out his experiences especially his love for Carrington to Gilbert at the Mill and that Cannan had a marvellous memory and reproduced them word for word in his book. I can't believe that Mark didn't know that he was writing it ... The book is so exactly like Mark, the way he would describe people, and his general behaviour, that I have often thought that it was a better memorial to him than an official life.'

16. December 20th, 1915. 'Bird of time' from Fitzgerald's *Omar Khayyam*. 'The Bird of Time has but a little way to fly—and lo! the Bird is on the Wing.'

17. Kathleen was working in a munitions factory at the time.

18. S.B.C., 150.

19. Hankin and Lillah were friends of Gilbert at this time, and he was already an inveterate theatre-goer.

20. Shaw to Granville-Barker, December, 17th, 1908. *Letters to Granville-Barker* (ed. C. B. Purdom), 142–143.

21. Letter to Ottoline, October 26th, 1915.

22. Undated letter to Ottoline.

23. C.L., 94.

24. *The Really Interesting Question and Other Papers* (ed. Paul Levy), 28, 29.

25. *Ibid.*, 30.

26. Mrs. Lily Tobias, the novelist, remembers travelling with Gilbert by train to Cardiff where he made an excellent speech against conscription (1916). She described him as handsome with extremely good manners, a quiet gentle person.

27. Galsworthy Diaries, University of Birmingham.

28. *The Divided Self* (by W. S. Stewart), 18.

29. G.L.S., 116–117. Letter from Gertler to Carrington August 14th, 1916.

30. *Ibid.*

31. A.D.M., 152–157.

32. G.S.L., 254.

33. *Ibid.*, 256.

34. *Ibid.*, 233.

35. *Memoirs and Correspondence*, 218.

36. G.S.L., 254.

CHAPTER 8

1. Undated letter probably written in autumn 1914.

2. Mrs. Igor Vinogradoff told me that her mother, Lady Ottoline, always spoke affectionately of Gilbert. The reference to conceit appears in M.E.M., 245. The last of Gilbert's visits recorded in Ottoline's Visitors' Book was

September 11th to 13th, 1915. He had, however, stayed at Garsington five times in the three preceding months.

3. C.U.M.

4. *Fantasia* was published several years later, but in part reflects earlier beliefs of a similar nature.

5. Letter from Mrs. Kostenz to the author, April 30th, 1976.

6. *The Release of the Soul.*

7. C.L., 49.

8. G.S.L., 137.

9. As far as I know, the play was not published or performed in this form, but a similar one, *Pierrot in Hospital*, appears in *Seven Plays*.

10. In a letter, January 15th, 1920, from the Bellevue Stratford, Philadelphia, Gilbert wrote to John Drinkwater: 'Please ask Kathleen to stop hating me—she can't go on with it if I don't hate her—and to write me an affectionate letter appointing a day: any day next week for dinner.' His plea was successful; a second letter addressed to Kathleen (undated) confirms that a lunch was arranged for January 29th in New York.

11. Letter to author from Sir Felix Aylmer, June 5th, 1969.

12. Alexander Ivanoch Kuprin was a Russian author, some of whose work was translated into English by Koteliansky and Middleton Murry.

13. Letter undated but Noel Carrington who sent me a xerox believes it to have been written in March.

14. L.C.L. Lawrence to Koteliansky, March 12th, 1917.

15. June 14th, 1918. L.C.L., 557–558.

16. Mark Gertler wrote to Carrington that originally Gilbert had wanted to live with Mary and still have his girl—to which Mary objected (February 1917) G.S.L., 140.

17. S.U.D.

18. S.U.D.

19. S.U.D. It was Una Trowbridge who led to Macedonia the party of volunteer nurses, which included Kathleen Bruce.

20. D.J.M.B., 218.

21. D.J.M.B., 219.

22. January 25th, 1918.

23. C.L., 94.

24. *My Brother Evelyn*, 119.

25. *The Early Years*, 110–111.

26. *My Brother Evelyn*, 122.

27. Letter from Edward Craig to the author, June 26th, 1975.

28. Mackenzie's choice of the name Rodney for Gilbert in *The South Wind of Love* may well have been inspired by Gilbert's choice of Rodd in *Mummery*.

NOTES

CHAPTER 9

1. Report in *The Star* of that date.
2. M.E.M., 246 'She (Mary) always said she would retire from his life if he fell in love with anyone his own age.' Gwen was younger but the age gap not so great as that between Gilbert and Mary.
3. August 30th, 1918.
4. Letter to Pinker, dated August 1918.
5. Letter dated August 1918.
6. S.B.C., 128.
7. I have not been able to identify *The Free Lady* and cannot find any work published under that title.
8. Letter undated.
9. February 11th, 1919.
10. February 26th, 1919. The handwriting suggests some uncertainty about the date on Gilbert's part.
11. Letter dated February 26th, 1919.
12. July 2nd, 1919.
13. *My Life and Times, Octave Four,* 221, 222.
14. Sometimes they took a fourth person along, e.g. Koteliansky (G.S.L., 174).
15. S.F.F., 74.
16. *The Priest of Love,* 312, 313. Letter from Lawrence to Amy Lowell dated February 13th, 1920.
17. Letter dated January 15th, 1920, written from Bellevue, Stratford, Philadelphia.
18. R. E. Jones, the American stage designer. Letter to Kathleen Drinkwater wrongly dated 19th January and almost certainly written on January 16th, 1920.
19. March 24th, 1920, C.L., 624, 625.
20. Compare *My Life and Times, Octave Five,* 177–178.
21. In collection of poems specially written for Gwen.
22. These and following despatches were published in *Letters From a Distance.*
23. Gwen taught him to ride during the earlier visit to Africa.
24. August 6th. The paper heading: 'Highfield House, 62 Fitzjohns Avenue, Hampstead' is deleted and replaced by 'c/o Brown Shipley, 123 Pall Mall, London, S.W'.
25. Letters from the Hon. Vera Birch to author, May 5th and 15th, 1969.
26. Date indecipherable.
27. May 2nd, 1922 from Hotel Wagram, Paris.
28. July 28th, 1922.

29. August 6th, 1922. He wrote to Pinker: 'Better send the cheque along and I'll take over the Newbury allowance as from August. Many thanks for looking after it for so long.'

30. September 11th, 1922.

CHAPTER 10

1. Nevertheless he dedicated his next novel, *The House of Prophecy*, to Gwen and the baby.

2. M.B.T.W., 253.

3. September 27th, 1922. L.C.L., 720.

4. M.B.T.W., 253. *Time and Eternity*.

5. January 5th, 1922.

6. Section 2, column 2, page 6.

7. Horace Brisbin Liveright (1886–1933), American publisher and producer. See: *My Brother Evelyn*, 116–117.

8. Letter to Eric Pinker, March 2nd, 1923.

9. *The Priest of Love*, 344.

10. *A Portrait of Barrie* (by Cynthia Asquith), 157–158.

11. Contained in an unpublished collection of poems written for Gwen mainly while Gilbert was in South Africa.

12. Letter dated February 2nd, 1924 from Gilbert to Henry: ' ... I know nothing about Bury Street except that you were in the sitting-room when I was shanghai'd and that my property is missing. Gwen and my mother tell different stories but, and I have stayed here only to give them time to get under cover, I don't hold *women* responsible.'

13. Undated letter from Violet Cannan to Gwen's husband.

14. Undated letter.

15. February 28th, 1924.

16. Undated letter.

17. March 5th, 1924.

18. Letter to Secker, October 12th, 1923.

19. Letter (undated) from Grace to Gwen's husband.

20. *Time and Eternity*.

21. March 3rd, 1924.

22. *Life for Life's Sake* (by Richard Aldington), 204.

23. Letter dated May 15th, 1969 from Vera Birch to the author.

24. Undated letter.

25. Letter from Henry Cannan to Board of Control dated May 8th, 1924, and undated letter to Rita Cannan. Also letter from Edwin to Gwen, April 25th, 1924.

26. Letters from Nicholas Davies to the author, November 13th, 1974.
27. D.J.M.B.
28. See *The Autobiography of Bertrand Russell*, Vol. II, 72.
29. Letter to the author, March 3rd, 1969.
30. *The Buildings of England: Surrey* (by Ian Nairn and Nikolaus Pevsner), 314.

Index